# ABOUT T

'He can vividly conjure up images and feelings of periods which remind us of episodes in our own lives—like a kind of cultural photographer' says Australian Prime Minister, Paul Keating, about Glenn A. Baker, who occupies a unique niche in Australian entertainment and public life. Music expert, intrepid traveller, radio and television presenter, magazine and newspaper feature writer, author and effusive enthusiast, his face and voice have become extremely familiar over the past twenty years, as has his capacity to elucidate upon his favourite topics with accuracy and humour.

An active travel writer for almost a decade, Glenn's features have appeared in *The Australian Magazine, Good Weekend, Australian Gourmet Traveller, Mode, Vogue, Cosmopolitan, Penthouse, The Bulletin, Signature, Ita, The Age, Sydney Morning Herald, FMG, Airways, Silver Kris, Sawasdee, The Peak, Quest, Expressions* and many other publications. He was the travel presenter on TV's *Good Morning Australia* in 1991 and *The Midday Show* in 1992, and is presently preparing episodes for the international series, *Baker At Large*.

This is Glenn's twelfth book, his previous titles including *Sydney In Black & White* (with Robin Morrison), *External Combustion* and *The Beatles Down Under*. He was born in 1952 and lives in Sydney with his wife, six children and an abnormally large record and book collection.

As the world's worst traveller—anxious from the minute I leave the house—I admire Glenn A. Baker's aplomb in foreign parts as much as his vivid writing. I'm bound to steal some of his copy and put it in a novel one of these days, but I'll never get that airport poise . . .

Peter Corris
Novelist/Biographer

Unlike Glenn A. Baker, I have never been kicked by a waiter in the Cosmos Hotel and I have not seen the land dive on Pentecost Island. But I have done the Hermitage and the Vatican Museums in under an hour each, and I have almost crashed into Guadalcanal. And like Baker I have always missed the Nude Teenage Drum Majorettes. *Perpetual Motion* is a great way to keep moving between stops.

Gareth Evans
Minister for Foreign Affairs

Glenn A. Baker's talent for finding the unique, the off-beat and the amusing in his frenetic travels gives the reader a roller-coaster ride around Planet Earth with the verbal velocity of Tom Wolfe and Hunter S. Thompson.

David Elfick
Film Director

Forget *60 Minutes*, Glenn A. Baker makes 'em look like a bunch of stay-at-homes! Can you imagine the poor, out-of-the-way beauty spot—unsuspecting, bothering nobody—and suddenly Glenn A. steps off the bus with pith helmet, Hawaiian shirt, terry-towelling shorts and the strains of *Sgt Pepper* bubbling from his Walkman? Talk about Close Encounters . . . Godzilla takes one giant step into the Time warp. 'Officer it was . . . well . . . frightening.'

Ray Martin
*The Midday Show*

# PERPETUAL MOTION

## TRAVELS WITH GLENN A. BAKER

ALLEN & UNWIN

First published in 1993
Allen & Unwin Pty Ltd
9 Atchison Street, St Leonards, NSW 2065 Australia

National Library of Australia
Cataloguing-in-Publication entry:

Baker Glenn A., 1952–
Perpetual motion: travels with Glenn A. Baker
ISBN 1 86373 429 5.
1. Baker, Glenn A., 1952– .—Journeys.
2. Voyages and travels. I. Title.
910.92

Set in 10/12 pt Palatino by DOCUPRO, Sydney
Printed by Southwood Press Pty Ltd, Marrickville, NSW

# FOREWORD

## GLENN A. BAKER IS A SYDNEY WRITER

(the enigmatic footnote to one of Mr Baker's
popular newspaper features)

Before fifty there is time for everything, and if you haven't read
all the novels of Bulwer Lytton or George Meredith, it doesn't
seem to matter. There will be plenty of time later. In some
comfortable chair, under a rosy lamp, beside a crackling fire—
sometime in the future—the untasted pleasures of literature will
at last be yours. It is the same with travel.

You may never have been to the Antarctic, or Ecuador, or
Sumatra, or Helgoland, but before you reach the critical watershed
of two score and ten, you know you'll probably get around to
them one day. But as middle age yields to a mental and physical
condition we resolutely refuse to give a name to, but which braver
men have described as the Beginning of the End, a realisation
dawns upon us. It is not an unpleasant realisation either. We
suddenly wake up one morning and know for certain that we
will never read all those books, never visit those far away places.

Surely one of the least publicised delights of the 'Autumn
Years' is the knowledge, albeit forced upon us by dwindling time,
that we need never read this, taste that, go there. We are exoner-
ated. We are off the hook—reprieved. It is almost as though we
were back at school and we had presented our teachers with a
note in our mother's holograph:

*Please excuse Barry from the excursion to Central Borneo.*
*He is too old.*

Herein lies the vocation of the travel writer. As Des Essientes,
who cancelled his trip from Paris to London and read the works

of Dickens instead, knew, we can travel vicariously; with more comfort and safety and without painful injections, in an armchair.

Unfortunately, a bad travel book can be as disagreeable as an uncomfortable journey. It can even induce nausea. The book in your hand now is of a different order. It is amusing, it is personal, and it reflects the lively curiosity of an impenitent globetrotter.

Mr Baker is a mercurial man. To many Australians he is a celebrated broadcaster, to those in the know he is one of the world's greatest *afficionados* of rock music, with an encyclopedic knowledge of its ephemera. He could, at the drop of a hat, tell you who was the stand-in second guitar on the B-side of an obscure 1965 45 r.p.m. by The Easybeats, or reel off all the important gigs ever played by the group Paul Keating used to manage. He is, of course, a record producer of flair and imagination who has already published two compilations of songs and sketches by the present writer, and his albums of nostalgic Australian radio theme tunes and vintage commercials are already collector's items.

It is, however, as an entertaining and evocative guide to the World that he engages us here. In reading again those voyages to Venezuela and Turkey, Zimbabwe and Pentecost Island, I am astonished that we have never actually crossed paths. Sometimes, it is true, the manager of an exquisite and remote resort on the Coburg Peninsula, or some hunting lodge in the Hungarian forests, has asked me if I know Glenn A. Baker. 'He was here only last week!,' they invariably exclaim in their several languages.

One day in the future we will meet on a desolate beach in the Bahamas or some Corsican cove. He striding along the shingle, I in my wheelchair. For Mr Baker is not the perfect travel writer whose exotic world pictures can save you the trip. When he describes somewhere, whatever your infirmities, you've got to go there.

Barry Humphries is a Melbourne writer.

# CONTENTS

# ACKNOWLEDGMENTS

Travel writing can not be initiated or accomplished without the courtesies and assistance provided by a large number of organisations and individuals, to whom I extend my appreciation and sincere thanks:

Lorelle Baker for so admirably holding down the fort;

Bob King, Susan Skelton, Susan Wyndham, Ken Boys, Pauline Turner, Patrick Gallagher, Barry Humphries;

Qantas Airways, Ansett Australia, Garuda Indonesia, Japan Airlines, Singapore Airlines, Aerolineas Argentinas, American Airlines, Gulf Air, Cathay Pacific Airways, British Airways, Aer Lingus, Finnair, Northwest Airlines, Air New Zealand, Air Zimbabwe, Air Pacific, Air Vanuatu, Philippine Airlines, Turkish Airlines, East-West Airlines, Turtle Airways;

Adventure Associates, Zimbabwe Travel Bureau, Japan National Tourist Organisation, German National Tourist Office, Irish Tourist Board, Southern African Tour Operators Association, Trans Turk Travel, Hong Kong Tourist Association, Korean National Tourism Corporation, Orbitours, Argentina Government Tourist Office, Macau Tourist Information Bureau, Abercrombie & Kent, Fordham Communications, Corpcom, Destinations International;

Sheraton Hotels, Hilton Hotels, Southern Pacific Hotels, Ramada International Hotels, Inter-Continental Hotels, Regent International Hotels, Forte Hotels, Oberoi Hotels, Beaufort Hotels, Select

Hotels & Resorts Intl, Small Luxury Hotels of the World, Turtle Island Lodge;

Jennifer Lionetti, Tony Hill, Helen Goodall, Ken Morton, Delphine Troughear, May Chiu, Barry Matheson, Dennis Collaton, Mike McDowell, Georgina Finn, Roger Henning, Gordon Steptoe, Peter Hook, Peter Gisbourne, Mark Williams, Peter Blunden, Arthur Hullett, Simon West, Mark Grieve, Mark Leonard, Ray Martin, Gary Burns, Paul Melville, Phil Kwok, Larry Writer, Charlie Lockhart, Alice Ghent, Susan Sams, Chris Marais, Phil Abraham, Andrew Conway, Maggy Oehlbeck, Catherine Marshall, Jane Corbett-Jones, Kim Har Chew, John & Lynne Parche, Cathy Rossi-Harris, Mary Rose Trainor, Bruce Barnett, Neil Ainsworth, Janine Cooper, Sue Rose, George Negus, Phillip Adams, Gareth Evans, Peter Corris, Sian Griffiths, Julian Good, Martin Fabinyi, Heather Jeffery, Belinda Howell, Melanie de Souza, Melanie Baker, Alison Bell, Graeme Allen, Irene Irvine, Frank Gallego, David Collins, Wayne Shields, Jane Doughty, Rhonda Barton, Victoria Goddard, Yekta, Pablo King, Barry Mayo, Robyn Smith, Deborah Anderson, Richard Roseberry, Wayne Fay, David Ellis, David Hummerston, Bonnie Boezeman, Kathy Bail, Thomas Samels, Sharon Hannaford, Robin Usher, Ben Sandilands, Peter Cordingly and a few hundred others whose names have faded in the mists of time;

Amanda O'Connell for her patient and enthusiastic editorial coordination, Lynn Segal for her editing skills, Vanessa Radnidge for her proofreading, and Monica Joyce for her very public relations;

Susan Kurosawa for inspiration and David McGonigal for understanding the way things sometimes happen and for the title.

Glenn A. Baker is a member of The Australian Society of Travel Writers. He is represented for public engagements by Harry M. Miller's Speakers Bureau. He uses Apple Computers.

The features in this book have previously appeared (sometimes in different form) in the following publications: 'Bedlam And Breakfast', *Weekends For Two*, 1991, *Living*, 1992; 'Piles Of Fun In Kanazawa', *Sydney Morning Herald*, *The West Australian*, 1991, *Sawasdee*, 1993; 'Pondering The Playpen', *The Age*, 1992, *Living*, 1993; 'The Way Of The Irish', *The Peak*, 1993; ''Nam Now', *Australian Gourmet Traveller*, 1991, *Muhibah*, 1992; 'A Journey Through A World In Change', *The Australian Magazine* (USSR), *Cosmopolitan* (part of Berlin), 1990; 'South Africa On The Line', *The Australian,* 1993; 'The Savage Scribe', *The Australian Magazine,* 1991, *Listener, The Peak,* 1992, *Living,* 1993; 'The Man Who Never Came Home', *Rolling Stone,* 1993; 'Mayhem At The Manila', *Good Weekend,* 1987; 'The Back Route to Bangkok', *Sydney Morning Herald, Signature, 1989, Living,* 1993; 'The Ultimate Upgrade', *Sydney Morning Herald, Living,* 1993; 'Scars Among The Lotus Flowers', *The Age,* 1991, *Silver Kris, 1993;* 'Front Line Faith', *Good Weekend,* 1986; 'Panmunjom—The Cold War's Last Showdown', *Orient,* 1993; 'The *Bounty* Aristocracy', *The West Australian Magazine,* 1989, *NZ Sunday,* 1990, *Sawasdee,* 1992; 'Jamaica Jerk-Off', *The Age,* 1992; 'Venezuela—Beyond The Paths Of Plunder', *Australian Gourmet Traveller,* 1992; 'Turkey—Edging Into Europe', A compilation of pieces published in: *Penthouse, People, Follow Me Gentlemen, Silver Kris, Australian Gourmet Traveller. The Bulletin;* 'In Search Of The Wild Man of Borneo', *Good Weekend, The Age,* 1985, *Expressions,* 1993; 'Freefalling For Fertility', *The Australian Magazine,* 1990, *Silver Kris,* 1990, *The Peak,* 1992; 'Samurai Sleaze', *Follow Me Gentlemen,* 1990; 'The Good Life Guaranteed', *Good Weekend, Sunday Mail Magazine, West Australian,* 1988; 'Don't Cry For Argentina', *Good Weekend,* 1986; 'The Opening Of A Forbidden City', *The Age, West Australian, Vacations, Sawasdee* and *Quest,* 1991; 'Kariba!', *Club Marine, People, Canberra Times, The Age, South China Morning Post,* 1988-93; 'Turtle's Tear Factor', *Australian Gourmet Traveller,* 1989; *M Magazine,* 1992; 'Paradise is Doing Nothing Atoll', *Good Weekend, The Western Mail Magazine,* 1987; 'Tasting The Spice Islands', *Traveller,* 1987; 'Victoria—Northern Australia's Forsaken Settlement', *Silver Kris,* 1991; 'A Twenty-Second-Century Preview', *Penthouse,* 1991; 'Living For Death In Torajaland', *Singles, People, Off Duty, Been There Done That!,* 1986–91; 'Five Ovens—No Waiting', *People,* 1988; 'Mount Bromo Dawn', *Sunday Telegraph, Adelaide Advertiser, Off-Duty, Signature,* 1985–89; 'On Okinawa', *Away* 1993; 'The Troglodyte Realm of Cappadocia', *Mode,* 1989, *The Peak,* 1992; *The Age,* 1993; 'The Hidden Macau', *Sun Herald,* 1993; 'Blues, Bluegrass And Bourbon', *Sun Herald* U.S. Supplement, 1991, *South China Morning Post, Living,* 1993; 'Prancer, Dancer, Rudolph And A Man Called Claus', *Sawasdee, The Australian Way,* 1991; 'Flying Wry', *Australian Penthouse Living,* 1993; 'One Flew Over The Penguin's Nest', *The Peak,* 1993; 'Adventures In Abu Simbel' has not previously been published.

# BEDLAM AND BREAKFAST

I am, if I may be allowed a small boast, an intuitive traveller, able to sense and sidestep impending catastrophe with nimble skill. In the three score and more countries that I have descended upon in the capacity of writer, telecaster or simple stickybeak, I have generally avoided or survived muggings, seditious acts, noxious substances, fetid food, homicidal drivers, undocumented strains of disease and airline seat occupants so boring that the hostesses pay children from coach to take them their meals.

Which is not to say that I have been spared all discomfort or dismay. I recall in indelible detail a night and a day in a stifling room of a government-run hotel on stilts above a Hanoi lake; my photographer violently ill from food poisoning next door and both of us driven to the threshold of madness by ineffectual air-conditioners carefully tuned to duplicate the sound of a jet aircraft engine during reverse thrust. Outside our rooms a Vietnamese attempt at creative landscaping offered a flea-bitten monkey manacled inside a filthy cage more suited to one of Monty Python's Norwegian blue parrots. If it hadn't been my birthday I might not have been quite so defeated by the whole Kafkaesque mosaic.

In comparison to that, it was but a mere irritation to dine at a small lodge in the Blue Mountains, west of Sydney, where every dish of every course was accompanied by a small dollop of vile, red fish eggs which could not, by any fair stretch of the imagination, be termed caviar. Or, during my younger years of journeying abroad on the whiff of an oily rag, to stay in a London hotel room so miniscule that it was not possible (and I do not steal this from

1

Groucho Marx) to lay down on my bed or indeed even close the door if my suitcase was in the room.

There have been commercial aircraft which took off while I was trying to locate my seat, an Indian taxidriver so impenetrable that I had to throw his hat out the window to coerce him to stop, a Thai host who became dangerously offended when I declined to partake from a bowl of crisply deep-fried whole day-old chicks, and a Chinese meal in an Argentinian outpost secured only after I had oinked like a pig, chirped like a chicken, mooed as a cow and pantomimed sweet and sour sauce in a manner that I'd best not detail here.

More speed humps than hurdles, these incidents (if I may be permitted to mix my metaphors) serve to spice the travel broth. However, even the most accommodating palate knows when to spit the chilli and my moment of regurgitation came in Moscow at the infamous Cosmos Hotel, an imposing edifice built by the French to accommodate all the citizens of Southern Siberia, should they choose to drop by Moscow one night. It is the city's equivalent of Times Square, Grand Central Station and the lounge level of the Sydney Entertainment Centre, with a bank of poker machines at one end of the foyer and a clutch of attractive (and apparently inexpensive) working girls at the other.

It is said that the Russians had the hotel built for the Moscow Olympics, though their own amusement seems more likely. At any hour of the day or night there seemed to be at least 2500 people milling about the grand entrance, not one with any apparent direction or purpose. It seemed enough just to be there. Outside in the snow, kept from the guests by a veritable battalion of vigilant door guards, innumerable traders braved arrest to barter rabbit hats, military belts, flags, campaign medals, beluga caviar or carved dolls for Kylie Minogue cassettes, sloganed t-shirts, baseball caps, packs of Marlboro, Walkmans or felt pens with coloured ink. The comrades were definitely committed to commerce; I'd been to Arab souks with less activity.

The guards were supposed to provide a demarcation line between street trading and the civilised order of an international hotel. Supposed to. What they effectively did was keep the small fry away from the grand game. Early in my stay an associate set out to the front desk (an expedition requiring a thermos flask and a compass) to exchange an American $100 bill for the regulation 60 or so roubles. Before his elevator had travelled from the sixteenth floor to the lobby, a persuasive university student had given him 700 roubles for it. The student slipped away into the lobby throng like a Le Carré agent at a letter-drop, fearful of apprehension. He lacked the necessary camouflage—a waiter's uniform.

Let me explain that, for all intents and purposes, Russians don't eat; at least not where they can be observed. To the naked eye there are no cafes, restaurants, snack bars, sandwich bars, pastry shops, hot dog stands or bagel carts. No kebabs sizzling on street corner charcoal braziers, no roasting chestnuts in converted oil drums. No anything. At a tourist hotel, if one has a spare hour to engage in subtle hostilities with an artfully insolent waiter, it is possible to secure a barely digestible plate of boiled stodge. Otherwise, one's nourishment is directly related to one's foresight.

I'd left Heathrow with a brown paper Harrods carry sack containing cereals, biscuits, cheese and crackers, raisins, milk, orange juice, health food bars and fresh fruit forced upon me. Just an amusing piece of extra hand baggage in London, it came to be known as a 'Red Cross parcel' in Moscow. I lived out of mine for four days. Each morning I poured a measure of orange juice with the exacting eye of a Changi prisoner. Either that, or endure a trip to the breakfast room for a cold boiled egg, even colder gruel and a piece of curling cheese. That's if it was actually open; some mornings the staff didn't bother to unlock the place.

There was a dining room and it sometimes had at least one of the dishes listed on the ornate and elaborate menu. I succeeded in securing a seafood salad one night. It arrived at my table upturned from a can, with the indentations of the steel ridges set plainly in the glutinous mass. It was followed by a brown and brittle substance that I would have liked to have sent out to a laboratory for analysis. It did not conform to standard animal, vegetable, mineral groupings as I have always understood them.

By the third night I'd begun to fathom the system. First of all, I was eating in the wrong dining room. There was a small, less frequented food hall over the other side of the Cosmos. When my photographer and I found our way there, things improved dramatically. Meals of three distinct courses, edible if not exotic, arrived and were consumed. There was a drink, there was laughter and good humour, there was a bill.

The roubles required for this modest repast, at the official rate, made a blow-out at Bilson's look like a bargain. But a series of stumbling semaphores on the part of our waiter, ranging from rolling eyes, to very wet 'pssssst' spurts, to a strenuous kick to my shin beneath the tablecloth, led me to the unmistakeable impression that roubles were not the desired currency in this particular culinary establishment.

'You pay in dollars?' he beseeched, in a whisper as soft as sandstone. To my query as to the number, he raised two fingers. 'Two hundred dollars!' I spluttered. He looked at me as if I were an inept KGB operative sent to ensnare him before concluding that I was a garden variety imbecile and wearily explaining 'No, two dollars'. 'Each?' I thought he would weep. 'No, for both.'

I know a bargain when I'm offered one, even if it does take a moment or two for the finer details to filter down. Armed with pure understanding, I reached for my billfold and began peeling off greenbacks, depositing them with a flourish upon the table. The sudden death of his mother could not have occasioned more honest grief. His complexion paled, his hands shook, his eyes darted about in frenzied reconnaissance activity. 'No, under the plate!' he squeaked, when he had recovered his composure. 'Oh yeah, sorry.'

Paying the waiter discretely was one thing, running the gauntlet of the cashier's desk was another. Or so I feared. In fact, the process turned out to have a certain rhythm to it. As we stood to leave, the cashier suddenly developed a bout of coughing and had to disappear behind a curtain until we had passed her possie. (No prizes for guessing where one of the two one-dollar bills ended up.) To be honest, until we actually left the dining room, I was convinced that the whole piece of crude theatre had been a ploy to extract a tip. I still expected to pay the bill. I would have, if anybody had been prepared to accept my roubles.

Up in the rooms of the vast Cosmos Hotel, the system was a little more subtle. Pleasant women staffed each floor, logging the comings and goings of all guests and attending to the security of the rooms. A pack of Marlboro each day, or even a block of western chocolate, was a sound investment. It was really no different to tipping an American bellboy for the spine-shattering task of carrying your hold-all from the elevator to your room. These knowing ladies kept the peace and ensured that about the only place in the hotel that one didn't have to contend with bedlam was in bed!

# PILES OF FUN IN
# KANAZAWA

I keep promising myself that I'll abandon the obligatory scan of
the Calendar of Events whenever I arrive in an unfamiliar country
or city. It's never been worth the frustration.

I always seem to arrive in town the very day after the annual
Nude Teenage Drum Majorette Memorial March Past. Or I'm
eagerly scanning a river bank six weeks after the Elk's Lodge
Dragon Boat Regatta and Fund Raising Fish Fry, or I'm in position
down by the town square some months after the final embers of
the Pumpkin Harvest Bonfire have been extinguished.

The only time I ever seem to witness a highlight of a distant
port's social and cultural calendar is by accident. I had once been
in Bombay less than an hour, offloaded from a faulty aircraft en
route to another part of the subcontinent altogether, when I found
myself swept along in a loud and colourful train of humanity
toward Chowpatty Beach, where I was almost deposited in the
putrid water along with a garland-draped effigy of the elephant-
trunked Ganesha, the munificent God of Wisdom. By the time I
discovered the reason for the joyful clamour, it had been reduced
to the strangled moans of beggars trampled in the rush.

Given my track record for successfully scheduling arrival and
occasion, I shouldn't have bothered to consult the weighty guide
to the Japanese castle city of Kanazawa when I found myself
approaching its precincts on 21 May. No doubt I would be weeks
or months away from the Fish Cleaning Festival or the ancient
*mushi-okuri* ritual to rid the villages of mosquitos ('farm boys beat
big drums and march with torches through the rice fields').

However, I gave in to habit, consulted away hopefully, and rang up a jackpot that just about sent me off to the nearest Pachinko parlour to try and further my good fortune. There actually was an entry for 21 May; one of only three for the second half of the month. It read: 'The haemorrhoid-curing Buddha is on display at Sanboji in Higashiyama'.

*Oddly, the haemorrhoid-curing Buddha is not on the society's city checklist (Bob King)*

Although I had been hoping for an event that would allow me to partake of complimentary rice cakes and sushi, distributed by beaming and demure samurai-descended geishas slumming it in the local park, I am not a churlish man given to looking a gift Buddha in any of its inflamed anatomical regions. Off, I instructed my driver, to the Sanboji temple. After all, the next display was not scheduled until 21 September, by which time I would no doubt be off missing a Saharan camel race meet by a matter of hours.

Winding through the almost impossibly narrow Kanazawa streets, I consulted *Kanazawa: The Other Side of Japan* by Ruth Stevens, a veritable treasure chest of practical information concerning arcane Nippon practices. 'The temple found itself in business,' she informs, 'during the Edo period when a dying parishioner dedicated himself as a Buddha to help fellow-sufferers of the then untreatable malady. His five-tiered grave, in a corner of the front garden, was visited by an increasing number of people plagued by piles. As their prayers were answered and the word spread, the temple began dispensing medicines and incantations. Today, the priest will chant the sutras and hand out a soothing salve and a packet of red pills made of shredded paper brushed with holy words.'

I mounted the temple steps in reasonable expectation of encountering a shuffling, fidgeting queue before the merciful Buddha. Such, in the land of advanced technological and medical achievement, was not the case. There were but a few aged petitioners, all so removed from apparent discomfort as to appear absolutely beatific. There was to be no casting aside of sticks and offering of fervent thanks to the heavens on this occasion.

The Buddha itself, a jolly little number mounted aloft behind glass and away from the ever-drifting incense smoke, gave no visual indication of its highly specialised powers. Had I not been made aware by the Kanazawa Calendar of Events, I would not have readily attributed any curative capacities to it. Soothing salve was nowhere to be seen. Had I been a sufferer, my disappointment would have been truly unbounded.

As it was, unable to disguise my crestfallen state, I attracted the attention of a priest, who informed me that on days other than 21 May and 21 September other merciful acts were on the agenda. I again consulted Ms Stevens, who advised, 'The altar on the right is crowded with pictures of grateful people cured by Sanboji's other service—a general purpose Buddhist exorcism, in which a mysteriously gifted person takes on the ills of the supplicants. Until she recently became ill herself, the exorcist was a spiritual old woman whose success was legend among local temples.'

That did it. If even the general purpose exorcism was on hold, there was little point in continuing to darken the tiny temple's (rather ornate) doorway. I left Kanazawa promptly the next morning. A guidebook for a nearby town promised a memorial service at a university hospital for the souls of rabbits, mice and dogs used in their experiments. It only appeared on the Calendar of Events once for the year, so it would have been a terrible shame to pass it up. I've never quite got over missing those Nude Teenage Drum Majorettes.

# PONDERING THE PLAYPEN

Perhaps it was because I don't often avail myself of bus services that I was the only passenger who seemed to find it amusing. There above the driver on bus eight from Waikiki to the Ala Moana shopping centre was the stern, stencilled warning: 'Federal law prohibits operation of this bus while anyone is standing forward of the standee line'.

In any other circumstance I would have nominated the Standee Line as something John Wayne once protected from marauding Mexicans or Indians. But I had, the night before, been asked to 'deplane' by a flight attendant on an American aircraft and that very morning a CNN newsreader had earnestly announced that some exclusive visual material from one of the world's flashpoints had come into the network's possession and she would be 'efforting to bring that to you by eleven o'clock'.

Now, I don't know about you, but when I am on American soil, I often find myself actively efforting to cling to familiar parameters of sanity. Katherine Hepburn once observed that being an actress was akin to spending your whole life in kindergarten. I would have thought that just being born American was sufficient. When you own all the toys, the playpen is yours.

I was in Hawaii to relax on the golden sands, suck a pineapple and admire the fabled sunsets. Well that was the idea, if not the eventuality. Unfortunately, the amateur anthropologist lurking within seized the upper hand.

Admittedly, Honolulu is not the optimum city by which to judge a civilisation; its garish assault can almost make one pine for the demure charms of Surfers Paradise. But extremism is nigh on a virtue in a nation which seems to draw much of its spiritual enlightenment (to say nothing of a blueprint for behaviour) from an endless stream of 'action' movies which worship at the altar of two mighty cinematic gods—the car chase and the firearm.

*Terminator 2* was showing around the clock to full houses at a Waikiki cinema across from my hotel. Down on the beach, where topless bathing is unthinkable but the 'buttfloss' bikini is not, a hundred tanned arms held Stephen King novels aloft. The All Elvis Shop, Bionic Burgers, Orson's Chowderette and a pistol-shooting gallery tucked away behind a large stars 'n' stripes all seemed to be full of gormless youths maintaining the rage of the Gulf War via t-shirts emblazoned with slogans ranging from the stern 'Do What Must Be Done!' to the rather more strident 'Fuck Iraq'.

I sought refuge in the sanctuary which ne'er faileth—a bookshop; although the comfort there derived was decidedly minimal. I really do find American bookstores depressing. Instead of the familiar racks of Picadors and rows of Penguins, one confronts layers of supermarket-style stacks in ascending height. The first layer is comprised of thick historical novels, easily discernible by their raised, gold-embossed, script-lettered titles and airbrushed depictions of a supple, sweating, black slave, naked to the waist, or a frail woman in a bonnet observing a whipping or lynching.

Behind them come the self-improvement tomes that Americans devour with unquenchable appetite. Sturdy journals with titles along the lines of *Understanding the Profit Potential of Your Dreams, Mastering Migraines, Close That Deal Right, Learn to Legislate, The Pre-Nuptial Contract Manual,* and *Winners' Diets.* All of which begs the inevitable question—if Americans are so obsessed with self-improvement, why do they remain the most infuriatingly insular people on earth? It doesn't bother me that they have a World Series in baseball in which there are only two countries participating, and I've become accustomed to the regular sincere question about why, being an Australian, I speak such good English, and I can even smile when I'm told that Australia is that little country next to Germany. But it does require a serious show of will to suppress a scream when told, as I once was by a Californian acquaintance to whom I'd announced my impending departure to Sydney: 'Hey, that'll be one helluva drive!'

Plainly, the *Crocodile Dundee* impact has worn off. I'm convinced that what we need is a quick Mouse That Roared conflict with our American friends. Then we can join the slender ranks of nations that all Americans recognise instantly (and which a few can actually identify on a map)—Vietnam, Korea, Iraq, Iran, Grenada, Panama and Japan chief among them. Actually, I think I may have come near to starting one.

I'd resisted the clutches of the Terminator, fled the bookstore and stepped over the standee line at a car rental office. With the alacrity of an adept alien I was soon hurtling across the island of Oahu on a freeway which bisects pineapple plantations and deposits one somewhere near all the places that Jan & Dean sang about, when I was coming to grips with certain aspects of puberty that rendered me unconvinced that a Woodie was an ornate American panel van used to transport surfboards.

It was an expedition that could have been conceived by Gary Larson and filmed by Roger Corman. For there, stalking the freeway and the arterial roads and the beach tracks and everywhere else I ventured, were beasts from the bowels of hell. They call them Bigfoots—lurching four-wheel drive Tonka Trucks come to life, with tyres taller than my rented car, maybe even taller than me. The drivers were whooping and laughing, mostly as they were attempting to drive over me like tanks in the desert. At one point I was sorely tempted to invite them to 'detruck' but I wasn't sure if they could survive our atmosphere. I contented myself with snapping around their ankles and escaping before they could lumber toward me in an enraged (certainly engorged) state.

That these motorised tarantulas can be driven on public roads is a testament to the constitutional right of all Americans to engage in the pursuit of happiness. And all power to them. Like I said, it's their playpen. The unavoidable thought that the toys are becoming as lethal as the popular culture seemed, amid all that fun, so unworthy as to be almost churlish.

# THE WAY OF THE IRISH

If the Republic of Ireland has an emblem it is surely not the shamrock, nor is it a pint glass of Guinness. Its national symbol is the pram. The country is rife with baby carriages, pushed less with pride than with grim determination by young mothers singly, two and three abreast, and sometimes in flotilla formation.

Ireland is perhaps the only white, Western nation still producing children with any real vigour. Not that it has a great deal of choice in the matter. The only vending machines to be found on the walls of pub loos in emerald Eire dispense combs.

Ireland is a church state as surely as North Korea is a police state. The Catholic faith is enshrined in the constitution and the Vatican does a remarkable job of maintaining the faith from afar. You can buy prophylactics and porn within a five-minute walk of the Sistine Chapel, but in Dublin the newsstands are bare of even the vast array of English men's magazines that clutter W.H. Smith stalls. Nothing even slightly titillating is tolerated. Breasts are for suckling, not for display on the covers of glossy periodicals.

I was staying at the Shelbourne Hotel on St Stephen's Green when the Bishop of Galway scandal broke. While the revelation that the powerful cleric had a teenage son living in the United States occasioned a few newspaper paragraphs and some lowly-ranked television news reports in most parts of the world, it occupied the front page and four full pages of the *Irish Times*; more coverage, according to the hotel's bemused commissionaire, than the Gulf War.

I initially mistook the obsessive interest, which continued unabated for a week, as sympathy and concern. In fact, it was an

11

opposite emotion. The story of the Bishop's peccadillo broke soon after the furore which arose when a London-bound aircraft was turned around mid-flight to prevent a young woman from obtaining an abortion in the UK. It was seized upon by many with a mixture of scorn and contempt as a justification for the extraordinary malaise of cynicism which seems so much a part of contemporary Irish life.

There is more irritating petty theft in Dublin than in any other European city. A visitor is constantly advised, by posted signs, publicans, new friends and complete strangers, to firmly anchor purses, handbags and cameras. There is at least one hired, uniformed security guard in every downtown Dublin shop; not just in jewellers and hi-fi houses but in small shops selling donuts, jeans or cards. 'We do it,' said a young woman in the grounds of Trinity College, set aback for a moment by the naivety of my question, 'because we're all so bloody cynical. We do it because those who control our lives do much worse, because it's all we can do.'

Not all. Adolescence is a critical time in Irish life; a time when an almost traditional choice is faced; to leave for London or America or the other distant shores upon which the Irish have washed up for centuries, or to stay and grow old in mute acceptance of a life that is warm, enveloping and enriching on one hand and narrow, stifling and often impoverished on the other.

Ireland's best are skimmed off like cream each year. More than two million have emigrated since 1900—more than half its present population. A garrulous bus driver told me about his economics course at Dublin University. Of the 26 graduating students, 23 were poached by the one Californian corporation and exported like horses to a stud. 'They knew which ones to leave behind,' he observed with forced humour, slapping his steering wheel.

But what else, pray tell, does Ireland have, after its culture and its people? It has been accused of being a Third World country masquerading as a First World nation and as harsh as the judgement may be, there is no escaping the sum total of the oft-mentioned 'fifteen centuries of faith and poetry and eight centuries of strife'. The Irish have a per-capita income less than half that of France and their country is one of the least industrialised in Europe. When you cross over into Northern Ireland—admittedly flush with British funds—the contrast in the quality and maintenance of everything from roads to houses is striking.

Of course, if you want freeways and flash cars you can go to

Germany. If Ireland's present is bleak, its past is sufficiently intriguing to draw and satisfy two million tourists a year. It is not true, as an over-zealous publicity campaign once boasted, that every Dublin cab driver can recite great slabs of Joyce. But every one of them can take you to the pubs, unchanged beyond a few new advertising posters, where he sat in the corner and drank, arm-wrestled, railed, observed and brought Bloom to life.

The spirit which imbued Joyce, Wilde, Beckett, Yeats, Swift and Shaw is not domiciled in libraries; it pervades the very character of the thousand-year-old Dublin and its people. Nowhere else on earth is there such an acceptance of literature as a part of the very fabric of life. On a Literary Pub Crawl I accompanied a moon-lighting actor as he stood before ancient bars, statues, the pre-served doorways of Georgian houses, and colleges, loudly and unselfconsciously singing and intoning glorious verses of rebel-lion, romance, drunkenness and humour. There is no better way to be introduced to this city of illustrious ghosts, shabby and elegant in equal proportion.

Vincent Caprani, the author of books on Dublin lore and rem-iniscences, has written of a time, two hundred years ago, when 'Dublin Ballads! One a penny. Latest songs, penny each!' was yelled on the same streets. 'Ballads, broadsheets and doggerel were crudely printed on single sheets of cheap paper and hawked about by ragamuffin vendors who, as often as not, recited a stanza or two of the current "hit" as enticement to the purchaser. Many of the ballads and rec-im-itations—with an insouciant disregard for metre and the laws of libel—commented on topical matters; sporting and social events, public affairs, courtship, politics and murder trials. Very little escaped the pen of the old ballad makers.'

Such is the Irish affection for well-crafted words that there is even room for the acceptance of worthy outsiders. In two weeks around Dublin and rural Ireland the words I heard most often had been penned, to the accompaniment of music, by a Scotsman living in Australia. The songs of Eric Bogle—particularly *And The Band Played Waltzing Matilda, The Green Fields of France, Leaving Nancy* and *Now I'm Easy*—have touched a nerve with a people not unfamiliar with expressed notions of justice, regret, tragedy, acceptance, isolation, poverty and family ties.

There *is* a basis for Irish jokes. The Irish are by no means stupid but they are surprisingly innocent and untouched, and they do exercise a parallel logic as confounding as it is endearing. I saw

13

a courteous sign at Dublin Airport, greeting arriving passengers, which instructed: 'Persons not familiar with escalators please use nearby lifts & stairs'. I'm not sure if it was meant to be an Irish joke. Nobody but me laughed. Just as I would laugh in a small gift shop in Sligo when I enquired on behalf of my children if there might be a toy leprechaun available and felt a soft tap on my right shoulder. A small, old and wizened Irishman with threadbare clothes and a tiny hat sitting askew had materialised by my side and with (I swear) twinkling eyes announced cheekily, 'A leprechaun sir, at your service'. He lived, I was informed, under a mushroom a few miles from town.

There are persistent, slightly intimidating and oddly disturbing child beggars living on the streets of Dublin and other Irish cities, and there are towns inhabited by true 'Bog Irish' folk—freckled, red-haired, big-boned, hunched and shuffling men with cold stares, or girls with spindly, chalky-white, shapeless legs and vacant expressions. There are places that seem a century, rather than one air hour away, from modern London, where progress has been tolerated rather than welcomed. There are peat bogs and stiles and decaying stone cottages; ingrained hatreds and beguiling hospitality; and more human history than you can digest in a lifetime. All within an island of such physical beauty that it can scarce be described. There is no green as intense as the green of Ireland's surface nurtured by a mild, humid and ever changing climate and largely left untainted by those who tend it.

The Irish are generally content to let well enough alone. The traditions that are worth preserving flourish effortlessly. Particularly those that involve a high emotional content and can be accomplished with the accompaniment of alcohol. To understand how deep this consciousness runs, it is necessary to visit an Irish pub, party, wake or any other excuse for a social gathering. All it takes is a few casual notes on a tiny tin whistle. Then, before you realise it has happened, somebody has lifted a fiddle to his chin, another is ferreting behind the bar for his accordion or his Uileann pipes, while yet another picks up the beat on his goatskin bodhran. Within minutes the room is awash with the pure surging joy of natural, unfettered and unpretentious music. Song titles are shouted, whoops of recognition hit the ceiling and the gathering is united in the gutsy singing of age-old words. It is an exhilarating, sometimes exhausting experience that can be repeated night after night throughout the entire isle in a thousand locations. It is the way of the Irish.

At O'Donoghue's Pub in Dublin, just along from St Stephen's Green, the proprietor stands on the bar to hand over Guinness pints and snatch crumpled banknotes. This sodden wooden pen, the size of a Shelbourne guest room, is where The Dubliners—whose sketched faces adorn one wall—began their international rise. Most nights there are about ten musicians sitting around a small table near the doorway, chatting amiably or musing on personal matters. Their renderings rely on a degree of osmosis. From the midst of conversation a lone voice will arise, imparting a moving lament or air. Some of the other musicians may pick up the melody or, as often as not, will give the singer his space. Five minutes later, it may be a jig or a reel that is causing the pub's glasses to shake.

The essence is that it is not a performance as such. Musicians have no 'set list' and nothing specific is expected of them. What they give forth is an expression as natural as conversation, as free-flowing as the Guinness that is trucked in from the St James Gate Brewery down by the River Liffey. And as a language it is, at least as far as age is concerned, universal. The violinist may be eighteen, the piper eighty-eight. Sons play with fathers and even with grandfathers, working over tunes they all first heard when the men of music met in their homes and chronicled the joys and despairs of Irish life, simultaneously tickling the funnybone and pulling at the heartstrings.

Not all of Ireland's musical focus is on the traditional. A ten-minute walk away from O'Donoghue's is the Windmill Lane Studio owned by the rock group U2. There, the walls of an entire street have been covered in intricate graffiti by fans on pilgrimages from a score of countries. It is no accident that the rock group perhaps most capable of commanding a following of intense loyalty, understanding and commitment in the world today, is Irish.

The world's lines of distinction are smudging. Not only are Western cities beginning to look very much alike, you can be in Singapore and not know you are in Asia. But Dublin remains as Irish as Joyce's often impenetrable prose, or busty Molly Malone's barrow. Nothing is ever so modern that it can obscure the reality of Irish life. Not even an ultra-hip FM rock radio station which, in between U2 and Guns'n'Roses tracks, inserted a revved-up advertisement for a millinery shop offering unbeatable prices on confirmation and christening dresses. All those pram passengers eventually have to grow up.

# 'NAM NOW

*When I journeyed to Vietnam in July 1990 it was very much a case of good timing. The emerging country was serviced by just two international airlines and foreign writers were very thin on the ground. Within just a year, another half-dozen carriers had landing rights and it seemed as if everyone who ever held a pen was Vietnam-bound.*

The first place I asked to be taken was the American embassy, a building as deeply television-etched into the psyche of my generation as the Dakota apartments in New York. Night after night, during the tense days leading up to the 1975 Fall of Saigon, the world's attention was dominated by the graphic images of thousands of fearful South Vietnamese clamouring for access to the embassy compound and, ultimately, the helicopters embarking from the roof. Ten deep, they surged at the steel gates, some attempting to distract the attention of guards while their friends scaled the wall; those less wily reduced to just weeping and pleading.

The embassy is still there, intact. So too are the walls and the steel gates. You can walk right up to them, the mad clamour of a decade and a half ago as loud in your ears as you wish it to be. You can even shake the gates that separated desperate people from the escape they believed they'd been promised. But don't shake them too hard. These days, entire Vietnamese families sleep in single hammocks strung between the steel railings.

Up the road a piece is the Presidential Palace, where the late Neil Davis secreted himself behind a tree and photographed the crushing of the front gates by a Vietcong tank. No families slumber on or near these gates; even the Amerasian children who conducted a poignant silent vigil in the park across the way for many years have been moved on.

In the centre of Ho Chi Minh City young boys play soccer in the streets, not idle ball kicking but serious tournaments, with parked cars as goal posts and play which frantically bursts across intersections clogged with bicycles and pedestrians. Their shouts reverberate down lanes and side streets which, two decades ago, housed bars, brothels and sexual freak shows in numbers sufficient to render today's Bangkok a convent by comparison.

The carnal history of their appropriate playing field means nothing to the young footballers, born long after salacious Saigon became socialist Ho Chi Minh City, and the pimps turned their premises overnight into quiet restaurants and religious icon shops. Certainly, the kids know of the war the Americans waged in their country—25 million bomb craters are hard to ignore—but the battle tales their parents relate are drawn from literally hundreds of years of war and myriad enemies, including the French, Japanese, Chinese and Khmers.

For all their openness, hospitality and almost childlike eagerness to be accepted into the world community, the Vietnamese are, unmistakeably, a warrior people, with a core of iron. There is no shy lowering of eyes or looking away when you fix your gaze upon them. Eye meets eye, not so much in defiance as in honest curiosity. Having driven out every invader who attempted to subjugate them, the lean, resourceful and genuinely kind Vietnamese are not about to start displaying any undue obeisance.

That they are a people apart, even from other Asians, is immediately apparent. The American-imposed total trade embargo which followed the 1975 Fall of Saigon effectively isolated the 67 million people from others like them. While Singapore, Indonesia, Thailand, Japan, the Philippines and Hong Kong are, in many ways, as 'western' as Los Angeles, Vietnam has yet to be submerged in garish neon, fast food, corporate logo t-shirts, rock 'n' roll cassettes, violent Hollywood films, slavish fashionwear and mass-produced consumer goods nobody really needed in the first place. Life is much more basic than that—millions of bicycles, markets abundant in natural produce, fields frantic with the activity of farmers and their ducks, strikingly elegant women with a predilection for brightly-coloured hats and bonnets, and multitudes of buoyantly optimistic children.

Those who come expecting images struck by writers Michael

Herr and Tim O'Brien or film directors Francis Ford Coppola and Oliver Stone are destined for disappointment. All that left with the last chopper from the embassy roof. The western influence that does permeate Vietnamese life is the type that Singapore, for one, has assiduously eradicated since World War II. Tropical Saigon and, particularly, four-seasonal Hanoi remain redolent of the twilight of colonialism. The ambience is a mixture of aged European grace and the exotic east, like pages of Greene or Maugham come to life. In Hanoi, a city of languid green lakes with purple pagodas, cluttered trading alleys, elegant though tarnished French villas and rusted trundling tramcars, tall leafy trees flank wide, uncrowded boulevards, while government buildings, all in shades of muted yellow, sit amid cool green precincts.

In Saigon, the French colonial architecture, so perfectly exemplified by Notre Dame Cathedral and most of the old hotels (notably the venerable Hotel Continental) sited around the shaded plazas, offers a sort of tropical baroque so soothing to the eye that one is in danger of being skittled by a bicycle while gazing upon it. No misguided conception of progress, so far, has torn down or built over this exquisite charm. Indeed, there is no progress to speak of. They even seem to have run out of yellow paint.

Which is why the Socialist Republic of Vietnam now has a serious program for foreign investment and a promising five-year-old tourism industry—all under the banner of *doi moi*, 'renovation'. The Soviet Union's decision to cease, from the beginning of 1990, its $3 million a day subsidisation of this far-flung and frankly superfluous member of the Eastern Bloc, left Vietnam with little choice but to move into the capitalist orbit; for all the misgivings of a few hardliners who have yet to concede that communism has become a meaningless ideology. No longer interested in the meagre rouble wads of Aeroflot loads of loyal Siberian factory workers sent on Indo-Chinese holidays as a reward for improved quota performance, Vietnam now wants dollars, deutschmarks, yen, lira, pounds and francs in vast and constant quantities.

What it offers in return is an emotionally rewarding 'adventure' destination—a country bearing many of the scars but little of the bitterness of a protracted war. Although the Vietnamese will patiently indulge visitors who wish to dwell upon the past, they choose not to themselves. Since 1975, survival and rebirth has been the Vietnamese lot. The daunting task of environmental

*Proud emblem of war surviving in Hanoi (Bob King)*

rehabilitation, in a country which lost 2.2 million hectares of forest and a full fifth of its farmland to bombing, and which was sprayed with 72 million litres of herbicide, has been tackled as a national imperative. In 1985 and 1986 alone, students planted 52 million trees and built more than 800 000 hectares of tree nurseries. At Ma Da in Dong Hai province, the Vietnamese have become the only people to successfully replant a tropical forest. As General Vo Nguyen Giap, once commander-in-chief of the North Vietnamese Army, and now drafter of the National Conservation Strategy, expresses it: 'The soldier now comes to another front, the environmental front.'

The once great Giap is not the only old soldier helping lead his country to recovery. The government's tourism operations are largely staffed by former Vietcong officers, guides of quite impeccable experience able to come up with the most astonishing inside aspects. Who better to crawl with through a Vietcong tunnel complex  than a man who once lived beneath the ground like a hunted rat? Who better to sail the Perfumed River with and view the crumbled walls of Hue's Forbidden City than a man who possibly let loose the mortar bombardment on the Imperial Citadel? Compliment your driver on his skills and he may well tell

19

you, as mine did, that he gained them on the Ho Chi Minh Trail and the roads into Laos.

One particularly beguiling guide, a 35-year-old mother of two, related dispassionately to me how she grew up on the seventeenth parallel and lived in a forest for ten years, hiding in a small hut or down tunnels while the daily torrent of bombs fell. It was she who first made me aware of the absence of recrimination or anger; an absence evident in the almost incredulous testimonials written by American veterans in the visitor's book of Ho Chi Minh's Tomb in Hanoi. Warned off by their own government, they are arriving in increasing numbers, slipping in sheepishly and departing confidently, with more than a few personal demons put to rest. 'They can't get enough of Americans,' recently observed writer Joseph R. Yogerst. 'It's the only place I've been to in recent years where the people flash a smile and their eyes sparkle the second you tell them you're a Yankee.'

At Ha Long Bay near the Chinese border, Vietnam's answer to the Grand Canyon or Cappadocia, I sailed in and out of the hundreds of prehistoric, bizarrely-sculptured pinnacle mountains jutting out of the sea while a pert young thing told me, 'Two years ago we were not able to talk and be friendly with visitors from capitalist countries, and when we got off the boat we had to tell our director everything they spoke about. Now we can be friendly with everybody and nobody cares what they say. That is better, I think.'

So much better and so much more comfortable for all concerned now that the barriers to a free exchange have been effectively broken down. Some 22 000 visitors came in 1987; 210 000 arrived in 1989; a million are expected by the year 2000. They come for magnificent Ha Long Bay, for the long stretches of white sand beaches near Danang ('China Beach'), for the unexpected tranquil beauty of Hanoi, for the textured, slightly rebellious Saigon, for the rich diversity of Vietnamese food with its French overtones (right down to breads and pastries), for the infectious, knowing laugh of Saigon's 'reformed' bar girls, for the sheer thrill of flying into Tan Son Nhut airport—once the busiest in the world, for the drive through the high Pass of Clouds on Highway One, for the sumptuous seafood spreads in the waterfront restaurants of Vung Tau, for the 'wheel of death' acrobatic circus erected in some dusty field, for the chance to sit on the balcony of the Huong Giang Hotel in ancient Hue at sunrise and watch the mist over the Perfumed River and to walk in the central highlands and spot the forest ox, douc langur monkey, tigers, Java rhinos and elephants, and for the real privilege of catching the guileless smiles of a people who are only interested in the future.

A future looking rosier every day. Vietnam's exports to noncommunist countries in 1989 doubled in value to almost one billion dollars, eclipsing, for the first time, trade with traditional communist allies. The same year, a bumper grain harvest of 21 million tonnes made Vietnam a significant grain exporter for the first time. Each night, in the bar of the Saigon Floating Hotel, the five star, Australian–run oasis of comfort which has probably done more to open Vietnam up to western tourism than any government endeavour, fast-talking Thai, Malaysian, Taiwanese, Australian, Singaporean and Hong Kong entrepreneurs rub shoulders with Italian delegations who have dropped by to announce $100 million low-interest loans, or low-key Americans risking Uncle Sam's wrath (it is still a treasonable offence under the Enemies Act for a US company to do business in Vietnam) to undertake scouting missions in reasonable expectation of a big thaw. Like the Shanghai and Leningrad of old, Saigon is a window on the world and just being there is exciting.

Apart from the Saigon Floating Hotel, accommodations in Vietnam are still relatively spartan. The mattresses are hard and the air-conditioners rattle. The internal carrier, Air Vietnam, flies only in the early morning and has been known to start taxiing while passengers are still finding their seats. Yet there is no real element of discomfort or danger and one's passage through the country—all of which is open to visitors—is no more daunting than through a dozen 'western' nations I've visited. The eagerness to improve is so intense that by mid-decade the current impediments could well be a distant memory.

'This is a beautiful, tropical country with incredible God-given gifts and very enterprising people,' enthuses Saigon Floating Hotel manager, Patrick Imbardelli, an Australian who has sensed the promise of a former battlefield which has buried its dead, dusted off its charms and opened its doors. Like its oft-eulogised Tiger Ladies, those seemingly fragile, willowy women who control their lovers, husbands and families, Vietnam has the cunning to survive during the bad times and flourish during the good.

# A JOURNEY THROUGH A WORLD IN CHANGE

*This observation of a crumbling USSR and a breached Berlin Wall came out of a January 1990 visit. Although it was written briskly upon my return, the frantic pace of change in Germany rendered the second half redundant before I could place it for publication. The first (Russian) half appeared in the* Australian Magazine *that year, while the remainder is published here intact for the first time. It certainly does not represent the Germany of today but it does capture, for me at least, a brief, tumultuous and momentous snatch of contemporary history. I consider myself fortunate to have been there as the Eastern Bloc was unravelling.*

Tchaikovsky drank some bad water and died of cholera in a house not far from my Leningrad hotel. Not while I was in residence, mind you; though the decor can't have changed much since his demise. My plumbing seemed safe enough but I was definitely worried about the soap. I had initially mistaken the suspicious, brittle, brown pellet for a doorstop. When it proved to have the lather potential of English toffee, it was so employed.

The comfortable Hotel Baltiskaya is on the seedy end of Nevsky Prospekt—Leningrad's Champs Elysees, *sans* the shops and the lights. Handy to the street moneychangers and fur hat traders, it seemed to have more guests clogging the stairs than there were rooms to accommodate them. It eventually came to my attention that most of them were going into one room, a small function hall with a couple of television monitors at one end beaming an endless loop of soft porn videos, such as *Emmanuelle*. 'This would have been unthinkable just a few months ago,' explained an almost embarrassed manageress, 'but now, I think anything is possible.'

Almost anything is. Clearly, things had changed since my first Russian sojourn, ten months earlier. Then, transactions were agonisingly slow, the quality of consumer goods appallingly poor, and the shortage of basic commodities simply scandalous. It was all part of the grey, stubbornly resilient fabric of Soviet life. This time around, nothing had actually been improved but the cloth was fraying at every edge.

The confusion is palpable. Soviet citizens are accustomed to knowing what is right, what is wrong, what is permissible, what is forbidden. But since *glasnost* and *perestroika*, the lines have become so blurred as to be useless. Each day, the edge of the envelope is stretched in a thousand tiny ways, by protesters, rock musicians, writers, would-be entrepreneurs, indeed almost the entire spectrum of society; all with one eye over the left shoulder waiting for the axe to fall. When it doesn't, they move forward another small step, emboldened and adrenalised by their small victories.

At the Hermitage Museum, the security guards are hesitant to enforce the long-standing no photography rule, just in case it doesn't exist anymore. Police shrug and walk away from a thick crowd of curious men gathered around a tobacco kiosk displaying a series of small colour reproductions of *Playboy* centrefolds. At a street demonstration, state security men choose to avert their eyes from placards declaring, '73 Years on a Road to Nowhere,' a sentiment too universal to be challenged.

To test the mood I stood in a snowdrift at Pushkin, outside Catherine the Great's obscenely opulent summer palace, and asked a conservative, middle-aged Russian if communism was dead. He bit his lower lip for thirty seconds, mustering sufficient personal courage to say, 'Yes, I think it is.' The young are usually not quite so hesitant. While we watch the socialist states fall like the dominoes they were once meant to be insidiously tumbling in Southeast Asia, and bite our own lips at the breathtaking pace of reform, impatient comrades decry the crab crawl of meaningful change to their standard of living.

They know, my but they know, how the rest of the world has deified their brave leader. But while Mikhail Gorbachev may be a saint bar the canonisation abroad, at home he enjoys guarded admiration at best. His own people will start chanting 'Gorby, Gorby' when their roubles will buy something worth having. Or when they can actually spend them in their own country. Real anger is mounting over the proliferation of outlets which accept only 'hard' (foreign) currency. Not just the tourist-slanted Berioska shops with their supplies of Pepsi, Marlboro, Sony Walkmans, rock cassettes and assorted sweets and nibblies, but the fancy restaurants and boutiques with their sneering doormen.

Instant mobs are lately to be found outside the doorways from which the privileged can be seen emerging laden down with bags of booty. The thick glass door of the ritzy Rifle jean shop near Moscow's Red Square, where the prime exchange rates for a dozen currencies are digitally displayed beside a caged cashier's office manned by the runners-up from the last Miss USSR quest, is marred by a splintered web, spreading out from a hole about the size of a large rock.

It is a mistake to presume a compliant nature on the part of the Russian people. They have a strong sense of justice and an even stronger determination to reorder their own society without necessarily tumbling headlong into a capitalist embrace. They have an innate dignity, an endearing curiosity and a surprisingly good natured humour. Moving among them is a warm and often entertaining experience. Certainly it was when I marched along a railway platform at midnight with a porter and a university student, the three of us loudly singing Beatles classics with all the gusto of football fans on a winner's rampage.

I had arrived in Leningrad at the Finland Station. So did Lenin, in 1917, when it was known as Petrograd. He was delivered to the 'Venice of the North' in a sealed German railway carriage, keen to ferment revolution. I made do with a twin-berth sleeping compartment in my keenness to observe another revolution. Seven years after Lenin's arrival, the city was named in his honour. I fear I shall have to wait rather longer for my statue to be erected in Bakergrad.

I wasn't the first venturer to ease myself into Soviet life through Leningrad, the city to which change has come most naturally. This is the late twentieth-century equivalent to prewar Shanghai—a trading port on the rump of a vast, secretive nation quietly open to the evil influence of foreign devils. In its glory days as St Petersburg it was one of Europe's finest and most exciting cities. At some point in the future, it may again assume such importance. If attitude counts for anything, it's almost there.

I attempted to absorb the artistic ambience of Leningrad over three nights. The first was spent at a rather perfunctory performance of the Kirov Ballet on Theatre Square, which was over and done with in a mere ninety minutes. I think I saw the reserves; the first eleven were probably touring Australia. At the Leningrad Jazz Club on Zagorodny Prospekt (the sole such establishment in the USSR) the following night, I caught old 'soundie' films of Billie Holiday, Duke Ellington and Louis Armstrong on a suspended television monitor and a supperless supper show by an energetic trad outfit with a plump, almost vivacious sweetie labouring phonetically through *My Melancholy Baby, Sweet Georgia Brown* and *Summertime*. The owner, Roman Kopp, was such a dead ringer for Lenin that I almost broke out into a nervous sweat when the bandleader declared from stage that he was playing (as roughly translated to me) 'music to make us feel good because our life is so unpleasant'.

The culmination of my micro-excursion into Soviet cultural life was a rock concert at the Gaza Palace of Culture near the Kirov works plant. Having missed the first 35 years of rock's evolution, young Soviets appear to have made a conscious decision not to bother with what they may have missed, but to instead rush headlong toward the precipice of what is about to unfold. Their acrid, unsettling music erupts from a churning cauldron of frustration and bitter anger. It challenges, it accuses and, occasionally, it entertains. One rabid band, Red Spider, uses two buxom strippers. I sat through the earnest howlings of two amateur outfits, Clips and Catshouse, before pushing my way through a wall of denim jackets emblazened with Sex Pistols' logos (a sole concession to nostalgia) to the relative calm of a frozen Leningrad night.

Later that evening, I came down from Leningrad to Moscow on one of seventeen sleeper trains departing before midnight (so as to allow the good public servants on board to claim two days' travelling allowance from the state); the ticket price for which graphically highlights the morass that is the Soviet economy. Booked with Intourist in Australia, they cost around $230. Picked up at the rail station with currency exchanged at the same 'official' rate American Express uses to bill Soviet purchases back to you, they cost around $30. Bought with roubles traded on the street, where the exchange rate is up to 24 times the 'official' level, they will set you back around $2.

Try another example. A full three-course meal for four, of spicy Georgian food with drinks, at an upmarket Leningrad rouble restaurant, came in at around $3, all up. A few days later, a table of assorted cold meat and fish entrees at a Moscow cooperative, hard-currency restaurant occasioned a credit card bill for a party of visiting Australian businessmen of around $600. No rhyme, no reason.

Cooperative is merely a coy way of saying private enterprise. Cooperatives operate outside the all-enveloping state system. Restaurateurs have to go down to the markets and pay the same prices as housewives for their ingredients. Officially disdained, they have nonetheless become a vital force in the Soviet economy, with over 750 000 members nationally.

This year, coops are expected to contribute up to twelve billion roubles to the state. They will also contribute greatly to the growth of organised crime, as a consequence of the burgeoning protection industry which has grown up around them.

As leading criminologist Gennadi Khokhryakov sees it: 'The new threat is that the coop movement could go the same way as the shadow economy during the stagnation era; under covert criminal control. Organised crime is much older than the coops and the police are laughably ill-equipped and under-trained for the battle. The gangs can rest assured in the knowledge that patrol cars' daily petrol allowance will barely go 60 miles in a chase!'

Crime? I asked myself facetiously. In the workers' paradise? Verily yea! One of the most commonly-employed cold war deceits was the righteous finger-pointing by the Soviets at the decadent west. Yes, of course America and its running dog vassal states were awash with consumer goods, but they were also diseased by rampant crime; while the well-ordered socialist world was safe and quietly productive. It was, of course, a monumental lie on both counts.

The Soviet Union may not have many consumer goods but it sure as hell has crime—organised, disorganised, underground and above ground. In 1988 there were 16 710 premeditated murders in the Soviet Union, a country where there is no right whatsoever to bear arms. A Soviet citizen has, officially, a four to five times higher chance of dying a violent death than a citizen of Japan, Britain or France. And just as staggering is the suicide rate. Around 25 to 30 occur in Moscow each week. In 1984, the national total was 81 417, amounting to 30 per 100 000 of population. The US level in the 1980s did not rise above twelve, in the UK not above ten. This is a dangerous place to live.

We were not the only ones deceived by the masterful manipulation of reality on the part of propagandists. 'The discovery that organised crime is widespread in Soviet society caught us psychologically unaware, fumbling even for words to describe it,' admits criminologist Khokhryakov. 'Moral attitudes have reversed somehow. Profiteers and extortionists are quite often looked upon as benefactors and the ones who fight them as the villains. Criminals have stopped thinking of themselves as social outcasts. A poll among senior school students even revealed that one in five wanted to be a professional criminal.'

Such a revelation seriously saddens me; for as much as I have come to believe that young Russian women are the most beautiful in the world, I have concluded that Russian children are the most enchanting. Sting, the rock star, once wondered aloud in a popular song if 'the Russians love their children too'. Plainly he had never visited Moscow and certainly had not seen a popular television show featuring row upon row of Soviet children in a choral cavalcade of extraordinary vigour and charm. Uncommonly handsome, with a radiance that stopped everyone in the room, these obviously well-loved ankle-biters would have reduced Ivan the Terrible to mush.

However, there are exceptions. Outside Moscow's National Hotel, where a tourist can swap a pack of Marlboro through a car window for a large jar of black caviar, I was assaulted, and I mean it in the literal sense, by a girl less than two years of age. This determined gypsy beggar child, ceaselessly chanting 'rouble, rouble'—doubtless the entire extent of her infant vocabulary— proceeded to wrap herself around my leg in the manner of a spider monkey in a Balinese field temple. Fearful of causing this demented babe injury, I pressed some coins upon her and carefully unwrapped her limbs. Two paces later she had adhered herself to the same leg with even greater determination and volume. Eventually, I was forced to run clumsily and dangerously across the icy surface to the nearest door; an ignominious escape to which not even India had ever forced me to resort.

The desperation for roubles amazed me. Who'd bother? The locals will give you so many in exchange for any other currency that you sometimes think they must have mattresses full of the stuff. You can't take them out of the country with you, you can't use them to pay for anything useful, like your hotel room, a small bonfire of them wouldn't even keep you warm. They certainly don't figure in the schemes of all the bright young men who wear lapel badges proclaiming their involvement in a 'Joint Venture'. That's the current Soviet buzz-word. Everyone who's anyone has one going, with the Americans, the Finns, the Brits, the French,

27

the Japanese, the Canadians, or the Germans. Trendier than coops, and more common than potatoes, joint ventures are emblematic of the new Russia. They are also a convenient foot-in-the-door for the likes of McDonald's, who have just opened for business on Pushkin Square, opposite a large Coca Cola neon sign.

The heady mood of reform that descends upon one in the Soviet satellites or even in relatively casual Leningrad can swiftly evaporate in Moscow. Down by the red walls of the Kremlin, where the faithful queue for hours in respectful silence to view the embalmed Lenin, there seems nothing flimsy about the Party's power. Here you watch your step and watch your words even more closely. It may be nine-tenths paranoia but old fears die hard.

So do old rebels, as I walked across Gorky Park to duly investigate. The temperature had just hit –30 degrees centigrade and I was in pain. Nobody else was silly enough to wear shoes; they all skated by me with an air of superiority I frankly did not appreciate. I was calling upon Stas Namin, a former Soviet pop star who had sold twenty million records in his prime. The controversial grandson of a former Politburo member, the 38-year-old impresario, although refused permission to travel abroad for fifteen years, deftly survived anti-rock music purges for two decades to become a powerful symbol to Soviet youth. Now he is able to import western heavy metal acts like Motley Crue and Bon Jovi, and export his own bands, such as Gorky Park, virtually independently of the state apparatus.

Namin considers himself fortunate to have escaped Sakharov-type treatment during the dark years, when 'unauthorised' rock bands could suddenly find themselves on cold trains headed north, faced with a few years of humming pretty much the same tune. Although much is made of the protection afforded him by family connections, he doesn't buy that particular theory. Not in a country where once, as he put it to me, 'politicians who outlived their usefulness were usually taken out and shot'.

The Stas Namin Music Centre boasts a recording studio, rehearsal rooms, cabaret restaurant, an amphitheatre out the back and a Hard Rock Cafe that has nothing at all to do with Peter Morton's international chain. The cafe is a spartan but cosy room which I shared with Annie Lennox and Peter Gabriel on my first visit and Frank Zappa on my second. For it to even exist is a testament to Namin's charismatic power, which is as tangible as his long mane of black hair, tied in a ponytail. It will only be cut, he insists, when communism collapses in the USSR.

He confidently predicts that his long overdue visit to the hairdresser will come to pass in 'two, maybe three years'.

*    *    *

Crossing the border at Checkpoint Charlie was definitely a mistake. I could have talked my way through, down by the Brandenburg Gate at Friedrichstrasse Railway Station. I suppose I wanted a touch of romance. What I ended up with was an hour of frustration.

Checkpoint Charlie is actually a misnomer. The American border station which it denotes checks nobody at all. It's there to shout encouragement when daredevils in low-slung sports cars charge the boom gates, as one lovesick lad did in the early 1960s. The actual process of checking is left to the more austere post on the East Berlin side where the Germans of communist persuasion still look at you as if the entire degeneracy of the free world is your doing.

My host had made the mistake of advising the East German officer that I was a writer intending to engage in that very pursuit as a consequence of my visit. The suspicious soldier demanded to see my permit to write. My host was enraged on my bemused behalf, angrily pointing out that such things, in the new age of pan-German enlightenment, had been consigned to the dustbin of history. And on it went, for the better part of an hour, until I began to wonder if the exercise was worth the trouble.

My first thoughts remained the most cogent: when they chased the rats out of this cage they changed the locks. The inmates have definitely taken over the asylum and, no matter which angle you view it from, it's all over bar the fireworks. If I needed any sign from above to bolster my conviction, it was made manifest in the form of the crane which enabled workmen to remove the large emblem from the Communist Party headquarters on Warderstrasse, on the very afternoon that I was strolling by. It was a profound moment in twentieth-century history and I was the only one watching. It almost made up for my absence on 9 November, when the hated wall began its conversion to swiss cheese.

The wall. The almighty bloody wall. A frontier between two currencies. A nine-inch division between the superpowers. You look for it from your aircraft and you ask your cab driver to go

*A disgraced East German
Communist Party stripped
of its emblem, East Berlin,
January 1990
(David McGonigal)*

by it on the way to your hotel. When you actually touch it you feel like a fully-fledged citizen of the world. It doesn't remotely disappoint. Not even walking across the infamous Glienicker Bridge is as purely exciting as finally laying eyes, hands and chisel on its textured surface.

You can spend a day at the wall and wonder where the hours have gone. For what interest be lunch or ablutions when one of the great human dramas is unfolding before your very gaze? There are lines of forlorn eastern cousins in drab clothes and nasty Bulgarian shoes lining up with their identity cards to pass into a realm where their own marks won't buy them a decent sandwich. There are professional souvenir brokers, oblivious to 'No Chisel' signs, taking to the wall with diamond-tipped industrial drills and making away with enough chunks to satisfy the London boutiques for another day. There are busloads of tourists clambering through large holes in the wall, only to be waved back by guards of strained amiability who would have shot them all dead a half a year ago.

It seems somehow indecent that those emotive televised scenes of surging waves of divided Germans dismantling the hated wall with their bare hands should be overtaken by the almost carnival atmosphere of aggressive enterprise. The Berlin Wall memento business is brisk indeed. Some of the overnight entrepreneurs work all day at ground level with hammer and chisel, while the more determined of their number erect ladders and scaffolding. The best wall pieces are sold from picnic tables and the bonnets of cars to the busloads of tourists who pay up to ten marks ($7) for a chunk. Some inventive merchants cast them in perspex and fit them out as jewellery. Even the roughest chips are instant currency outside of Germany. Offered a choice of a string of pearls or a chunk of Berlin Wall, most people with any sense of history at all will unhesitatingly opt for the masonry.

At a number of popular points, the once-feared edifice is in danger of collapsing through lack of structural support. Berliners on both sides are so intent on seeing the evil construction toppled that every blow struck by a tourist—many of whom rent tools from the clever capitalists on the western side—is considered a contribution to the cause. Even a few of the stern-faced communist border guards are plainly amused by the unofficial but enthusiastic assault by thousands of eager human hands, day and night, week in and week out. An assault that is having an effect—some sections near the Brandenburg Gate have now been replaced by wire fencing.

There is one sobering section of wire which has been in place since the height of the cold war. Sited at the rear of the Reichstag building, parallel to the wall, it bears white crosses marking the deaths of those who failed in their attempts to reach the west. Although few have risked their lives since the liberalisation of border crossing restrictions in the 1970s, hardly a month passed during the 1960s without some dazzlingly daring stunt being hatched by desperate freedom-seekers.

The Checkpoint Charlie Museum bears graphic testament to people's ingenuity and courage. Its irregular rooms and passage-ways display the hot-air balloons, winches and pulleys, cable drums, petrol tanks, false-door panels, tunnelling tools, amateur flying machines, homemade submarines, and reinforced vehicles which were employed in the more spectacular escapes in the years immediately following the partition of Berlin. Perusing the jumbled array of photographic images of bravado and death helps considerably in coming to grips with Berlin's endless paradoxes and perversities.

Berlin cannot fairly be called a crossroads city, for it is not really on the way to anywhere in particular. But it has the same urgency and relentlessly international flavour as Istanbul, Jerusalem, New York and Hong Kong. Psychologically shaped for 28 years by a wall which dissected, surrounded and dominated it, the vast city of Berlin—the largest in Germany—is steeped in tension, decadence and subtle intrigue. Beneath its sleek German prosperity, it is a city of exiles and extremists. One writer described it as 'a dangerous melange of artistry, politics and design extravagancies; red-gashed mouths in smoky nightclubs gaudy and melancholy'.

Berliners tend to carry themselves with a certain aloof disdain for the rest of the world. Indeed, for many, Berlin *is* the world— the centre of the artistic, intellectual and political universe. You can scoff at the idea from the outside but it is very hard to disagree once you allow yourself to be enveloped by the extraordinary ambience of the schizophrenic city by the Spree.

History is omnipresent. Few residents will willingly direct you to the undistinguished mound of dirt that was Hitler's bunker, but everything else is on ready display, from the imposing Reichstag to that indelibly media-etched bridge, where screen spies from Richard Burton to Ian Holm have been exchanged for commie infiltrators. Even the street names evoke atmosphere— Bertolt Brecht Platz, Freudstrasse, Marx-Engels Platz, Jungstrasse, John F. Kennedy Platz, Einsteinstrasse and Kaiserdamm.

Passing through the street checkpoints or using the U-Bahn or S-Bahn trains to enter East Berlin through the busy Friedrichstrasse Station is still akin to Dorothy clicking her red heels and going to Kansas. It is another Berlin, another Germany, another world. You know you have passed from a West Berlin Metro Station to an East Berlin one (via sealed ghost stations which haven't seen a commuter for almost thirty years) by the magazine covers on the platform stalls—they change from full frontal nudes to observations on the writings of Marx and Engels.

It is good for the soul to tear oneself away from the neon glare of West Berlin's heavily thronged Kurfurstendam central thoroughfare, distance oneself from the wan, anorexic teenage junkie prostitutes huddled for warmth under the bridge near the Zoo Station, and enter the East Berlin time machine. Without being as harsh and affronting as Moscow, the old heart of the great metropolis of Berlin is the west of thirty years ago frozen in time. The pace is calmer, the manners more pronounced, the window dressing endearingly twee, the affection for fine arts obvious and the consumer curiosity limitless.

Ian Walker, the author of *Zoo Station: Adventures in East and West Berlin*, once observed that 'journeying east is like retracing your steps. You remember as a child drawing cars like these with curved roofs, bulbous bonnets, enamel radiator grilles like jagged smiles.' It's all rather like a few hours at your great-aunt's; thanks for the tea, the cake and photo album but, my is that the time, we really have to be going! In a word, East Berlin seems innocent.

It also seems very old, and I don't mean the buildings. The greying of Europe is profoundly evident in both Berlins, which are awash with (mostly female) pensioners. And not without good reason. During the devastating years of World War II, the population of Berlin was reduced from 4.3 million to 2.8 million. Jews, once the cultural pacesetters of this vital city, are so thin on the ground that there are only 500 of them remaining in East Berlin, almost all of them aged.

It may well be this ageing factor which accounts for the exceptional radicalism of Berlin's young. There are gravity-defying coiffured creations atop West Berlin punks which would have drawn stares in London in 1976. Fashion is almost a political statement, intertwined as it is with a darkly conscious alternative arts scene. Visual, musical and literary creators from all over the world seem able to conjure up their most disturbing and dynamic works within the confused conflagration of capitalism and communism that is contemporary Berlin.

West Berlin is Germany only to the extent that New York is the United States. It is a city apart which almost celebrates its decadence. It has eaten, drank and made merry under an effective state of siege since Adolph breathed his last, with a mounting standard of living that is now almost absurdly high. If the true measure of a country's wealth is the food hall of its leading department store, Germany has no contenders. In Berlin's giant KaDeVe emporium I counted more than 100 varieties of sausage alone. A glutton would have been daunted.

Michael, a West Berlin librarian, told me of an elderly man from the 'other side' who walked through the store in the days immediately following the opening of the wall. 'He moved slowly, looking carefully at all the goods. Then he went to the main door, turned around and, with a face full of terrible anger, yelled "They've been cheating us for forty years!" Most East Germans still walk through our shops like they are in museums because they just can't afford anything. Their eyes are like glass. It is very sad really.'

The good citizens of the Soviet Union don't have their enormous economic disadvantage constantly rubbed into their faces quite in the manner of the East Germans. Reunification became inevitable long before the wall came down and the party chiefs were disgraced. It was kindled when nightly television images of the bountiful west began to be beamed eastward. Those comrades who managed to chug across the border in their tiny, two-stroke, plastic-bodied, smoke-belching Trabants might well have got the impression that something was amiss when they had to slug it out on the autobahns with the latest from Porsche, BMW and Mercedes.

That the two Berlins started on the same footing is the one inescapable reality in an almost surreal world. That the East Germans managed to lose so much ground in four decades is testimony to the colossal shortcomings of, among other things, Stalinist planning systems. Nobody was better at socialism than the Germans but they still couldn't keep up. Now, for all intents and purposes they have given up. The young are voting with their feet and the old are placidly awaiting change.

Just what kind of a world they will inherit from the upheaval is open for conjecture. For all their disillusionment with communism they, like their Russian cousins, are not exactly rushing headlong into an embrace with capitalism. It was, as I recall, a West Berlin resident who expressed to me an open admiration for the sense of community and lack of blind materialism which exists on the other side of the wall. If this goes, along with the shackles, a deprived people will lose far more than they expect, or deserve.

*Stas Namin's prediction came to pass well ahead of schedule . . . and not without significant contribution on his part. News film of the coup against Gorbachev captures him imparting certain promises of retribution to trembling tank drivers at Moscow barricades; an act which did not go unnoticed by the citizens of the city, who are now inclined to view him as a figure of somewhat more importance than your average rock'n'roll promoter. Apparently, he still has his hair.*

# SOUTH AFRICA
# ON THE LINE

Open apartheid wasn't the only thing that got lost in the shuffle when the South Africans let Nelson Mandela out of prison and set about wooing foreign cricketers, footballers and rock bands. The strict Calvinist morality that had so tightly bound the country for so very long began to unravel. Not quite to the stage where there are Afrikaner television shows equivalent to *Chances*, *Sylvania Waters* and *Sex*, but to the dubious level of moral evolution where *Basic Instinct* is in the cinemas of the cities and on the tongues of the white adult population.

Slightly naughty thrills are the order of the day and the principal beneficiary is the phone company, Telkom. In a country where 93 per cent of the white population is literate but only 32 per cent of the black, telephone instruction is booming. At a hefty tariff of up to six rand ($3) a minute, callers can dial some 11 000 services and secure advice or engage in communication on matters ranging from the terrestrial to the celestial.

Entire newspaper pages are full of garish display ads for the lucrative phone services, the most entertaining being in *The Sowetan*. While Sexwise and the Sex Doctor predictably offer to counsel callers on any matter from celibacy to spectacular satisfaction, other services offer exotic excursions into the unknown. The heavily-advertised Sangoma—pictured as a sort of well-decorated Whoopi Goldberg—claims 'Hear me throw the bones and tell everything about your future—your ancestors guide you with the power of the moon'. Sangoma is able to determine your future in English, Zulu, Sesotho, Xhosa and Venda but don't try to argue the toss with her if you're on a fixed income.

35

If the bones bode well and you want to receive further illumination, you can dial Godfrey Moloi who promises 'Call me and I will tell you why I bought my coffin'; or Brenda, who will reveal 'Why I was accused by Kaizer Ngwenya'; or the Dream Doctor, who wants to know 'Are your spirits unhappy?'; or Phil Kumalo who will tell you 'How to obtain a taxi licence'; or Kansas City who offers 'The truth about the death of my wife'. One enterprising organisation encourages callers to 'Sing on the phone! . . . And you can make a recording', and not only that, 'You will be heard by people in the recording business'.

South Africa is, at least at the moment, fascinating in the way that all unleashed and uncertain countries are. It is also very schizophrenic. International media coverage of the staggering levels of township violence (3500 deaths from black communal clashes in 1990 alone) and of massacres in the 'homelands' create an erroneous impression of a country in flames. Yet there is remarkably little evident friction in Johannesburg, Pretoria, Cape Town or any of the other places which attract foreign visitors. There, blacks and whites eat, drink, travel and work together with roughly the same level of amiability as in New York or London. Even if you arrive with your antennae twitching, ready to smugly pounce on any infraction of civilised behaviour codes, your pointing finger is likely to droop from inactivity.

What is instantly striking are the similarities of South Africans to Australians. Leaving aside the undoubted residual huddle of neo-Nazi whackers who are too busy hatching loony plots to bother encountering tourists, the sunburned and scruffy white masses like to yell at the football, drink beer in pubs, barbecue any available piece of meat, tell bad jokes and watch a lot of television. They even eat meat pies. For all the emphasis on their sandbagged intransigence, most of them never enjoyed being pariahs and, after the delirium of being allowed to participate in the Barcelona Olympics, don't seem inclined for a moment to recircle the wagons. Self-purging is carried on daily in the press, with surprisingly frank and bold revelations of Special Branch and defence force excesses during the 'dark years'.

While the country hasn't exactly thrived in isolation (certainly not culturally), it has kept itself relatively spick and span waiting for the day that we all came back. It is a modern, well-functioning, western nation with spectacularly good roads (full of more Mercedes Benz and BMWs than I've ever seen outside of Germany), excellent hotels, spruce shopping malls, clean and attractive cities, a deservedly admired Blue Train, and the best-run public game parks on the continent. It may be difficult to buy a decent book (pulp reigns) but you can turn your dollars into so many rand that it is possible to actually laugh when paying the bill in a good restaurant, of which there is no shortage.

While Johannesburg, the world's most heavily populated city with no water frontage, is worthy of not much more than a transit stop, Cape Town—where the Indian and Atlantic oceans meet—can take your breath away. Not just imposing Table Mountain, the artfully restored working harbour, and choppy Camps Bay, but the entire Cape of Good Hope peninsula, where exists a lush, green, rich, chocolate-box-lid world so enveloping that it was almost impossible for me to comprehend that, an hour or so before driving through it, I had been in the shanty township of Khayelistsha where the hospital closes down each night to avoid armed assaults.

Whales were frolicking off Hout Bay and baboons were clambering over cars near Fish Hoek when I made my way down to Vasco da Gama Peak on Cape Point through a vast nature reserve which has more indigenous plant species per square metre than any other place on earth. The Cape of Good Hope was named over five hundred years ago, before Vespucci and Cortez discovered the Americas. Cape Town itself, the nation's 'Mother City', is a year older than New York and 130 years older than Sydney. It is as important a destination in Africa as the Nile or Victoria Falls, and as essential for anyone who likes to consider themselves well travelled.

Or well informed. The good citizens of Cape Town are not denied the pleasures of telephone edification so popular in the dusty northeast. The *Cape Times* carried ads for Party Line Dating, at the top-of-the-line R5.97 per minute, and, better still, Personal Palm Readings. (Now that's a walk on the wild side. Just consider, for a moment, the margin for error inherent in describing your handprint over the phone to a perfect stranger.)

Sadly, what started as a community service descended fairly rapidly into a smorgasbord of smut and extortion, with the myriad sex and gambling lines occasioning the greatest number of complaints from conservative civic groups, bad losers and parents facing quadrupled phone bills. As I was leaving the country, Telkom was muttering about suspending the offending services and perhaps the entire system. That sent a shiver through me because . . . how do I tell you this . . . Sangoma had warned me that the rather fortuitous bone throw conducted on my behalf would only be binding if I called her back for confirmation, every week, from wherever I was in the world. Doesn't Telkom realise that it pays not to mess with cosmic forces?

*Courtesy* Living *magazine and the artists*

# THE SAVAGE SCRIBE

Tom Sharpe was busy at the stove in the kitchen of his Cambridge home. A man easily distracted, he had ambled over to prepare some tea but was now earnestly explaining how one goes about inflating a condom with the aid of a standard domestic gas ring. 'I spent hours here one night proving that it could be done,' he assured me. 'I went through packets of them!' All in the name of literary research, mind you, not deviancy; though Sharpe's deviations are among the more imaginative in that stratum of British bentness quaintly called eccentricity.

It was 1974 and Sharpe was writing *Porterhouse Blue*, his anarchic assault on Cambridge college life. Zipser, a callow research graduate poorly handling a lustful preoccupation with Mrs Biggs the Bedder, had found himself in felonious possession of two gross of purloined prophylactics. It was nearing midnight and 'Beside him on the carpet a pile of empty packets grew and with it a pile of foil and a grotesque arrangement of latex rings looking like flattened and translucent mushrooms.' By 1am, a cold, wet and exhausted Zipser had managed to flush 38 down the toilet. Clearly a more efficient means of disposal to avoid apprehension was required. Thus entered the gas ring and an assembly-line release of 250 buoyant balloons through the chimney. Alas, 'as each porcine sensitol-lubricated protective emerged from the chimney stack, the melting snow ended its night flight almost abruptly'.

The resultant fiasco was fashioned into one of the most memorable scenes in the high-rating British television production of *Porterhouse Blue*, the second of three Sharpe works to be brought to the screen in all its outrageous, savage, absolutely tasteless glory (*Blott On The Landscape* and *Wilt* being the others). 'Tom Sharpe serves up the loudest laughs in literary comedy,' declared a serious London newspaper reviewer in 1984. 'He is the great post-Waugh humorist, the Wodehouse who dares plunge into the bottomless vulgarity and hysteria of our times.' In the same year, the *Guardian* acclaimed his 'rich comic vision' and his 'sublime orgiastic satire'. *Time Out* insisted that he 'is the funniest novelist currently writing'. The *Listener* called him 'a danger to his public'.

The driver of the taxi I hired at Cambridge station recognised the address and all but asked me my business with 'Mr Sharpe'. I told him I had a troublesome grandmother and needed some advice on how to dispose of her. If he blinked I didn't see it. Without so much as a glance at me, he nodded sagely and kept driving.

Not that one would need to come to the source for specific instruction. Sharpe's eleven novels, which enjoy combined global sales in excess of ten million, are eminently instructional. His dizzying farces, careering across the soft spine of contemporary morality like a scud missile over Israeli airspace, offer details of dispatch dazzling in their diversity; although the blessed relief of death is generally denied to the left-wing academics, pompous landed gentry, venal officers of public order, scheming feminists, greedy capitalists and gormless civil servants upon whose hapless heads he gleefully heaps almost unimaginable embarrassments and humiliations.

Sharpe doesn't so much hang his characters slowly as play out sufficient rope for them to accomplish the task themselves. After ensuring that all their perverse peccadillos are given full rein, he sits knitting by the gallows. This is not a man overly burdened by sympathy for the wretched of his own creation. He is perfectly willing to skewer on their own stupidity, dangerous fools from any niche of society. In *Ancestral Vices*, Walden Yapp, Professor of Demotic Historiography, is unable to restrain his umbrage when Lord Petrefact, the president of Petrefact Consolidated Enterprises, refers to a 'roast dwarf of a pig'. 'The term "dwarf" has perjorative overtones' he is advised, 'whereas Person of Restrictive Growth or PORG for short, does not'.

'I have a strong feeling against any "ism",' Sharpe explains. 'As soon as you start pumping that stuff out, either the guillotine or the gas chamber is just around the corner, mate. Show me religious fervour and I'll show you someone who should be put to breaking rocks. What's wrong with dwarf? Things like PORG and ploughperson's lunches are the pretensions of bloody people who can't do anything. You find these buggers at techs and universities. They're absolutely no good as teachers because all they want to do is sit around in a fucking committee all day and talk.'

Sharpe doesn't bestow these opinions upon you as soon as you meet him. It takes at least five minutes, just enough time for you to take off your coat and sit down. At the front door of his neat Cambridge cottage he is piousness personified, a tall wispy-haired gent with all the solicitous demeanour of a vicar. However, there's no lulling you into a sense of false security, there isn't the time. After perfunctory introductions, his South Carolina wife and various of his three adult daughters are placed on the other side of a closed door and the dear old man with twinkling eyes becomes the seditious satyr his millions of readers know and most definitely love.

Little old ladies of not inconsiderable number are prone to write fan letters to Sharpe, which leaves the 63-year-old author more bemused than amused. 'They really do adore me,' he laughs. 'They come and ask me to sign their books. Apparently, I can raise the sick. Someone came up to me at a book signing once and said, "A friend of mine was having a breakdown so I gave him one of your books. I saw him smile and then he began to laugh." There was a headmaster who wrote to tell me that a small group of retired blokes met in a pub near Blackpool and one of their number went missing and nobody knew what had happened to him. He came by after six weeks and they asked him where he'd been. He told them "I was reading one of that bloody man Sharpe's books and I busted an ulcer laughing. I've been in hospital!" '

Notwithstanding that he was a lecturer in History and English at Cambridge College of Arts and Technology from 1963 to 1972, I did venture an opinion that sedate Cambridge seems an unlikely place to house a man able to conjure at whim race riots, carnal catastrophes, terrorist sieges, awesome arsenals and a home-brew that induces irrepressible erections. 'I do walk past houses thinking "What goes on inside?",' he admits. 'I'm not a voyeur but I'm always fascinated. It's just that I can't believe that my street is full of people who don't do peculiar things because I've met too many who do. Everyone's a little bent, I just don't know which ones they are!'

Sharpe hasn't always lived in Cambridge and he has not always written satire although almost everything that shaped the first thirty years of his life provided essential ammunition for that eventual pursuit. His was a childhood and adolescence of the great British public school system, the Royal marines and all those things which turn spotty youths into pillars of the empire. It took him very little time to realise that he wasn't having a bit of it.

'My father was fifty-six when I was born and was packed to the gills with Victorian attitudes, particularly hypocrisy,' he relates. 'He was looking forward to his retirement but instead he had this ghastly brat on his hands. He wanted to go abroad every year so he dumped me in Northumberland—probably the wildest county in England—with people who worked on the waterworks. They had nothing to do, no television, so they talked and told long, often obscene stories every night, with this five-year-old sitting in the corner listening to every word. My father told some good ones too and my mother had a devilish sense of humour and a fierce pride. When she was in hospital dying, this Catholic nurse came to turn her over and said "Come on me darling". She said, "I'm not your darling, I'm Mrs Sharpe!" Her last words to me were, "You wanted me to go and now I'm going."

'I suppose I had a usual happy childhood although it did occur to me very early on that authority justifies having itself set against and that you can take it as a maxim that everything authoritarian is wrong. I would sit in my classroom and look at my queer schoolmasters, who were usually about to thrash me for doing something bloody horrible, and think: how am I going to get rid of you, mate? It's very odd, you know, the number of people who die of tetanus. Now if he were to sit on a drawing pin covered in manure, nobody would know, would they?'

In 1951, Sharpe ventured to South Africa, where his mother's family had held some sway for generations. It was not to be a happy intermingling of cultures. Within a decade he had been deported, after a political farce that rivalled the fiction it inevitably inspired. The exact sequence of events is difficult to assemble but began in 1957, when, after bouts of social work and teaching in Natal, he was running a photographic studio in Pietermaritzburg.

'There was a bit of a recession, photography wasn't doing all that well so I got a part-time job teaching English at the tech. I also wrote an anti-apartheid play called *The South African* which had been put on by a little try-out theatre group in London that I think thought I was black. Anyway, along came the Special

Branch, who ransacked my house and said I was a communist. You see a communist, under the 1951 Suppression of Communism Act, was someone so declared to be by the Minister of Justice and he did not have to have read, heard or even know anything of Marx, Engels, Lenin or anybody else. It was a blanket cover. Then I got sacked from my teaching job on the orders of Education Minister Vorster, who later became Prime Minister.'

After the sacking, a local newspaper ran a banner headline proclaiming 'Sharpe is a Confirmed Liar'. Sharpe slapped a law suit on the editor and two weeks later a deportation order arrived, curiously predating Sharpe's writ by two days. 'I sued the Minister of Justice, demanding to know why I was being deported and made them come back about three times with their bloody warrant,' he detailed. 'My father was extremely right wing and when the police arrested me they said "We don't understand you, your father is very right wing." Where did they get that from? Not from me, they obviously got it from MI5, who trained all their interrogators.

'Finally, they threw me in prison for the weekend, then drove me down to Durban, stuck me in another one there and then put me on a ship. When the ship got to each port in South Africa, they'd keep everyone on board until I was dragged off by two Special Branch men in pork-pie hats with feathers to be locked up again. I arrived back in England at the age of 33 with just £400 to my name, thinking I could at least still write serious plays.

'You see, in the Britain of my youth you were brought up with the notion that good literature is always serious and meaningful. You are inhibited by your own education. I did read Conrad, I did read Mann but it was when I dispensed with that, that I found what I was, which was some sort of clown. I started writing this serious story about a white woman who lived next door to a police station and what happens when she rings up and says "I've murdered my black cook". Of course, the South African police wouldn't allow you to say that. You can't have murdered your cook, there's no way. Of course it was an accident. From that point the lunacy began to take off and that's how I discovered I was a clown. I was somebody else before that.'

Armed with his new-found talent, Sharpe wreaked the most glorious revenge. His first two books—*Riotous Assembly* and *Indecent Exposure*—for all their side-splitting excess, are the most damning indictments of aberrant Afrikaner behaviour ever published, far more devastating than a dozen *Cry Freedoms*. Once he hit his stride, Sharpe had reduced the lower uniformed ranks of the Republic of South Africa to their base elements, particularly as regards breaches of the Immorality Act with Bantu women. The prose was so purple (though always impeccably literate) that a major American publishing house paid an advance for the rights to the books but refused to publish them on the grounds that they were racist. 'I wasn't allowed into the States for a long time because they thought I was a communist as well as a racist, but it's all right now,' he reveals. 'Unfortunately the Americans do *not* know what irony is, they haven't a clue.'

It wasn't until he had a half dozen books in the marketplace that Sharpe began making money from writing what he cheerfully calls 'gallows humour'. Now his semi-retirement lifestyle is conveniently augmented by income from screenplays fashioned by such current literary darlings as Malcolm Bradbury. It has been a long time since he actively taught students, although his experiences trying to drum the humanities into first year butchers' apprentices one afternoon a week at tech did provide him with an invaluable base for the Meat One classes in his three *Wilt* novels. 'All people who teach English are mad about D.H. Lawrence,' he mused, 'but I had some difficulty with that. My mother used to shut her eyes when people kissed on television! I went to one of the highest Anglican schools in England where we sometimes had five services on a Sunday and although we heard a lot about faith, hope and charity, we sure as hell never heard a fucking word about sex. So I'm afraid I've never actually experienced this total coming together of the spirits, this total ecstasy. I don't know about you, but I've never had a union of two minds and two bodies while I've been shagging. I'd say it was jolly difficult, actually.'

Sharpe doesn't dwell a great deal on the difference between good and bad taste, in fact he doesn't acknowledge the distinction. He insists that every black incident in his books has a parallel with real life as he saw it in the marines or in 'the last Stalinist regime on earth,' South Africa. 'Don't ask me where I got my attitudes, I don't know. I just find some things bloody unjust.' After detailing a particularly disturbing story he once heard about an eighteen-year-old Jewish kid being tortured by the South African police he asked me angrily, 'Does that rival my books for farce or what?'

Still, he carries his concerns with such irreverence that Amnesty International's membership very likely doesn't increase in direct proportion to his sales. Any Tom Sharpe novel is peppered with snippets of arcane information which he collects like lint on his crumpled work clothes. When I quoted back his line that Shelley had a phobia about elephantiasis, he countered with the choice nugget that one of the executioners's privileges when Mary Queen of Scots lost her head was the right to necrophilia. 'You read things!' was his only defence.

Reading has occupied the bulk of his time since the mid-1980s, when serious angina caused him to lay down his pen and abandon his copious intake of pure snuff. Being carted back from Europe on a stretcher, spending a month flat on his back and being unable to walk a hundred metres without pain for three months, almost ended his career. Now coming slowly back to writing, he views the entire incident with the sort of jaundiced eye that would have done his mother (whom he buried at sea) proud.

'I was on Spanish television doing some bloody chat show; you know,"Why is there so much sex and violence in your books?" sort of thing. It started at 9.30 and went till midnight. All the time I had this pain in my arm and it was getting worse. I'd stretch my arm and hear in my ear from the control room, "These chairs are very uncomfortable aren't they?" I wanted to say "it's not the fucking chair it's my chest!" It started to spread down the other arm as well and it did cross my mind that this was all being televised.

'By this time the Spanish crew was showing signs of anxiety because I was clearly unwell. While I was waiting for the ambulance they said, "Why didn't you tell us, we would have stopped the show". I told them that the thing that reconciled me to it was the thought that if I did die, at least I had the consolation of knowing that my daughters, when they got fed up talking with their husbands, would be able to say to them "Let's watch Daddy dying again, shall we dear?" When I put that to the Spaniards they were quite appalled.'

# THE MAN WHO NEVER CAME HOME

I'd no sooner raised my glass—to drink, not to toast—than he issued the oddest of pleas. 'Whatever you do,' he asked, with all apparent sincerity, 'don't wish me a long life. I couldn't bear that. I'm trying to get it over and done with as quickly as possible.'

I had gone to Vietnam to find the Australian soldiers who 'went troppo' after the war and embraced the country they'd been sent to obliterate. It turned out there was only one, there had only ever been one; but he was more than enough. I felt fortunate that Graham Greene hadn't got to him first.

John Sanders did come home, for many years. But the army only transported back the physical man; his spirit was beyond their reach. The reunion of the two was inevitable, it was also latently tragic. After realising that he couldn't live anywhere else, he came to live in a city where he suspects he'll die.

Until you dig persistently deep, there is nothing at all pathetic or depressing about John Sanders. He is captivating company, albeit low-key, rarely guilty of consciously seeking sympathy and as honest as a child. I found his friendship in Saigon not just welcome, but essential. He hasn't imposed himself upon the city; he has been absorbed by it, and now moves about its precincts with all the assurance of a pedicab driver.

More than fifteen years after the fall of Saigon, the city (now officially known as Ho Chi Minh City) still has the tone of the Vienna of *The Third Man*. The bars and brothels which serviced American soldiers might have been transformed into sedate souvenir shops and icon factories, but certain back rooms still have ample supplies of the contraband that brings in greenbacks, from

Cuban cigars and Russian caviar to Veuve Clicquot champagne and pornographic playing cards. It is not hard to appreciate the heady appeal of the place to soldiers of fortune. 'Hanoi lives by the rules,' *National Geographic* recently declared. 'Saigon lives by its wits.'

So too does Sanders, former private investigator, Commonwealth policeman, insurance agent, and activator for the rights of the half-caste children left without hope when the final chopper lifted off from the roof of the besieged American Embassy in 1975; though he'll readily admit that he's not terribly successful. 'I'm Vietnamese until 2 am, then I get lonely,' he told me one steamy night, over a feast of ginger crab of which he partook not a morsel. 'I have some good days and I have some bad days. I mostly have bad days, I suppose, but there are some really good ones. When you understand that you've got to pay for your friends and you've got to buy your love, you get by. It's not a bad arrangement I suppose, at least I know where I stand. And when it all gets too much I can go to my room and spend a week there without moving. I just sit and ponder, drink, listen to some Chopin and write poetry. After a few days I'm right again.'

Sanders' room is just that, in fact it's barely that. Reached by squeezing past pallet-loads of crates of imported commodities in a dark warehouse down by the Saigon docks, the tiny cubicle in which he resides has space for a bed, a chair, an air-conditioner, a cassette player, an open suitcase and him. After a few claustrophobic minutes, I left him to it, convinced that he'd probably have stoically endured the infamous 'tiger cages' on Con Son Island.

That is, had he been fighting with the North. It's something the son of a career soldier, a major, has actually thought about more than a few times. 'I have a lot of mates here who are ex-VC,' he related, 'and they are the people here who are more genuinely friendly and warm towards me. My landlord was a VC officer and sometimes he talks about the war over a bottle of local brandy. There are a lot of parallels: he's the same age as me, we joined the army at the same time, we're both married and separated with three kids and neither of us have much hope for the future. By the end of a long night we both wonder which side we were on. It's like, "Hey, remember that time when we were ambushed; oh, hang on, you guys were doing the ambushing!" Had I had the benefit of wisdom, age and maturity back then, I probably would have been at the forefront of all the protests. I may have even preferred to have been on the other side.'

John Sanders turned nineteen on board HMAS *Sydney*, which sailed from Adelaide on 16 December 1967 (the day before Harold Holt disappeared), and delivered its cargo of eager young warriors of the Third Battalion to Nui Dat and other base camps two days after Christmas. In the main, these were not nervous conscripts, but regulars and volunteers, brimming full of piss and vinegar, barely able to wait to show Charlie a thing or two about the great Aussie fighting spirit. John lost his virginity at the Flower Bar by the beach at Vung Tau and set about severely testing an implicit belief in his own immortality by serving as a forward infantry scout; the war role ranked next to 'tunnel rat' in its contribution to the occupancy of padded cells.

'I was very, very young, I had something to prove and I was never, ever scared,' he said, through a broad, rare grin. 'I did a bloody good job because I considered myself the best forward scout that ever lived. I was just so confident that I was invincible, that nobody could kill me. The truth is, I enjoyed every moment of it. I'm a soldier and I guess I'll always be a soldier. In fact I was so gung-ho at one stage that a mate and I were going to knock off a jeep and go into Cambodia.'

John's glorious career as a hot-shot scout came to an inglorious end in just six months. He was shot twice, once by his own side in the knee and a month later in the shoulder and body during an enemy ambush. By the time he'd recovered, his unit had been posted home so he was sent to a reinforcement unit in Malaysia for eighteen months. Although he met a Malay woman whom he would soon marry, these were not the happiest moments of his young life. So intent was his desire to return to the war that he regularly went AWOL, got into brawls and generally caused so much distress to his superiors that they decided he might as well go back and get his stupid young head shot off.

'I came back as a machine gunner and went straight out to "the Horseshoe". The first night I watched *Woodstock* on the hill. I spent thirteen months there but didn't see much action. Australia lost heart for the war before the Americans did. By that point we were just stuffing around in the jungle waiting for the Yanks to tell us to go home. Which was something I'd decided I didn't want to do. I loved the place. It probably all came out of that initial feeling of comradeship in adverse circumstances, but there was also a strong empathy with the people and the country. It began to feel like home.' Such feelings can be dangerous.

With a son due to be born (he had married during a brief R&R

trip back to Malaysia), Sanders re-enlisted and swung a posting to his wife's homeland, where he lived for four years. At the end of his stint there he tried to get a job on an oil rig but the army refused to discharge him anywhere but Australia, and he was forced to come back to a place that he no longer considered home and raise a family like all the other dutiful vets.

'I came back to Kentucky Fried Chicken shops and other things that weren't there before,' he explained. 'The people had changed, it just didn't hold the same interest for me as when I was growing up in Armidale. I began to feel, like I do now, that I'd done everything there was to be done, that there was nothing more. I changed my political views and I was disillusioned with the military and with Australia.' In time, he settled into a numb acceptance of ordered life back home and joined the federal police, serving for six years as a plain clothes officer, with such assignments as guarding Gough Whitlam. Then, after a year driving trucks, he set up in business as a private investigator doing, as he now terms it, 'all sorts of tricky things'.

'I was a dick for eight years, with a lot of that time spent in the Griffith area looking into social security and car frauds. My clients were also solicitors and doctors from interstate whose wives were flying into Sydney and they wanted to know who they were meeting and where they were going. Actually, their suspicions were mostly true, or they were when I finished with them.'

During these years, Sanders maintained contact with some of his old war mates but derived little comfort from the associations. Although he participated in the 1987 'Welcome Home' parade for Vietnam vets, he did so with considerable misgiving, having long stood very much outside the close-knit veteran community. 'I couldn't find any affinity with them and, in the end, they gave me away and I gave them away. I didn't feel that I was dealt a hard blow being sent over here. I didn't feel that we needed any recognition. I never accepted all that Agent Orange stuff, I thought it was nonsense; even though I had this rash around my groin that I couldn't get rid of for ten years. I never felt I was afflicted like my mates, no way. To me, they'd gone back to Australia and given up on life. I watched the deterioration of some of them and their families as they drank themselves to death and became no-hopers.

'What put it into perspective for me was coming over here and seeing these poor bastards who got absolutely nothing. They not only had to live through it but they have to live with it now. Many of them had to suffer in re-education camps after the war and now can't do a thing for themselves. And I compare that to these bloody whingeing Aussies back home.'

Early in 1988, John Sanders became part of the first contingent of Australian soldiers to revisit the battlefields of Vietnam. Of those who chose to face up to their past, none was more profoundly affected than he. A journalist travelling with the group concluded that John found what he wanted and quoted him saying, 'I just wanted to go back for some reason or other. Now I know the reason. Things get lost and it takes either a shock or an emotional disturbance to hit the spot you were looking for, even though you didn't know you were looking for it. Going back to those places meant we were able to say goodbye; it pulled some heartstrings out there, it was really spooky. I think everyone agrees that we had no moral right to be here but a lot of us are thankful that we had the opportunity. Henry Lawson said "Our fathers taught us how to fight and not care what the cause might be". It doesn't matter what you're fighting for as long as you're fighting.'

The fighting spirit of John Sanders, who never rose above the rank of private, was indeed rekindled by this cathartic exercise, though not in the manner he may have expected. Walking through the streets of Saigon, weaving his way through the bicycles, motor scooters and odd ancient Renault and Peugot cars, he came face to face with the human reality of a long and debilitating war—the 50 000 adolescents and adults who are known as *con lai*, the half-breeds. When he became aware that between 700 and 1200 of the outcast Amerasian children were in fact fathered by Australian servicemen, and were deemed not to exist by our government, he sold up his business and threw in his lot with American activist John Rogers, who had established FACES (Foundation for Amerasian Children Emergency Support) with the financial assistance of Bill Cosby.

The plan was to identify the fathers of as many children as possible and discreetly advise them of the existence and state of their progeny. John thought his efforts would be seen as a service; instead, they were viewed very much as a nuisance by the settled, respectable former hell-raisers. Even though he travelled back and forth between Australia and Vietnam, bringing over veteran tours at the same time that he was attempting to rally media interest and community support by arranging visits by television crews, he never really chipped away at the brick wall.

'I couldn't interest anyone much in coming up here to see these kids with no fathers. Nobody at home would wear me. Not many of the men I wrote to wanted to meet their children,' he said incredulously. 'It can obviously come as quite a shock. I couldn't even get the veterans' organisations interested because they couldn't see that it would help in any way with their class actions. I didn't want money for the kids and I didn't want to bring them to Australia, it's too late for that. I just wanted some little agreement on responsibility so that I could go to the government and say "I've got the veterans behind me". I don't know, it leaves me a bit sick. It happened, so why not bloody own up to it!'

If John needed a last straw, he'd found one. His marriage had failed, his business bored him and one day he told himself that Australia no longer offered him anything he thought was worth having. So he cashed in his superannuation, gave half to his wife and boarded a plane for Vietnam. Ironically, the man who had gone to bat for part-Asian children was prepared to leave three of his own, to be raised by their mother Kim in the NSW town of Camden.

'I'd never forgotten the place and it was obviously always my desire to come back. I'd made a pest of myself in Australia over the *con lai* kids and been granted a service pension because I was classified as unemployable, a mental reject. They're probably right. I can't live in Australia, I can't cope with the attitudes of the people mainly.'

Once he had given an undertaking to the Vietnamese authorities that he would not interfere with their politics (something which had eventually brought about the expulsion of American *con lai* lobbyists) the city of Saigon was his. 'It can be so exciting here,' he enthused, in a rare moment of consistently positive thought. 'I love the intrigue, I love the idea that people here are fucking suspicious of me. They probably think I'm up to no good but they won't kick me out of the place because they want to find out what it is! Ordinary people here like me and come to me. They sometimes look at me as somebody who has some wisdom they haven't got.

'The Vietnamese have so much potential but they don't feel that they've got any future, so they're out to survive any way they can. They really don't know anything but war. They've forgotten how to do a lot of things—business, government, foreign affairs.

But they know how to bloody fight and they're not scared of anything—and they feel really good about it. I can live among that.'

The question is, can John Sanders live? Some weeks before we met, he'd become so ill through an excess of rice vodka that he was packed off to a Singapore clinic for treatment. 'I've drunk too much over here and I never eat, I don't feel I need it,' he told me. Still, he's a sociable drunk. He plays a lot of tennis with his VC mates and has actually learned to dance since he's been in Saigon. One memorable night I watched in amusement and a little admiration as he sang *Love Is A Many Splendoured Thing* at the Queen Bee Karaoke Bar, a glitzy Japanese eatery where every patron fired off a warm first-name-basis greeting in his direction.

I liked seeing him happy because it was so disturbing to see him sad. That usually came late at night, when all men are left alone with themselves. During one particularly engaging conversation, I asked him about the two close mates who had died during his fighting stint and we took an abrupt turning. 'Something happened then that I'm not very proud of,' he murmured. 'I had to kill somebody who surrendered to me. It only happened once—shit, you wouldn't want it to happen any more than once— but it still bothers me.' The silence he then fell into was so consuming, so apart from his normal diffidence and snatches of distraction, that I wanted to leave.

'No, I'm not often happy,' he finally responded, to a facile, tension-breaking question. 'There's no sense of purpose to what I'm doing. When it all disintegrated at home I came back here, to find something. It's not working, it won't work. But it's all I've got, so I've got to stick with it.'

Ha Long Bay, Vietnam (Bob King)

African cultural expression, Zambezi River, Zimbabwe
(Bob King)

*Left* Guardians at the gate of the Temple of Rameses II, Abu Simbel, Egypt (Bob King), and *below*, Pram flotilla, Republic of Ireland (Bob King)

*Above*, Torajan rice barn house, Sulawesi, Indonesia (Bob King), and *below* Elephant seals, Hannah Point, Antarctica (Glenn A. Baker)

Samosir Island in Lake Toba, Sumatra, Indonesia
(Bob King)

The Berlin Wall, January 1990 (David McGonigal)

*Right* Kavak National Park, Venezuela (Mark Leonard), and *below* Five ovens, no waiting, Spring Hill, Singapore (Bob King)

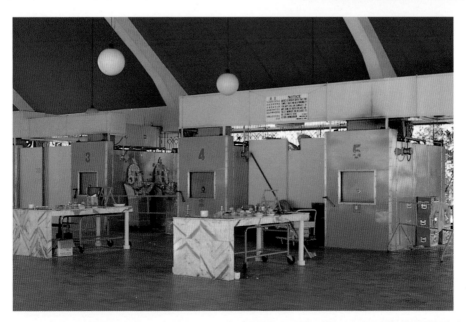

The troglodyte realm of Cappadocia, Turkey (Bob King)

A strident assertion by a passive people, The Maldives (Bob King)

Occupation: Elf, Santa's Workshop, Rovaniemi, Finland (David McGonigal)

*Above* Sunday afternoon, Buenos Aires, Argentina (Bob King), and *right* Traditional dancer, Okinawa, Japan (Bob King)

*Top* Strapping a
Pentecost Island land
diver, Vanuatu (Bob
King); *middle* Tom
Sharpe gesticulating in
his Cambridge study
(David McGonigal);
and *bottom* Moscow
Summit, 1990—(left to
right) the author, Frank
Zappa, Stas Namin
(David McGonigal)

# MAYHEM AT THE MANILA

It was almost too much to bear, even for one of the world's most celebrated innkeepers. There in the opulent grand foyer of the sumptuous Manila Hotel a noisy, clumsy revolution was unmistakably underway. Outside, buses and trucks had barricaded the surrounding streets and renegade troops armed with M-16 assault rifles, K-79 grenade launchers and light submachine guns were ringing the 74-year-old building. It was enough to make a grown man cry, even the normally unflappable Franz Schutzman.

Throughout Asia, Franz is known as a master storyteller; a larger-than-life character who mesmerises the unwary with an extraordinary catalogue of anecdotes and incidents drawn from 35 years as a consummate host and confidant. Of his encounters with potentates and personalities he has much to impart but he becomes curiously silent when the events of Sunday, 6 July 1986 are raised. 'I want to forget the whole thing,' he shudders.

As manager of the sumptuous Manila Hotel, Schutzman had become accustomed to the weekend pro-Marcos rallies staged for three months in nearby Rizal Park. Taking advantage of Cory Aquino's policy of maximum tolerance of political expression, Marcos loyalists strutted and posed under the direction of former cabinet ministers, mayors and influential businessmen.

That Sunday, events took a nasty turn when Ferdinand's running mate, Arturo Tolentino, gathered his followers in the driveway of the Manila Hotel. In a ludicrous ceremony staged primarily for the benefit of the international media, he had former Supreme Court Justice Serafin Cuevas swear him in as acting president.

While Tolentino was ranting against the 'illegal' Aquino government, an array of military officers—Brigadier Generals, Rear Admirals, Major Generals and Colonels—prowled the hotel corridors. After pronouncing a 'no surrender, no retreat' policy, Tolentino declared the hotel his new seat of government and led some 3000 civilian and military disciples through the main entrance.

Confusion and chaos reigned, as thugs and bully boys plundered the liquor and food stores. Some 250 guests were ushered out and transferred to other hotels, while a handful of obstinate resident journalists refused to budge. Staff were sent home and by Monday morning the emergency air-conditioning had shut down; electricity, water and telephone services having already been cut off from the outside.

By this stage, more than half the 400 military renegades had rejoined Cory's forces and the 'occupation' collapsed into absurd farce. Even Marcos publicly disowned the exercise from Hawaii. In the early hours of Tuesday morning, a humiliated Tolentino left in a convoy of ten cars, and by 6 am it was all over.

As Schutzman, 71, stood among the debris he realised that his precious hotel, possibly the best (of its kind) in Asia and listed as one of the twenty best in the world, had been looted by the invaders. Linen, silverware, china, paintings and imported liqueurs and foodstuffs had been stolen, consumed or destroyed. The doors to every room on one particular floor had been forced and plush carpets carried scores of burn marks. The total damages bill approached one million dollars.

It took 1100 staff exactly 24 hours to completely clean and restore the palatial hotel and reopen it for business. Not surprisingly, new bookings were considerably slow, compounding the hotel's loss. Chairman Feliciano Belmonte angrily prepared a detailed account of damages and forwarded it to Tolentino but is still waiting for reimbursement. Schutzman is probably just as angry but prefers to dwell on the positive aspects, such as the role which a number of senior officers played in personally patrolling and protecting valuable items and areas. 'That was a very Filipino thing to do,' he concedes. 'They are not, by nature, a violent people. We were lucky that there was no really serious damage done.'

Schutzman is in a rare position to judge human character, given his proximity to some of the most celebrated examples of it. In his plaque-studded office he willingly unfolds the mementos of an extraordinary life—the letters from W. Somerset Maugham, his framed ordination certificate as a Knight of the Order of San Silvestre, and photographs, most of them signed, of himself with Ava Gardner, James A. Mitchener, Orson Welles, Gloria Swanson, Jayne Mansfield, William Holden, Ernest Borgnine, Xavier Cugat, Liza Minnelli, Gina Lollobrigida, Sammy Davis Jnr, Lyndon B. Johnson, Pierre Trudeau, Kings Faisal and Khalid, and truly more stars than there are in heaven.

The man unconsciously drops names like a dog drops fleas. The Sultan of Johore was a close confidant; Chou En-lai once debated the tenets of communism with him during a long drunken night; he convinced Pope Paul that Conrad Hilton, a divorced Catholic, should be given the Order of Malta. But perhaps the most wonderful tale of all concerns the occasion he took the ageing Maugham to the rigid British Taglin Club in Singapore but was refused admission because the writer was wearing a dark suit rather than a tuxedo. 'I don't care who he is,' snarled the manager, 'this is a gentleman's club and gentlemen dress properly'. Franz pressed the point and gained admission. Maugham said nothing until a quiet lull in a stage presentation when he informed his friend, in a loud voice, 'Franz, when I look about me I understand why there is such a shortage of domestic labour in England'. Schutzman received his membership cancellation in the next mail.

Born in Java, the Dutchman worked as a prosperous Viennese music publisher and developed a taste for the better things in life before finding himself in the French army at the outbreak of World War II, and becoming a celebrated spy for the allies within a year. Sent to Rome, he was instructed to infiltrate Himmler's SD, the Reich's super intelligence unit that spied on fellow Germans. 'We knew that Himmler's key man in Rome was a poet who translated Italian books and plays into German,' he recounts. 'It wasn't too difficult getting a job in his office.'

After the war, he decided to try his hand at journalism in the turbulent Asian region. Attempts to interview rebel leaders in Indonesia and Malaya were thwarted by his Dutch passport and he found himself stranded in Singapore. With characteristic boldness, Franz put on his only clean shirt, marched into elegant Raffles Hotel and refused to leave until he had landed himself a job. Although he offered to wash dishes, the job was table waiting. Within six months Schutzman was managing the venerable establishment, a position he held for a decade. In *There Is Only One Raffles*, Ilsa Sharp observed, 'It was the beginning of a lifetime career for a distinguished and self-taught hotelier, who was at heart an adventurer, one might even say a buccaneer'. It was Franz who made the Singapore Sling famous by sending the recipe to hotels around the world.

Ironically, it was the same man who caused him to be expelled from Taglins who cost him his job at Raffles. Franz had offered Maugham a short complimentary stay at the hotel as a gesture of thanks for the use in advertising of a quote from one of his books. However, a Chinese businessman who had once been slighted by the Raffles manager bought the hotel and, as chairman, made Franz's life as miserable as possible. The final straw was a veto on Maugham's free stay. Schutzman paid the tariff out of his own pocket and resigned the next day.

He went on to manage the Nile Hilton in Cairo, Rome's Cavalieri Hilton, Toronto's Hyatt Regency, the United Nations Plaza in New York and, for a short time, an oil company ('the only kind of oil I knew was salad oil, but I learned'). In 1975 the image-conscious Marcoses spent $30 million reconstructing the Manila Hotel, which had once served as General Douglas MacArthur's headquarters. When unveiled the following year, there was really only one choice for manager.

Married twice, first to a Danish artist and then to an Italian senator's daughter, Franz Schutzman now lives alone, consuming reading material by the vanload and indulging his love for classical music. Softly spoken, impeccably dressed and uncommonly gentle, he maintains a rare relationship with his huge staff, who hold him in obvious affection. His eyes rarely miss a thing and he will just as soon pick up an offending cigarette butt himself as delegate the task to an underling.

As he approaches retirement and contemplates an easier life in the Majorcan sun, Schutzman feels justifiably irritated by the Tolentino occupation, which has set him the not insignificant challenge of winning back a lost clientele. But it is a task that doesn't even begin to daunt a man who once hit upon the ingenious idea of inviting every cab driver in Toronto to a lavish annual party, just so they knew which hotel to recommend to their passengers.

*Since the 1987 publication of this piece, Franz Schutzman has retired and the Manila Hotel continues to suffer from the tourism malaise that has inflicted the Philippines since the Marcos overthrow.*

# THE BACK ROUTE TO
# BANGKOK

It is a problem relatively small in comparison to those faced daily by the eight-countries-in-seven-days traveller. I was in London on a Tuesday with a perfectly valid KLM ticket to Bangkok on Thursday. The only problem was, I had to fly out on Wednesday to connect with a flight to Sydney. Not quite life and death stuff, but urgent enough to warrant rash action.

There are certainly worse cities in which to be in search of a cheap and instant air ticket than London. In fact, only Bangkok offers a greater array of bargains; which is how I got myself into such an inflexible position in the first place. A quick scan through the back pages of *Time Out* and one is within minutes of dashing into a cluttered office off Regent Street, brandishing credit cards or old pound notes to secure a seat on a jet departing any time from one hour thence to virtually anywhere on the planet.

For just £300, a shifty travel agent, who looked as if he slept on a camp stretcher in the back room, silently issued me with a passage halfway around the world. The ticket came stapled inside a colourful wrapper from Air Cortez, an airline apparently specialising—at least according to an American hippie purchasing a ticket to Kathmandu—in ferrying illegal labour across the US–Mexican border.

As it eventuated, I was spared the dubious delights of travelling Air Cortez, as the vouchers within nominated Tarom Romanian Airlines. Reading the flicker of panic in my eyes, the previously somnambulist agent hastily assured me that this particular Eastern Bloc airline was the only one using Boeing engines, rather than the Russian Kuznetzov Turbofan variety commonly employed by Aeroflot on its cross-Siberian jaunts. I was suffi-ciently dazzled by his knowledge of aeronautics to head for Heathrow.

From London to Amsterdam's Schipol Airport, the flight was all it should have been. But as we soared eastward—in more ways than one—the peculiar was followed by the faintly alarming. The dinner tray delivered to my seat from three rows away by deft wrist flick was truly a sight to behold. Watery borsch had been ladled generously into a bowl and even more generously around the perimeter of the tray. A chunk of heavy white bread, probably broken off the loaf by a chimpanzee in search of a banana, garnished the main course, as did an irregularly severed lump of crumbling cheese.

Terrified of being scalded by free-flowing hot beverages, I abstained. My request for Coca Cola generated a response appro-priate to its standing in most socialist states. My mood was greying but, with a change of aircraft due in the Romanian capital of Bucharest, I was confident that things could only get better. At the very least I would be able to wash from my hands the ink which had smeared when I attempted to read the full-colour (all of it foggy) in-flight magazine.

I could not attribute the dark, depressing tone of Bucharest airport entirely to the weather. Beyond the drizzle it was possible to sight, flanking the runway, a few score of Romanian soldiers, with bayonets drawn. It was not initially clear if they had been posted to deter illegal immigrants or to prevent errant Romanian citizens from stowing away in the odd unattended wheel bay. Subsequent events would eventually dismiss the likelihood of the former.

Bangkok-bound passengers were required to present them-selves at what appeared to be a transit counter, the progress toward which was roughly at the same speed as Middle East peace talks. My ticket and boarding card were not so much taken as seized from me by what must certainly have been a moonlight-ing prison wardress, then thrust back defaced with a smeared rubber stamp imprint and rude scrawl.

'What is this?' I ventured politely. 'Seat!' snapped the terror of the detention wing. 'Yes, I gathered that. But is it smoking or non-smoking, window or aisle? I do have a preference.' 'Seat!!!' bellowed Miss Permafrost of 1935, with a scowl of fearsome dimensions.

'Yes, but . . .' was all I was able to offer before I was less than politely grasped around the elbow by a dour armed guard and escorted to the transit lounge; whereupon I discovered that every establishment which might well have been placed therein to sell items of interest to transiting passengers was closed and locked with the sort of permanence usually reserved for condemned dwellings.

In fairness, it should be pointed out that the passengers were not entirely denied entertainment or diversion. Once one tired of watching fellow captives vainly argue with the airline staff, who were quite obviously filling the new plane up from last seat to first with mathematical precision and unremitting single-mindedness, it was possible to settle back and watch some television. A sole black and white set was proudly beaming highly detailed film reports on the peasants' recent agricultural reforms and improved crop yields. In honour of the arrival of so many western visitors, all other programming was suspended for the remainder of the evening.

Fully acquainted with the dynamics of agrarian science after about five minutes, I began to pace about the transit lounge, peering out a window here, and gazing at the odd official act there. By my third lap, alarm bells were obviously ringing somewhere because my old friend the guard was rushing forward with a look of schoolmasterly rebuke, which burst forth into outright hostility when he recognised me. 'Please sit, please sit, you worry people,' he snapped, directing me unmistakeably toward an empty seat.

A quarter of a lifetime later, the flight was called and the weary human cargo filed aboard. The darkest fear of all long-distance travellers descended upon me as I managed to translate the scrawl and recognise the letter 'B'. As the stark horror of a middle seat in the smoking section took hold, I stumbled down the aisle sobbing and thumping seat backs. As I reached my row and gazed down at two obese Romanian tractor salesmen clutching ring-bound catalogues, I decided it was about time this worm turned.

Clutching my hand baggage firmly, I kept on marching, chin erect in noble purpose, toward the front of the aircraft. There, I appropriated a row of three empty seats, draped myself and my bag across same, affixed a confrontational grimace and silently defied any of the flight attendants to move me. They huddled and whispered, abruptly looked toward me as one and huddled and whispered again. With a collective shrug they then went back to their marshalling duties and ignored me.

In Bangkok, ten or so hours later, I had one howling priority: a soothing balm for my distressed body and spirit—a plate of pork and noodles. Even laced with the best Thai chilli, it didn't entirely obliterate the memory of the borsch.

*Courtesy Rocco Fazzari* Sydney Morning Herald

# THE ULTIMATE UPGRADE

Not all addictions are chemical. Some are more insidious than cocaine or heroin. You only have to be invited once to sit up the sharp end of an aircraft to dread having to ever again fold yourself up like a piece of origami paper to occupy an economy class seat.

At home you may well be as selfless as a saint, totally unacquainted with avaricious behaviour and perfectly content with the simple and modest things in life. But as soon as you click those suitcase latches and ring the cab to go to the airport, an unseemly lust takes control and the pursuit of the Big U begins. That's U for upgrade.

It starts innocently enough, like a letter from the lotteries office. You present yourself after a one hour wait in the economy check-in line, ready to argue over being assigned the middle seat in a row of five, and are told, 'I'm afraid economy is terribly over-booked today. We'd like to offer you a seat upstairs in Business Class.' Suddenly you stand a little straighter, splash out a bit more at the duty-free shop, and cast a pitying gaze over the steerage passengers as you board.

From that moment on, you are insatiable. The Big U is not a privilege, it is your right! The only problem is, the dizzying rise in status can only propel you so high. There is, after all, only three classes on an aircraft. You need another fix, a stronger dosage. You need luxury that can't possibly be accommodated in an airborne steel cylinder. You begin having Suite Dreams.

I wasn't expecting the Marco Polo Suite of Hong Kong's legendary Peninsula Hotel, I really wasn't. But it was a Sunday night and all the other rooms and lesser suites were taken and, what the hell, they probably figured I couldn't do it much harm in 36 hours (given its size, Saddam Hussein's Republican Guard would be hard put to scuff it up very badly). It was plainly their charitable act of the week to give a hairy Australian scribe the chance to see how not so much the other half as the other .0000001 per cent lives.

I think I was supposed to be awestruck as I was given the introductory tour of inspection of the Peninsula's replica of a grand English country manor house but I'm afraid I had to manfully suppress a bout of the giggles (as in 'I just don't believe this, tee hee hee'). I nodded politely and followed dutifully and couldn't wait for the duty manager to leave so I could be let loose in the ritziest room in the colony (US$3000 a night, with a butler and Rolls Royce Silver Spirit thrown in). I wasn't planning to swing between the three crystal chandeliers but at least I wanted to be able to play with the dimmers on my own.

He swept me past the large polished Georgian dining table with ten ornate carved chairs, past the four antique embroidered K'ossu panels depicting the four seasons, and swept a proud arm around the master bedroom, decorated in cool shades of blue and green and incorporating a black and white marble bathroom with an environmental masterbath providing bath, shower, sauna, jacuzzi, sunlamp and warm breezes. In this very room, he boasted, had slept pretty much the entire Who's Who listings— movie stars, millionaires, prime ministers and presidents, royal personages, sports champions, authors, orchestra conductors, heart surgeons, fashion designers, media magnates and brewery bosses.

I caught a few of the names: Imelda Marcos (no problem with shoe storage space), Jimmy Carter (who could have lusted well beyond the confines of his heart in this opulence) and Tom Cruise. 'NICOLE!' I shrieked involuntarily, hurling myself onto the bed and burying my face in the pillow, whimpering audibly until it was pointed out to me that Tom had in fact been in residence with an earlier flame. He thoughtfully averted his eyes while I straightened the quilt and my appearance.

Finally left to my own devices, I conducted a swift inventory. I discovered twelve telephones, four television sets, three toilets, three laser disc players, a VHS video machine, a CD player, a cassette deck, a graphic equaliser and a butler's pantry with a closed-circuit TV surveillance system which allowed me to steal a march on any lesser mortal approaching my portals. The drapes were motor-driven and phone messages appeared on the TV screens.

When I took a moment's respite from my explorations at the oak writing desk beside the huge picture window with the peerless view of Hong Kong island, I tumbled upon an Icom Short Wave Communications Receiver with accompanying instructions for tuning into the BBC, Voice of Free China, Voice of America and sundry broadcasts from such lands as Spain, Saudi Arabia, Australia, Luxembourg, Canada, Germany, Italy and the 'other' China (you know, the big one next door). That discovery set me off again. Opening cupboards became more fun than tearing into piles of wrapped presents beneath my childhood Christmas trees. In one cupboard I found an Epson personal computer and a fax machine with a private line.

I resisted the urge to repeatedly ring for my valet but I did try a small experiment. I removed my dusty boots and placed them outside the main suite door. When I opened it again five minutes later they were where I left them but bearing a dazzling shine. A fellow could get used to this, I thought.

There had to be something wrong, some blemish; so I set about finding it. The soft beds were wide enough for a family of eight to roll over together and not wake each other up and there was certainly nothing amiss in the spacious guest bedroom decorated in warm tones of coral and peach and graced with a honey-coloured bathroom and an electronic safe. The various glass cases were full of the finest ancient Chinese pottery and the lounge area was sumptuously comfortable. Momentarily thwarted, I took time out to watch a movie and my perverse pursuit was unexpectedly satisfied.

In such surroundings I was hoping to curl up with the likes of *A Room With A View* or *A Passage To India* but as I shuffled through the dozen laser discs I realised that the bellboy must have been despatched to the local electronic emporium with rather inexact instructions. There was not a disc jacket without a firearm, contorted corpse or military insignia. At the flick of a television switch, the Marco Polo Suite became the Killing Fields, courtesy of such gory epics as *Delta Force 2, After Dark My Sweet, Diary Of A Hitman, Rebel Storm, Final Notice* and the truly intriguing *Stuff Stephanie In The Incinerator*.

But then, maybe the planet's elite actually fancy a spot of crazed conflagration when they lock themselves away from the rest of humanity. Maybe stately grand film epics went out with snuff boxes. What do I know about the obscenely rich? I was only one of them for a day and a half. Upgrades have a use-by date.

*Courtesy Alan Moir* Sydney Morning Herald

# SCARS AMONG THE
# LOTUS FLOWERS

The Perfumed River is not. I doubt it ever was; though legend and fable vigorously oppose my disbelief. I'd seen the blanket of green and the wild orchids in the clear morning, but at night, as I sat on the balcony of the Huong Giang Hotel and observed the residents of the nearby floating sampan villages conclude their day, the evocative odours which wafted by my nostrils seemed to emanate mostly from the family cooking pots.

To be honest, for all its significance as the pivot of Hue (pronounced 'way') life, the River of Perfumes (Huong River) is hardly in the league of great waterways. Just 80 kilometres long, three to four metres deep and 300 metres wide, it is not much more than a glorified canal. But what glory! Along its north and south banks are positioned towers, tombs, citadels, pagodas, palaces, cathedrals, temples, huge bronze dynastic urns, and the flagpole known to millions of television viewers in 1968 when the Vietcong raised their emblem upon it for 24 days during the Tet Offensive.

The scars of war have irreparably marked this cool, damp and foggy imperial city in the geographic centre of Vietnam. For the first ten days of the Vietcong's occupation of the Citadel, US and South Vietnamese forces withheld heavy artillery and aerial bombing attacks, hoping to spare the magnificent Nguyen Dynasty fortress-city which the Emperor Anh had commanded built in 1804, with the aid of French advisers.

When patience was exhausted, the desecration began. The air, sea and land bombardment of the 525-hectare city lasted for two weeks, heavily damaging the huge outer walls, the Imperial City, and the Forbidden City (or Great Within), where the thirteen Nguyen rulers lived and reigned. That which armaments failed to damage has fallen to the subsequent ravages of damp rot, rust, termites and neglect. Today, walking through its precincts, running one's hands along the mortar-pocked walls and wading through weeds to reach the shells of throne rooms, is very much a Pompeii experience. UNESCO has promised to aid the restoration but it will be decades before the sort of transformation that occurred at Java's Borobodur Temple comes to pass.

Hue will wait, its regal air untarnished. Grace, civility and calm are intrinsic aspects of the character of this architecturally overwhelming centre of arts, education and culture. Like Indonesia's Jogjakarta, it has long trained the nation's scholars and housed its treasures. When the Nguyens set up court in 1802 they were attended by their known world's finest musicians, astrologers, chefs and physicians. Indeed, from 1601, when it was first mentioned in Vietnamese history as a rude village, Hue has commanded a convergence of heavenly forces . . . and been responsible for the unleashing of some rather darker ones.

The principals of the Vietnam War almost constituted a Hue old boy's club. Vietnamese novelist Tran Van Dinh once observed that: 'My own school produced such revolutionary alumni as Ho Chi Minh (then named Nguyen Tat Thanh); North Vietnam prime minister-to-be Pham Van Dong; General Vo Nguyen Giap, the victor at Dien Bien Phu; and poet laureate To Huu. On the other side at Quoc Hoc: the future president of South Vietnam, Ngo Dinh Diem.' Today there are twelve schools of higher learning in the city.

As Vietnam opens its doors to any tourists with the hard currency to pay their way, it is to Hue that most of the visitors are travelling. Like Venice, Cairo, Jogjakarta, Beijing, Rome, Athens, Jerusalem and Istanbul, the tangible majesty of the remnants of ancient civilisations and colonial power bases exerts considerable attraction. That many of the more significant structures can be reached from the river and the pole-propelled sampans which ply it only adds to the appeal.

Of course, stone mandarins guarding elaborate emperor's tombs, Palaces of Supreme Harmony, and lotus-laden lakes crowned by the summer resting rooms of the earthly divine can lose their awesome ambience after a day or so of dutiful trudging. After one has flown from Ho Chi Minh City to the parched and uncomfortable city of Danang (home of 'China Beach') and then been driven along Highway One through the strategic Hai Van Pass (or 'Pass of the Clouds') with its Japanese pillboxes, unexploded French shells and American chopper pads, and past a series of coastal fishing villages and abandoned military barracks, archaeology may not necessarily be a priority pursuit.

Hue is a great deal more human than its reputation for ruins might suggest. At dusk, young women with lush long hair pedal bicycles over myriad bridges crammed with non-motorised traffic, while scores of noisy children splash naked in the river. When the sun descends, old boatwomen can be heard to sing the songs of old patriots who resisted the Chinese, the French and the Americans. Novelist Van Dinh also recalls his mother teaching him *Ve That Kinh Do*, a 3000 verse poem about the 1885 sacking of the city by French troops.

A racier, more vital Hue is to be found in the city's tumultuous markets and the old French sector around Le Loi street. Ferried about by eager cycle-cart drivers, you can find everything from dishes of hot peppered pigs' feet with beef noodles to fair-haired teenage Amerasians with tattered photos of marine corp soldiers at the ready. The city is by no means completely anchored to its past, despite the presence of sixty Buddhist pagodas and endless ornate roofs.

Sacked and sanctified, defended and discarded, Hue has played host to emperors and foot soldiers, artists and intellectuals, traders and Gulf of Tonkin fishermen. Its sky-blue porcelain is as renowned as its accomplished musicians; its serenity as famous as its tenacity. Hue is almost reason alone to visit Vietnam.

# FRONT-LINE FAITH

'At about 5 am we heard the helicopters, so we linked arms at the barricades. Some of our sisters had already been tear-gassed and the tanks were just a few hundred metres from us. We were willing to die but of course we were scared, our feet were trembling. We sang hymns and our prayers defused our fears.'

Such fear was not evident in the photographs flashed around the world of nuns, rosary beads aloft, kneeling before tanks and bayonet-wielding loyalist troops. Photographs which substantiated the tales of extraordinary personal bravery being filed by hundreds of foreign journalists.

Frail, improbably tiny Sister Consolation Ducusin smiles gently when I call her a 'revolutionary' and, although she declines to accept the description, makes no attempt to disguise the note of pride in her voice as she recounts her role in the People Power revolution which forced despotic Ferdinand Marcos from presidential office in the Philippines. 'We were not thinking of involving ourselves in a political matter,' she stresses. 'It was not that we were fighting for Cory and Doy, but for our country.'

Active in 33 countries with an official code of 'evangelism by means of special communication' (print and electronic media, audio–visual, etc.) the Daughters of St Paul sisters seldom attend rallies and demonstrations, even in Manila. In February 1986 they made an exception. 'We were uncertain of the future but we knew this was our last chance for freedom. We went without any thought of what our constitution says. Our superiors were the first ones there and it gave us the courage to follow.'

As volunteer poll-watchers, the sisters saw early evidence of what the Catholic bishops of the Philippines would soon officially describe as polls 'unparalleled in the fraudulence of their conduct'. Five members of the hundred-strong order were sent to monitor one area and three were sent away by the mayor. 'He did not like their presence,' says Ducusin, 'it disturbed his conscience. And by that gesture we knew that something was very wrong. When Marcos declared victory our faith was tested. We could not believe that this was what the Lord really wanted.'

On the evening of Saturday 22 February, the bold Radio Veritas carried the astounding and totally unexpected announcement that Defence Minister Juan Enrile and General Fidel Ramos had declared Corazon Aquino the rightful president of the republic and were calling upon the armed forces to defect from Marcos. Jaime Cardinal Sin, Archbishop of Manila, then broadcast an appeal for food to be brought to Camps Aguinaldo and Crame situated on the wide highway known as EDSA.

The rebels were sustained by more than food. The following day EDSA swelled with over a million people seeking to protect those who had dared defy the despised Marcos. 'The people who came were the middle class who you seldom see in the streets,' explains Sister Consolation. 'They came to give food and stood hand in hand with the poor, eating and singing with them. So many Filipino traits came out at that time. Our God-fearing solidarity was the source of our strength and the brotherhood was manifested not only in words but in deeds and the presence of each one of us.

'We were up all night, expecting planes to drop bombs on us. The planes and tanks never came but we were ready. In a barracks nearby we found five molotov cocktail bombs placed by infiltrators. We all stayed because of our faith. People Power was really People's Faith; that was what brought the invisible hand of God to this event. But I have to tell you that, as this was happening, we didn't expect Marcos to leave. We had many scenarios but that was not one of them.'

Freedom has a different meaning to every Filipino, many of whom will eagerly take you to the place where they stood during the height of resistance. For members of the press it is the capacity to not only report truthfully but to offer responsible criticism of the government without fear of being 'invited' to disappear off the face of the earth. To my cab driver en route to the Loyola House of Studies it is the long-denied right to drive past

Malacanang Palace, instead of being diverted by military barricades three streets away.

At Loyola, Father Tony Lambino declared, 'Most people here, without embarrassment, refer to God's action, providence and grace, even if it meets with criticism from those who want to explain what has become known as the "Aquino phenomenon" through scientific means. It had a lot to do with culture and religion, which are a potent force for social change. That is what made the revolution difficult to understand for those who operate from a different perspective.'

Part of the Philippines Catholic Church 'think tank', the 48-year-old priest, who could pass for 28, was perceived as a leading enemy of the Marcos regime, though he's not really sure why. 'In January a newspaper under government control came out with a list, compiled by NISA (National Intelligence Security Administration), of 30 names, which they called "Cory's Little Presidents" and described as top communist advisers. To my surprise I was number one, with a picture! I had given talks on liberation theology and, at that time, taking any critical stance was equivalent to being a communist. An aide to Enrile later told me that I was one of 150 on Marcos' arrest list, which was supposed to become effective soon after his inauguration. So it seems I escaped by just a few days. I had considered the possibility that it would occur but I did not think they would risk international protest by torturing a Jesuit priest.'

Lambino had offered a novena upon the anniversary of Ninoy Aquino's murder, and mass upon the death of Cory's mother. After celebrating the marriage of Cory's eldest daughter, he became a friend of the family. 'She felt at home with priests and would mention certain important events regarding the country but I never felt that I was her adviser.

'I was at EDSA every day; I would walk many kilometres to get there. It was always difficult to proceed because there were so many people. Taking into account the crowds around two television stations and Malacanang, I would readily believe there were two million. Those people knew they could die, they knew what they were in for. We felt that, at any time, the order could have been given to get tough. Then there would have been carnage. It happened so fast that our adrenalin was reacting to the situation. When the cry was given of "tanks are coming", the crowd ran toward them, instead of away, which would have been the normal human reaction.

'There was very little time for reflection then but now I ask myself, what would have happened if we had met the soldiers with jeers instead of prayers, throwing stones and bombs instead of giving bread and flowers? The Marcos soldiers would have been well prepared for violence but the way we acted took them completely by surprise. We had no idea then how universal was the attention being paid to our actions. Later, I had letters from Cairo, Madrid, the Bahamas and California which told me that the whole world was watching.'

Victory was sweeter than Father Lambino had expected. 'Without any doubt I was much prouder to be a Filipino than ever before. I saw TV announcers, who had always had to tell us the government version of events, break down and cry. When it was certain that Marcos had finally gone, I would greet every person I met by raising my hand in the victory salute.' That salute was usually accompanied by the phrase *Bayan Ko*, which translates as 'my homeland'. It is the title of an early 1970s hit by major star Freddie Aguilar, who was also prominent at EDSA. Considered radical for many years, the song included the lines 'My cherished Philippines, home of my sorrow and tears, I vow to set you free'.

Set free, the Philippines is recovering slowly from two decades of cronyism, corruption and cruelty. One set of problems has been replaced by another. 'Our struggle is not yet over', admits Sister Consolation Ducusin, 'but now we are more optimistic. Cory is more pro-people but still we have a pressing need for land reform. It is the poor and landless who are going to the mountains to join the NPA (New People's Army).'

Father Lambino believes 'it is not a matter of will Cory survive, but of how effective a president she will be. Not everything is solved but nobody can do magic by completely transforming a society. I don't close my eyes to the many things that still have to be done but the first step was for the people to rediscover their national pride and self-image; to evolve a basic hope for the future and be ready to pay the price for it.'

*When this was published in the* Good Weekend *late in 1986, Cory Aquino had more hopes and expectations laid at her feet than could be said to be reasonable or fair. Her term of office was stable, if unspectacular and, to many, largely ineffective.*

# PANMUNJOM: THE COLD WAR'S LAST SHOWDOWN

There was a full page of text on the document I was asked to sign but the essence of the matter was captured in the opening sentence: 'The visit to the Joint Security Area at Panmunjom will entail entry into a hostile area and possibility of injury or death as a direct result of enemy action.'

If I'd been asked to sign this indemnity before I left Seoul, I would have laughed it off as a necessary prop in an elaborate piece of well-rehearsed theatre staged for the benefit of gullible tourists; 100 000 of whom make the day-trip each year. But after being driven 60 kilometres due north from Seoul to the barren, intimidating 4 kilometres wide and 250 kilometres long swathe of no-man's-land on the 38th parallel known as the Demilitarised Zone (DMZ), where soldiers sit in idling trucks with their hands on the wheel so as to be deployed for combat within ninety seconds, the mirth had been sufficiently knocked out of me to allow a slight shiver as I scrawled my name across the bottom of the form.

It really doesn't matter if you think the threat of invasion is overstated, the South Koreans don't, and with good reason. On 12 January 1950, US Secretary of State Dean Acheson carelessly disclosed in a speech at the Washington Press Club that South Korea was out of the US defence perimeter. Reading a green light, communist North Korea prepared and unleashed a border assault on 25 June, which had them in Seoul in four days. It took sixteen members of the United Nations to drive them out of the city three months later. In January 1951, assisted by Chinese troops, they were back in Seoul for another brief stay. They've been relentlessly trying for a third visit ever since; on all fronts and at all levels.

In 1974 a US Navy commander was blown apart when he discovered a large tunnel aimed towards Seoul. The following year a second tunnel was found, cut into sheer granite, 50–100 metres below the earth's surface. Like North Korea's ceaseless bombast of abusive propaganda and provocative behaviour which has claimed the lives of over fifty Americans and 500 South Koreans in hostile acts since the end of the war, these subterranean shafts were dismissed as irritants.

Then, in October 1978, a tunnel located near Panmunjom gave the citizens of the prosperous south more than a few sleepless nights. This sophisticated piece of excavation was designed to allow 30 000 armed troops with heavy guns and equipment to pass through within an hour and exit just 44 km from Seoul. There are estimated to be almost twenty tunnels either complete or under construction at regular spacings along the DMZ. All are believed to have been initiated in 1972 when the North took advantage of a short-lived détente with the south.

I didn't know all this when I was whisked along the Unification Highway toward the border but I did notice, every couple of kilometres, large concrete bridge-type structures over the road, all neatly camouflaged with cigarette advertising. Nothing passes over these 'bridges' because they are filled with explosives, as are similar concrete towers placed alongside the nearby railway line. At the push of a button the arteries to Seoul can be blocked by tonnes of smoking rubble. Indeed, some theorists suggest that the mountains themselves (already dotted with bunkers) can be turned into synthetic volcanos if the city is again under threat. It seems exaggerated but, as one of Asia's great industrial powerhouse nations, South Korea has much to protect.

By the time the three-year Korean War had been suspended by armistice there were more than three million casualties and Korea lay in ruins. On the day the dubious document was signed, Commanding General Maxwell D. Taylor stated, 'There is no occasion for celebration or boisterous conduct. We are faced with the same enemy, only a short distance away, and must be ready for any move he makes.'

Just how short that distance is, and just how ready the South and its predominantly American allies remain becomes startlingly apparent as you cross Freedom Bridge on the Imjin River and become a part of the last great East vs West (or, more accurately,

North vs South) cold war stand-off. Communism didn't cease opposing capitalism when Gorbachev finally pulled the plug on the party. Panmunjom, on the traditional invasion route favoured throughout history by Chinese warriors, Japanese samurai, Mongols and Manchus, is as tense and confrontational as the Berlin Wall in 1961.

Over one million soldiers are in place along the DMZ, with their weaponry trained across the border day and night. The vortex of the barely restrained hostility is at Panmunjom, where guards stand at attention, glaring at each other across the Military Demarcation Line. Both sides parade their elite troops. The best South Korean soldiers serve their entire thirty-month tour in the DMZ. They need to be taller and heavier than the average soldier and must possess at least a first-degree blackbelt in any of the martial arts.

The guardians of the South march, those of the North goosestep. When one raises his fieldglasses his counterpart matches the move. They have slaughtered each other over incidents involving the trimming of a poplar tree, the defection of a young Soviet translator and a surprise attack on a US base camp; and participate daily in the potentially lethal game of charades. Visitors on the southern side are strictly forbidden to respond to any provocation and make any 'gestures or expressions which could be used by the North Korean side as propaganda material against the United National Command'.

Propaganda is an expensive and expert business in this part of the world. Within the desolate DMZ, where such endangered species as the magnificent Manchurian crane perversely proliferate, there are two villages. On the Southern side is Taesong-dong (Freedom Village), with its 100-metre high flagpole, which houses 43 families who were resettled after the war; and although spared military service, taxation and all night-time social activity, have a life not greatly dissimilar to most rural Koreans.

On the northern side is the considerably larger Kijong-dong (Peace Village), with 40 three- to five-storey buildings and a 160-metre high flagpole (probably the tallest in the world) with a 30-metre long flag. From this odd conglomeration of entirely inappropriate structures, a vast battery of powerful loudspeakers sing the praises of the reverend Kim Il Sung or otherwise blast propaganda into the south. Such volume would make living in the village unbearable but that is of no great concern because nobody actually lives there, beyond a few caretakers who change the tapes and raise and lower the massive flag. The entire village is a shell, a tribute to absolute absurdity.

No less absurd, however, than that which has long taken place in the spartan barracks-like shed which straddles the Military Demarcation Line (MDL) of the DMZ, and is one of the 24 large and small buildings in the Joint Security Area. This squat hut, the ultimate destination of the military-accompanied tour of inspection from Camp Boniface is Panmunjom's *raison d'etre*, so to speak. Here were conducted the longest truce talks in recorded history. The 27 July 1953 armistice was arrived at after no less than 1076 meetings over two years and nineteen days.

But that was but a beginning. During the last forty years of 'peace' the Military Armistice Committee (MAC) has regularly convened to engage in bouts of verbal abuse over alleged truce violations and to discuss and rediscuss a reunification that seems no closer than it was a decade ago. Between the end of the Korean War and March 1990, the MAC held 455 meetings which achieved three-fifths of five-eighths of not much at all; although for a time they served as an anemometer of superpower politics. From historical reports, some meetings have been as bizarre as the script to *Dr Strangelove*. At one, the United States was referred to as the 'US Imperial Aggressor' more than 300 times. No doubt with straight, even stern, faces.

The point of visiting the shed, where robotic North Korean guards eyeball tourists through the window panes, is to view the plain green conference table upon which lies, down the middle, the border between the two countries. The Korean Peninsula is bisected, at its waist, by a microphone wire. On either side of this wire are national flags (which, early on, grew in size from meeting to meeting until it was no longer possible to get them through the doorway and somebody sane set a height limit). Stepping past the table and the wire is the single means by which visitors from the south can actually stand in North Korea—and a naughty thrill it is too!

Panmunjom is far more than a propaganda showplace for both sides. Not only is it the only portion of the heavily fortified DMZ not separated by razor-wire fences or walls but, under the official control of the United Nations, it is outside the jurisdiction of both the South and North Korean governments. It is, in fact, the only ground link and the only channel of real contact between the two ideologically opposed nations.

This is where the crew of the seized USS *Pueblo* were finally handed back, where South Korean fishermen captured while working the East and Yellow Seas have been sent back home, where Red Cross delegations have crossed, where mediators for recent joint Korean soccer and table-tennis teams have broken ground, where members of the Neutral Nations Supervisory Committee go about their business (and sometimes defect), where the scandalously few reunited families have gone over to the other side for a precious few hours, and where the tragedy of the Bridge of No Return took place in 1953.

After the armistice, this bridge was the exchange point for all prisoners of war. As they were verified, the soldiers had to choose a direction, north or south, understanding that they would not be allowed to go back the other way. No doubt many of them presumed they would be isolated from parts of their families for a few years. None of them could have imagined that the enforced separation would still be rigidly enforced 40 years later. It was a choice for life.

The Koreans may be more efficiently and heartlessly divided than any other common people on earth. South Korean citizens cannot telephone or write to North Korean citizens who would know better than to try. Most of the families fractured by warfare do not even know if relatives are alive. There are tales of mourning Seoul mothers sending weekly letters to lost sons in the north via redirection services in China for decades, without knowing if a single one of them reached its destination. There have been minor breakthroughs. In 1983, the Korean Broadcasting System attempted a bold reunion program. From 100 952 submitted applications, all poignantly displayed in Seoul's Plaza of Reunion, the KBS brought together 952 people, including one pair of twin sisters apart for 36 years. Two years later the Red Cross enabled 151 family members to cross briefly at Panmunjom in the company of singers and dancers on a goodwill tour.

North Korea stands with Albania and Cuba as the last stubborn hold-outs of Stalinist ideology. But while there may be some shreds of bravado in Fidel Castro's defiant resistance to inevitable change, there are none in Kim Il Sung's. When Moscow turned the money taps off on nearby Vietnam, Hanoi effected a subtle but effective change of priorities and suddenly developed an interest in western trade and tourism. Kim's response was to launch a campaign along the lines of Let's Eat Two Meals! There are few medicines, little fertiliser, and plainly malnourished people. One kilogram of meat is available per household four times a year, an egg per person per month, and 445 grams of rice per male person a day (women are entitled to 150 grams). But they do appear to have, to the increasing alarm of the UN, a very impressive nuclear weapons program.

'They are told that we are terribly poor in the south,' explained a Korean businessman I met in Seoul who had been part of a delegation to the northern capital of Pyongyang. 'The isolation is total because if the people there were able to see what we have done here I don't think the regime could survive.' But it does, with the full intention of being the only communist state with hereditary rule. Deserted in droves by its once staunch allies (even the Chinese are frustrated by Kim's refusal to pursue economic reforms), North Korea hangs on grimly with a stand-still economy and about as much future as vinyl record albums.

All of which makes the gaze across the fortified and defended DMZ into the mysterious north all the more compelling. Not that the tourist flow is all one-way. On the southern side, visitors (none of whom are allowed to be South Korean) gather on a lookout platform within an octagonal pavilion atop Freedom House; on the northern side a lesser number of visitors stand on the balcony of a rectangular building called Panmungak. Both are the official two-storeys high but the latter was deliberately built on high foundations to look taller and the front side is one metre wider than Freedom House. It's the flag pedantry all over again.

The western alliance really doesn't need to pitch its message of moral superiority quite so stridently in these post-perestroika days but a good machine is hard to turn off. In the conference room at Camp Boniface (named after a captain axe-murdered a short distance away by North Korean soldiers), a fresh-faced young American PFC rattled through the history of the place and UN proprietorial policy like a Tokyo–Osaka bullet train before asking that we remember to sign our forms before getting on the bus for the descent into the jaws of the beast.

Oh yes, that form. I still have a copy because I was particularly taken by clause 2, which stipulates that visitors have to be 'dressed in appropriate civilian attire so as to maintain the dignity of the United Nations Command'. Apparently, the North Koreans can turn blue jeans, sloganed t-shirts and dirty sneakers into tools of insidious propaganda but are severely hampered by collars and ties. I had a school teacher who used to be able to do that but, gee, I never suspected he was a communist!

# THE *BOUNTY* ARISTOCRACY

*In April 1789, Captain William Bligh was forcibly relieved of his command of HMS* Bounty *by Master's Mate, Fletcher Christian, who took refuge with his followers on Pitcairn Island in January 1790. It may not have been the first British naval mutiny but it was undoubtedly the most famous and consequential. More than 200 years later, on Norfolk Island, that oft-eulogised event is the cornerstone of a unique society.*

It may have been delivered as a question by the small man with the salt 'n' pepper beard but it hung in the air as a statement that invited no reply. David Buffett, the closest Norfolk Island has to a statesman, was not about to let the accepted verdict of history interfere with his own.

'Wasn't it Bligh who was the criminal?' he queried, in that tone of assurance trimmed with polite indifference that is peculiar to Norfolk's 'islander' families; a Pacific gentry who have managed to reverse the accepted social aversion to criminality and all but deify a bunch of lustful sailors unwilling to abandon a tropical Eden. 'I can't say I have any affinity with criminal activities,' snorted Buffett, 'but it is difficult to judge in modern terms what happened in those days.'

Not that it hasn't been attempted. At last count there were over 2500 books and pamphlets dealing with the mutiny on the *Bounty*—that single act of violent emotion which spawned a people, a language, and a fully-formed, distinctive culture.

A *Bounty* heritage is the ultimate badge of honour on the tiny Australian protectorate of Norfolk Island; the very basis of social order and unbending arbiter of community standing. There are 'old families' on Norfolk who are still considered 'mainlanders' after many generations and can never hope to be fully accepted into the same inner circles as the 'islanders'. For it is understood that they are deficient in their family tree and, as the official *Guide to Norfolk* book states plainly: 'A mainlander gets to be an islander in exactly the same way that a dog gets to be a cat'.

The vital heritage factor is a real *Bounty* mutineer—one of those eulogised folk heroes who put nineteen men to sea in a longboat and whose blood now runs, questionably, in the veins of a Pacific elite. Their imposing and enduring surnames are as Norfolk as the pines. You read them on the huge tombstones down by Cemetery Bay and encounter them in every conversation. Life revolves around the exalted Christian, Adams, Young, Quintal and McCoy families; and, to a slightly lesser extent, the prolific Buffett, Evans and Nobbs lines. Like the Kennedys in Massachussetts, they call all the shots that matter.

After that single act of violent emotion in 1789, Fletcher Christian and his mutineers zigzagged across the Pacific, sailing 7800 miles in search of safe refuge. After visiting Toobouai on the Tropic of Capricorn and stopping in at the Society, Austral, Tonga, Fiji and Cook groups, they arrived at a spot where Bligh's charts indicated Pitcairn Island should be. Incorrectly charted, the island was as good as undiscovered. Eventually located, after a 200 mile search, the bountiful, virtually unassailable landfall proved to be a perfect haven. The *Bounty* was burned on 23 January 1790 and the fearful party of 28 awaited seemingly inevitable retribution.

Retribution which never came, despite the efforts of the Admiralty, which scooped up the stragglers on Tahiti and carted them off to London's gallows in Pandora's Box, leaving the nine Pitcairn hideouts to destroy themselves through lust, greed and jealousy. Fights with disgruntled male Tahitians over the voluptuous raven-haired daughters of Polynesia took their toll and, in turn, eight white Europeans met grisly fates. By 1800, John Adams was the sole survivor, the patriarch of a swiftly expanding and surprisingly resilient community, with Thursday October Christian (Fletcher's son) as his right-hand man. 'The young men born on the island were finely formed, athletic and handsome,' wrote Sir John Barrow. 'But the young women particularly were objects of attraction, being tall, robust and beautifully formed.'

Mutineer Adams quelled all disquiet, instituted Christian worship and morality, and presided, until his death in 1829, over an almost utopian society. Even when he was finally discovered by British sea captains, there was no move to wreak vengeance upon an almost saintly man who single-handedly established a functioning melting-pot society, the fruit of which flourishes on Norfolk Island today. So impressive was his reign that, when a whaling ship called by Pitcairn in 1823, an educated young man by the name of John Buffett was, according to Barrow, 'so infatuated with the behaviour of the people that he resolved to remain among them . . . as an able and willing schoolmaster, clergyman and oracle of the community'.

By 1856, the natural riches of Pitcairn were nearly exhausted and the 193 residents (with just eight family names between them), after representations to the British government, were offered resettlement on an island whose very name caused men's blood to run cold—the former penal colony of Norfolk Island, where barbaric tortures beyond even the imagination of Sydney Cove's gaolers had been regularly performed. It was a brutal uprooting for these people, who had been the first in the world to grant female suffrage and make education compulsory. But in June 1856, the bedraggled group made the 3700 mile crossing and set about re-establishing their most civilised of societies on a desolate isle where the screams of the wretched still whistled through the pines. In time, some families returned to Pitcairn, their offspring maintaining the tiny population that continues to occupy Britain's last remaining Pacific possession.

Today, Norfolk Island has a New South Wales postcode, uses Australian currency and receives ABC television. All of which is not nearly enough to render it a part of Australia. Sited in splendid isolation, 1600 kilometres northeast of Sydney and 1000 kilometres northwest of Auckland, this lone blob of verdant volcanic rock with a population of less than 2000 is no adjunct to the mainland. While willing to shelter under defence and economic umbrellas, Norfolk stubbornly keeps its distance. The people neither feel Australian nor have any desire to be integrated into Australian society. Their own remains far more attractive.

The glue which holds Norfolk culture together is its patois, a living evolving tongue, actively spoken by no more than 600 people (though known by more than 2000), which has survived two centuries of sometimes concerted destructive effort. This lyrical language, sounding to the uninitiated like a cross between pidgin and pig latin, was entirely oral until 8 June 1988 when Alice Buffett, former Minister for Social Services and Primary

Industry, published *Speak Norfolk Today*, the first serious attempt to establish a proper orthography. Since her groundbreaking work was unveiled, Norfolkers have tasted the exotic, almost naughty thrill of being able to write to each other in their own language.

When Alice's father spoke Norfolk in the school playground at the turn of the century, he had to suffer the penalty of writing out 'I must not talk gibberish at school' 300 times on the class blackboard. By the time Alice herself reached school age, the penalty was only marginally less harsh. 'I had to write out "I must not speak Norfolk at school" 50 times,' she recalls. 'We used to have to whisper it to each other. That's something that most of my generation remembers. Many of us came from homes where English was almost never spoken and it was terrible to be denied something that was so close to us. The only bright spot was that, when we went away to school in Australia or New Zealand, we had our own private language, which confused and infuriated everyone else.

'A colonising force will always try to stamp out local language and culture and England was no less guilty of that. Their reasoning, which did have some merit, was that, if we were to take our place in the modern world, we would have to speak English. Even when the British influence faded, Norfolk was still only taught to our children as part of a "Norfolk studies" subject. That only changed four years ago because there was a very real fear of it dying out. I realised then that, for it to be taught properly, I needed to establish a set of vowels that represented the exact sounds we make.'

Those sounds are lyrical, almost musical; with subtlety, precision, power and wit. Beryl Nobbs' equally pioneering *Dictionary of Norfolk Words* makes for engaging reading. One of the more interesting words is *up-a-tree*, which means pregnancy. The island's vernacular is full of such endearing phrases as *Mard es a tear-tear shoe*! (As silly as a shoe with a flapping sole), and *Car know-a yesteddy end des daye es de saem daye* (One would never know that yesterday and today is the same day!). 'The mutineers came from different counties of England, in fact from all over the British Isles,' explains Alice Buffett. 'Young was from St Kitts in the West Indies and spoke Creole. When you mix all that with Polynesian languages something unique emerges.'

The most astonishing aspect of the Norfolk language is that it did not evolve over two centuries but was basically up and running within thirty years. John Buffett found the tongue functioning fluently when he threw in his lot with the Pitcairners in 1823. Since then, the changes have been minor, and occasionally amusing. *Kushu* (on top of the world), one of the few words unknown on Pitcairn but common on Norfolk, popped up after World War I, when returning soldiers would say 'Compared to what I've just been through, I'm on cushy street, brother'. Alice Buffett accepts the changes stoically. 'I'd say "But that's not Norfolk," to my nieces, but of course it was. Any language stays alive by moving and absorbing. The only thing that bothers me is that the Norfolk and Pitcairn languages seem to be growing apart, which would be a terrible shame.'

Alice Buffett is a seventh generation direct descendant of mutineer Matthew Quintal, who connects, through marriage, with almost every major bloodline on Norfolk and Pitcairn. As such, she seemed a logical choice to comment upon the tiny community's most jangling closet skeleton. There are those who claim that most of the vital bloodlines on Norfolk are spurious, that many of the mutineers died before fathering children and that the mysterious survivor John Adams (who some theorists believe to be Fletcher Christian in disguise, but that's another story) bestowed the surnames of his fallen comrades upon his own varied progeny. 'That's always been a touchy point here,' understates Alice. 'It is only an assumption, passed on by folklore. Certainly children did come along that Adams embraced but it's not something that anybody really wants to talk about.'

What Alice and David Buffett are delighted to talk about is a famous relative who is not in the least ancient. In recent times, the Norfolk Buffetts have claimed a kinship with American rock singer Jimmy Buffett, the seafaring son of a son of a sailor who finally made it to Norfolk after an Australian tour in February 1987, and played an acoustic concert to a capacity audience one balmy night when emotions ran high and the chosen ones were finally able to see beyond their Pacific horizons. With his scented songs of the Caribbean, Jimmy gave a new dimension to the incredible saga. 'It was always somewhere in the family legends,' he says. 'My dad used to talk about having relatives in the Pacific but we just figured that he was covering himself for whatever he might have got up to while he was away at the war.'

'We haven't yet tracked down the common ancestor, but we're sure Jimmy is related, he has that humour,' says Alice. 'As soon as we met him we felt an affinity. So we threw a Buffett picnic for him, on Albert Buffett's property out at Steele's Point. We all went along, with our family trees under our arms and Jimmy went around and met everyone in turn. It was such a lovely day.'

The Norfolk sense of family, of belonging, is overwhelming. Guest house proprietor Mera Martin, 54, comes from the Christian line and speaks of her forbear with an unabashed pride. 'The older I get, the more I realise how precious my heritage is. The mutiny is not the important thing. What is important is the first merging, in this part of the world, of two completely different cultures. We were brought up by our parents to feel no shame and to be very, very proud of our ancestors. We believe it was the publicity given to the mutiny which made the public aware of the shocking conditions for seamen in the British navy and brought about change. Fletcher was no criminal, he was a hero. Nobody in their right mind would have wanted to go back to England after staying for so long in Tahiti.

'I suppose we're a bit like the Quakers of Boston. We're the older establishment and there's a terrific sense of belonging. I married a tourist after the war and went to New Zealand for 24 years. But I always spoke of Norfolk as home, taught my children the language and finally came back with my family fifteen years ago. Now so many of our young marrieds are coming back here to live because the quality of our life is so rich. If I have a family function, 56 people have to be invited before we even get to friends. If we left even one out we'd be in trouble!'

For much of this century it was almost a ritual to leave Norfolk for education or marriage and return later in life. The loss of its young is debilitating for any society and Norfolk suffered accordingly. But with the legitimising of the language and a new swelling of identity, has come a surprising retention. Joanne Christian Bailey is a beguiling nineteen-year-old with an islander father and mainlander mother who was sent away to school for three years but is now determined to stay put, despite a paucity of eligible young men. 'There are things that make us special. It's very Polynesian in a way. The families stick together like one family, and everybody looks after everybody else's children. There's a lot of caring and sharing.

'When I was at school in Sydney I stayed with my dad's sister's family in Kingsgrove. We all spoke Norfolk and every weekend all the islanders in Sydney would come over to have a big feast and carry on the culture. It was like a home away from home. I needed that because Sydney really did frighten me. I was so innocent I couldn't imagine crime. I would speak to anyone. After the initial amazement wore off I realised I just didn't like the place very much.'

At primary school, Joanne was taught about Norfolk's geography but not its culture. Now she feels protective about that which she was denied. 'It is up to my generation to carry it on,' she believes. 'I'll teach my children the language and the history. As more mainlanders come in and islanders die off, what we have is in danger of being lost. Now we have television and video shops, which I suppose had to come. But I remember when I was fourteen, the whole family would go for a walk down on the beach after dinner. Now the television goes on straight after we eat. I hope it's just a novelty that will wear off.' (One video that tends to stay on the racks is the 1962 version of *Mutiny on the Bounty*, in which Marlon Brando, as Fletcher Christian, is killed off before he fathers any children.)

David Buffett, twice the island's chief minister, shares the prevailing islander apprehension about the future. 'Our culture can survive,' he predicts, 'but not without some changes. Of late there has been a general recognition that our lifestyle is important and has things to offer that other lifestyles don't. Our isolation is a buffer against the bad elements of the outside world. We are behind the times but not so much that life is difficult. It probably works to our advantage.

'Tourism is obviously the industry, but it needs to be watched carefully or we'll go the way of the Gold Coast. Our environment is very vulnerable and there are pressures for change from both outside and inside. The islanders prefer a quiet life; they are not very upfront, pushy or entrepreneurial, so they fall prey to those people who are. People who walk away from disasters and leave us to clean up the mess.

'I can understand how the ethnic Fijians felt when they woke up one morning, realised they no longer ran their own country and decided to do something about it. There is a grave danger that the same thing could happen to us. The control of the islanders, from a purely numerical point of view, is becoming less and less. We're being outnumbered because, in the past, we were too kind and too hospitable—to the extent that we're now a minority in our own land. Current immigration policy doesn't necessarily give preference to island people. Every time Norfolk Island does that, the Australian authorities seem to have trouble with it. That's one area where we don't enjoy a completely happy relationship.'

Relationships are the ties that bind on Norfolk. There are few surviving communities in the world as closely-knit as the *Bounty* aristocracy. So closely-knit, in fact, that one subject that tends to raise its ugly head among outsiders from time to time is inbreeding. The *Guide to Norfolk* even devotes a section to it, highlighting the findings of Harry Shapiro, the president of the American Anthropological Association, who lived on Pitcairn and Norfolk in the 1920s and reached the conclusion that, when the gene pool is sound, there is no genetic deterioration of any kind. 'I don't know much about genetics,' declares a mildly miffed Mera Martin, 'but I do know what I see around me. The Pitcairners, particularly, are a very canny, intelligent people who can turn their hand to anything. I can't find any adverse effect from inbreeding, in fact quite the opposite. There are no silly or defective people on Norfolk Island.'

There are, however, some wonderfully charismatic and amusing ones. On a 3455 hectare island with plummeting cliffs and no natural harbour or anchorage, where access by sea is near impossible and aircraft are turned back at the first sign of squall, it pays to have a sense of humour. The real characters of Norfolk are found down by Kingston and Cascade Bay, where the supply ships are unloaded by lighter boats and the anecdotes fly freely.

The best comes from a salty old lighter pilot who was once given the honour of bringing the Queen to shore from the *Britannia*. It seems that the royal yacht was anchored offshore in heavy seas, unable, like so many freight ships before it, to unload its precious cargo. Finally, with the royal Pacific schedule in tatters, it was decided that Her Majesty would brave the elements and set off to meet her loyal Norfolk subjects. Seated securely in the best lighter, helmed by a man of impeccable experience, she was hurtled through the pitching, heaving surf, her fine British complexion even paler than normal. Not a word was uttered until the lighter came alongside the dock, where it was tossed high and dashed low. 'What do I do now?' beseeched the royal one. 'Fuckin' jump,' screamed the captain who, to this day, delivers the punchline in a reverential tone: 'And, bugger me, she did!'

*Norfolk now has a radar system for aircraft landings and planes are no longer turned back when the barometer drops.*

# JAMAICA JERK-OFF

A decade after the death of Bob Marley, the hero of third world emancipation struggles, kids in Kingston are jeering and throwing bottles at his former comrade in music, hero Bunny Wailer. All is not well in the home of reggae.

Bob Marley exhorted Jamaican youth to 'Get up stand up, stand up for your rights'. Shabba Ranks, the reigning king of the X-rated dance hall sound that has overthrown reggae as the most popular Jamaican music form, offers a different exhortation. His hit *Bow Down* orders women to kneel before men for oral sex.

Dance hall is an ugly sound created in a sometimes ugly city; a squalid metropolis cursed by one of the highest levels of police-related killings in the world. There were over 700 violent deaths in Jamaica in 1990, with more than 150 attributed to the police. Kingston is no longer a city of dreadlocked Rastas whacked on ganga. Crack has taken hold in the ghettos and many young Jamaicans couldn't give a soggy spliff for the Marley idealism of *One Love*.

All of which begs the question: why go? Well, why go to New York, which is even more dangerous, or to London, which was recently tagged Europe's crime centre? One goes because of the undeniable exhilarating 'edge' of cultures in decline or, more simply, because the good far outweighs the bad.

Jamaica remains a lushly overwhelming and immensely enjoyable tropical island, rich in culture, history and extensive natural endowments. Certainly Trenchtown, Kingston's ghetto area bordered by burned-down petrol stations, is out of the question for a walk after dark, but it is hardly alone in that distinction. I choose not to go wandering at night in Brixton, the Bronx, parts of Bangkok and Sydney's Hyde Park as well.

*Be it calypso, ska, bluebeat, reggae or dance hall, Jamaican culture is intertwined with Jamaican music*

I suppose it's all in the eyes of the beholder, and there've been a few notables in those ranks. Noel Coward adored the place and was buried on Firefly Hill, where he had been inspired to write the song *A Room With A View*. His neighbour, Ian Fleming, wrote James Bond novels during his annual winter residence. Errol Flynn spent most of the final dozen years of his life there after washing up in his yacht *Zaca* during a hurricane. 'Never have I seen a land so beautiful,' the great screen swashbuckler declared in his 1959 biography. 'Now I know where the writers of the Bible got their descriptions of paradise. They had to come here to Jamaica.'

It's hard to argue with him. Jamaica, at the top of the West Indian belt in the Caribbean has, as all the right travel brochures and guides will tell you, a sturdy mountainous backbone which keeps half the land hovering more than 1000 feet above the sea. The thick foliage which sweeps down to the fertile coastal plain and spectacular cliffs houses more than 200 species of birds and over 3000 varieties of flowering plants, 800 of which are found nowhere else in the world. In parts it is a perfumed Eden, in others a perfect replica of Scottish highland farms or Welsh grazing land. The high air is so pure that natives who have lived well beyond one hundred are in plentiful supply. There are Spanish forts, ganga plantations, buccaneer lairs, grand mountain mansions, waterfalls and innumerable beaches.

I doff my hat to them all but, to be honest, I came for the people—the two and a half million inhabitants who are as exotic as their flora and fauna. 'Out of Many, One People' goes the idealistic national motto in a country where there is essentially no native population or native tongue and the skin tones run from Nordic to Nubian. When Perry Henzel directed Jamaica's first feature film, *The Harder They Come* (ostensibly in English though it needed English subtitles), he made the observation: 'Jamaica's history is African, its culture is European, its politics are third world. We're producing a totally new breed of human being.'

This hybrid strain delivers flowers of great diversity, from women so astoundingly beautiful that Jamaica took out the Miss World crown three times in thirteen years, to glazed-eyed Rastas who ease around the streets to a languid, fluid reggae beat mainlined into the central nervous system by the various modes of mobile sound clutched to their ears. There are solid white plantation lords, fiery black preachers, monarchists, seditionists and gangsters. None of whom you could fairly describe as driven people.

I was most taken by the pace of a Kingston reggae record store I sought out one afternoon. Finally granted entrance after I had pounded on the door for five minutes, I had trouble making out the racks of stock through the thick ganga smoke. When my eyes became accustomed to the haze, I realised that an entire reggae band was rehearsing in the shop, leaning comfortably against walls and record bins. They had locked themselves into a particularly hypnotic off-beat, heavy on the bass, and were in a funky holding pattern that, for all I know, could still be bubbling away. Access to the records was next to impossible and the proprietor didn't seem to register my presence in his emporium, so I eventually decided to quietly slip away and leave them to their odd reverie, taking considerable care not to let too much of the pungent smoke out the door with me. I was light-headed for days afterwards.

You can go to Jamaica for Montego Bay, Ocho Rios and Negril Beach—hedonistic haunts for hippies with a few bucks and

Americans who've finally tired of Miami Beach—and you probably should because, like Bali and Phuket, they are young, racy, amusing and exciting. You can go to watch some of the most energetic and determined cricket played in any former British colony. You can go to trace the path of Spanish and British conquerors and chart the tragedy of slavery. But, I have to tell you, that I go to be jerked, so to speak.

No guide worth his badge will accommodate me and even cab drivers look askance when I ask to be taken to one of the corrugated-iron sheds by the roadside where a white face is rarely sighted. Indeed, it is often only as a result of great perseverance that I can consume jerk pork.

Jerking is a native cooking process whereby peppered pork, chicken or fish is cooked slowly under zinc over a fire of fragrant pimento wood. The younger and more choice the wood, the richer the taste of the cooked meat. You have to queue up outside the door of the shed to purchase a half pound or more wrapped in newspaper; available at regular cooking times like proper fish 'n' chips in England. It is then *de rigueur* to sit out the back or around the side on a bench with the local lads, eating this rare treat with your fingers while sucking on a bottle of Pepsi.

If you tire of the fairly limited menu of jerker stands, you can move on to ackee and sal' fish, peppered pigs trotters, mackerel and boiled green bananas with avocado and broiled shrimp in a coconut shell, solomon gundy (spiced pickled herring) or, the dish made famous by a Rolling Stones' album title, goat's head soup. Unquestionably, it's a banquet well worth dodging dance hall deviates and Kingston lowlifes to seek out. If your stomach leads you around the world as, I must admit, mine often does, Jamaica merits a visit. Of course, it helps to like reggae as well.

# VENEZUELA: BEYOND THE PATHS OF PLUNDER

They came. They saw. They rarely conquered. The constant theme of Venezuelan history has been a largely unrequited lust for gold, oil and fabled riches. Over the past five hundred years, the paths of plunder have been trod regularly by noble explorers, ruthless pirates and daredevil soldiers of fortune. Yet in their wake has emerged the richest and certainly least damaged country on its continent; a sparsely populated nation the combined size of France and Germany that is part of both the Caribbean and South America.

I came, primarily, to see Angel Falls, a cascade far higher than Victoria, Iguazu or Niagara. Like Caracas, the name enchanted me, conjuring rich images of ancient Indian folklore or the legacy of Catholic missions. In fact, it has as much to do with either as economy class has to do with comfort. The slender, single, kilometre-high fall was actually named after the American pilot who 'discovered' it, one Jimmy Angel.

It was a disappointment I could easily absorb, elbowed aside as it was by an astonishing array of splendours within a country that tries valiantly to compete as a tourist destination with the Caribbean cruise circuit to the north and frantic Rio to the south, but tends to be unfairly tarred with much the same brush as unstable Latin American republics.

Venezuela, plainly, deserves better. Like Argentina, it contradicts the media-etched South American mosaic of dust, flies and insurrection. It has a comfortable, cosmopolitan capital city of great aesthetic appeal, some of the oldest and least-explored mountains and rainforest jungles in the world (the inspiration for

Sir Arthur Conan Doyle's novel *The Lost World*), almost 3000 kilometres of relatively pristine coastline with impressive coral reefs and innumerable recreation islands, twenty-six remote and endlessly rewarding national parks, the bird-saturated and jaguar-haunted Los Llanos lowlands, the vast Orinoco River Delta with its surviving near-Stone Age cultures, and an evocative salsa-styled music which draws on the heritages of indigenous Indians, Africans, Spaniards and Latin Americans.

The image problem is hardly recent. The Spanish, to their great discredit, seemed to view their possession, as soon as it did not provide easy booty, with the disappointment and disdain of a lord of the manor who fails to bed a scullery maid. It was a half-hearted act of colonisation from the start; which seems to be 1498 when Columbus supposedly claimed it for Spain. In 1499, two tired officers of the crown landed on a swampy, malaria-ravaged section of the coast where sickly Indians built houses perched on stilts, and pompously named the place Venezuela (Little Venice). They were content to then sail home with an exceedingly large sack of pearls and, apart from some cartography the following year, it was not until 1520 that a serious attempt at settlement was made. With the inland Indians far more hostile and tenacious than their coastal brethren, achieving effective control over the new country was a slow and costly process.

Obsessed with the thought that the hinterland was rich in gold deposits, both in the ground and in caches hidden by Indians, the Spanish enslaved conquered tribes and then imported Africans to labour in barren mines. Gold did reach the coffers of Spain but it was from the Peruvian mountains and Mexico's central highlands. Venezuela was dismissed as a consistent dead loss, though not only for the Spaniards. Sir Walter Raleigh ventured twice up the Orinoco in search of the fabled golden city of El Dorado.

Fool's-gold dreams continued for centuries. It was while flying a prospector named McCracken into the Guyana Highlands on a gold hunt in 1928 that Jimmy Angel first came upon the *Auyan Tepui*, the table-top mountain of multi-coloured rock from which the falls that would later bear his name plummet. He missed them in the mist on that trip but vowed to return and locate the source of McCracken's legendary find of twenty pounds of gold; finally penetrating the falls' swirling mists and deflected rainbows in 1935. The much publicised discovery was no great shakes to the local Indians, who had been worshipping *Churun Meru* since prehistory.

The great irony is that, after more than four hundred years of outsiders begging Venezuela to give up its gold, this forgotten former outpost of New Spain was transformed from an economic backwater into a prosperous, relatively modern nation when the ground around Lake Maracaibo near the Colombian border began yielding up its oil in 1922. By the 1930s a forest network of over 10 000 wells was pumping up to two and a half million barrels of black crude a day. Buildings rose, roads spread and Venezuela joined the modern world. In a country of just eighteen million, oil revenues can go a long way; although uncontrolled spending and international oil gluts can also deliver the sort of economic problems that Venezuela is presently trying to overcome.

The impact of instant wealth was greatest in Caracas. In 1567, as Santiago de Leon de Caracas, it was a 25-block compound wedged between the Catuche, Caroata and Guaire Rivers, populated by sixty families. Even when it became the capital in 1731 it remained little more than a village. In 1800 there were just 40 000 residents. When the oil started flowing there were 400 000. Today there are over 4 000 000. It wasn't that long ago that cattle were driven down dirt roads where high-rise apartment blocks now stand.

Caracas is couched in a long intense valley, and has been described as a city in a bathtub—you have to climb in and out of it. The thirty minute drive from the airport at the coastal town of Maiquetia propels you upward through three mountain tunnels, one of them three kilometres long. As you climb to more than 1000 metres the heat dissipates and the soaring perspective overwhelms you. Wherever you stand in Caracas the mountains (Avila being the most dramatic) envelop you. Every window seems to open onto a sheer green face. And in an interesting twist, the middle class lives on the floor of the valley and the peasants in a maze of brick and corrugated-iron boxes on (some of) the mountain sides. For a change, the poor people have the views!

They also, along with their wealthier fellow citizens down the hill, have something that could well have been invented by the local tourism industry. I've heard climatic boasts from residents of more countries than I can count, but none were delivered with quite the conviction of the Caracas man who confided in me that he just turned down residency status in Canada and a prime position in his brother's prosperous firm there because he couldn't possibly leave 'the best weather in the world'. As it turns out, he spoke with fair authority. The mercury hovers around the

'Caracas Cool' (Mark Leonard)

24—27 degrees centigrade mark all year and there are no seasons as such.

The temperate climate is matched by a casual, slightly hedonistic city lifestyle. Walking through the heart of Old Caracas, with its parks, shaded plazas, street debating groups, market stalls, sidewalk cafes and lovingly restored colonial houses, civic buildings and cathedrals is as enriching an experience as South America offers, even if it sometimes seems that the entire panorama is part of a giant museum dedicated to one man, the secular icon Simon Bolivar.

Born in Caracas in 1783 and revered as the freedom fighter who liberated Venezuela, Colombia, Equador, Peru and Bolivia from the Spaniards, Bolivar is as omnipresent as Lenin, until recent times, was in the Soviet Union. Not even the United States' predilection for deifying such founding fathers as Washington and Lincoln comes close to the Bolivar submersion. Visitors arrive at Simon Bolivar International Airport and change dollars into bolivars, the local currency. A cab or bus then whisks them swiftly to Caracas, entering the city at the district of El Silencio, the landmark of which is Centro Simon Bolivar, a large government office complex with twin 32-storey towers, between which is the Plaza Bolivar. Once ensconced at the Caracas Hilton (easily the best pub in town) they may well go strolling down the old city's Plaza Bolivar and nearby streets to admire the imposing statue of Bolivar the warrior on horseback, and visit Bolivar's birthplace and the Bolivar Museum. A snack may be in order at El Dorado on Calle Bolivar. If they fly down to see the Orinoco River it will most likely be from the vantage point of the city of Ciudad Bolivar in Bolivar state.

All of which, it should be made clear, is an absolutely sincere expression of respect and admiration. This is not Iraq or the old Romania; mind police don't come around and remove Venezuelans from their beds in the middle of the night if their portrait of the great hero is hanging a bit skewiff. In fact, outside the historical heart of town, the cult of personality doesn't stand much of a chance amid the restaurants, boutiques, discos, night-clubs and shopping malls. More than half the population of Caracas is under the age of twenty and there is a vivacious mood in evidence that is prone to spill over into uninhibited revelry. Bullfights, cockfights and street dancing are certainly not out of the question.

They are, however, more easily found outside Caracas. Like the Brazilians, Venezuelans tend to concentrate themselves in specific (mostly coastal) areas, leaving much of their great expanse relatively untouched. The major road network is concentrated in the northern part of the country, with light aircraft used to reach the far-flung Amazonas and Gran Sabana regions. For that reason, being outside Caracas can sometimes be like visiting another country, with local festivities, religious celebrations and social patterns varying dramatically.

The incredible enthusiasm which the Venezuelans display for promoting tourism has placed virtually the entire country, the fifth largest on the continent, within relatively easy access. One tour company offers over a hundred structured trips, ranging from a half-day tour of Caracas to six-day Autana River expeditions in the heart of the Amazonas, and a 22-day sweep through the entire country. Easily the most popular are those involving a fly-past or hike to the base of Angel Falls, which remains in rugged isolation.

If you have a full day and a reasonable reserve of stamina, you can, with the aid of a scheduled commercial, and then a light, chartered flight, venture past the Falls to the village clearing of Kavak in the Kavak National Park. From there, local Indians take you walking and swimming upriver, through stream beds, across waterfalls (which you can swim through and sit behind), and against strong flows with the aid of a strategically anchored rope, to the awesome Cave Kavak. Here you pass through a narrow entrance gorge into a deep, steep water cavern fed by a thundering waterfall and frolic in the fierce spray, venturing in and out of the tumult at will. After a meal of seasoned grilled meat you can fly back to Caracas by way of the city of Ciudad Bolivar, on the Orinoco River.

A less strenuous journey can be taken, again by light aircraft, directly north across the Caribbean to Los Roques, an archipelago of 340 coral key islets, many with shallow internal lagoons. This is where prosperous citizens of Caracas (the ones who live on the base of the valley) come to frolic on weekends. Miami is only two air-hours away and the mood is decidedly tropical. A sea biology station has been established among the tiny outcrops to monitor the sea turtles, black salamanders, iguanas and pelicans which inhabit the area.

With the oil boom behind them but a workable infrastructure in place, the Venezuelans are faced with the challenge of maintaining a modern, functional and prosperous nation that can sidestep the sad economic malaise of many of their neighbours while still keeping the axes from the jungles and bulldozers from the beaches. There has been democratic government since 1958 and, although the gulf between rich and poor is still wider than most western visitors find comfortable, the country exudes an air of confidence and capability. Gold and rumours of gold still draw adventurers but not nearly as many as the beaches, rivers, mountains, forests, birds, food and overall vivacity.

# ADVENTURES IN
# ABU SIMBEL

The man at the Egypt Air ticket desk in downtown Aswan didn't like my credit card. He'd probably had the sort of day that turns Pharaohs to stone and precisely what he didn't need, a few minutes before five, was me. His intransigence was breathtaking; he could have instructed groups of trainees in the finer aspects of never giving an inch.

He stabbed his finger at the expiry date, or the second half of it anyway, ignoring the month, which happened to be about seven hence, and declared that my plastic had expired. It was the same sort of insane interpretation which leads border officials to refuse you a two-day entry onto their precious piece of soil because your passport only has six months of its lifespan remaining.

I procured pounds and refused to remove myself from his sight until he'd issued a ticket for the next morning's flight to Abu Simbel, near the Sudanese border. I wanted him to know that I was not a tourist to be trifled with, that after four days of languid Nile sailing aboard one of the 250 luxury, multi-deck cruisers which ferry visitors of immense number between Luxor and Aswan, depositing them at all the temples through which Peter Ustinov pursued villains in *Death On The Nile*, I had sufficient reserves of energy to stand there all night. By six, I thought I was going to have to do just that.

It was really the only thing that went wrong in Aswan, well, apart from the temperature, which seems to hover around 40 degrees centigrade in any of the months that have even a nodding acquaintanceship with summer. This crossroads town for the ancient caravan routes between Egypt and Sudan is the one essential destination after Cairo. Here, the Nile is scattered with rocks and islands as its shape is contorted by the mighty Aswan High Dam, which increased the town's population tenfold from its modest 50 000 base thirty years ago. The caravans have been replaced by Nile boats, shuttle aircraft and daily air-conditioned sleeper trains, but the crossroads feel remains. Even though, with the exception of Abu Simbel, there is almost nowhere else to go but back from whence you came after you have reached and enjoyed Aswan.

Enjoyment is rife in Aswan, particularly on the part of adult western women, most of whom seem to have been raised on exotic tales of dusky Nubian slaves and harem guardians. One particularly impressive specimen of the race—slaves no longer—with skin blacker than a coal seam, glinting white teeth and a finely structured face that could have been reproduced on a postage stamp, energetically rowed his felucca across to Elephantine Island on a windless day with such athletic assertiveness that the females in my party abandoned all pretence of decorum and whimpered audibly while chewing the hems of their garments. They would have started on his had the crossing been any longer.

Nubia is geographically indeterminate, rather like Lapland. Apparently, in the tradition of all fabled lands of riches, it has always been so. 'Nub' was the ancient Egyptian word for gold, and the area of the first and second cataracts of the Nile, where the harsh desert came right to the river's edge, was well endowed with the precious substance—to say nothing of copper, diorite, pink and black granite, ivory, cattle, and suitably savage foot soldiers for Pharaoh's army. Apart from periods when interlopers such as the Hyksos were calling the shots, it was an integral part of the great Egyptian empire. Almost every Pharaoh erected a temple or a monument there and boasted of his far-flung domains with pride. No doubt it was Cairo's California, with the kings eagerly exhorting 'Go south young man' to their subjects.

More so than gold, Aswan granite was the prize of the possession. To more fully satisfy the edifice complex of the self-glorifying Egyptians, the stone was quarried and shipped down the Nile to ancient Thebes (now Luxor) and Cairo. At the Unfinished Obelisk one can view what would have been the largest single piece of stone ever handled. Abandoned by Hatshepsut's quarrymen because of a fault line, this 42-metre long piece of part-polished granite would have weighed around a million kilos, had it been eventually removed from the parent rock and fashioned into a soaring monument to human vanity.

Talking of which, I did make the morning plane to Abu Simbel, the second greatest man-made marvel in Egypt after the Pyramids. My adversary at the ticket office had resisted the temptation to wipe me from the computer. By midnight I would be wishing that he hadn't.

Boeing 767s lob onto the parched and desolate earth of Abu Simbel each day as part of a well-oiled tourism procedure. Passengers walk through a tiny airport and onto a fleet of modern buses which whisks them down the road to the temples of Ramses II and Hathor. Two hours later they retrace their steps, strap themselves back into the Boeing and are on the verandah of the Old Cataract Hotel ninety minutes or so later, sipping gin and tonics (without ice) and digesting the day's delights.

Such was not destined to be my experience, for, sadly, some sand got into the oil of my day's machine. Rather a lot of it, actually. The sandstorm which struck the minuscule outpost as I was waiting to depart was so ferocious that it was reported by British newspapers, caused the cancellation of war games and was even given some sort of ranking by the regularly sandblasted Egyptians (the fifth worst this millennium, or something like that). But although I spent nine hours largely confined to a plastic chair, nibbling stale wafers and reading a guide book which included such essential phrases as 'a museum is a building where old and interesting objects are kept,' my journey to Abu Simbel was certainly not in vain.

Ramses II was the third Pharaoh of the Nineteenth Dynasty, about 3000 years ago. He reigned for 67 years, fathered 92 sons and 106 daughters, and fair filled the land with imposing monuments to guess who. He ordered the poet Pentaur to inscribe the walls of his various vast temples with hieroglyphic depictions of gripping tales of his battle bravery. After stirring translations are delivered by guides in Luxor, Karnak and Abu Simbel, one could be forgiven for thinking that he was so rarely by the homefires that he must have fathered his children by some primitive means of artificial insemination. Not quite so. Ramses the Great, as he preferred to be known, only ever fought one battle, against the Hittites at Kadesh, and that ended in a draw and a treaty.

To perpetuate his person, Ramses embarked upon a building project at Abu Simbel as audacious as the Pyramid of Cheops in Cairo. While almost every historical Egyptian edifice is freestanding, the good king set his slaves to work carving an awesome facade out of the side of a mountain in the middle of the Nubian desert. The greater of the two temples consists of four colossal exterior statues of Ramses II—each twenty-metres high and four metres from ear to ear—topped by a series of carvings of sacred baboons. Inside, the Great Hall is supported by pillars 31-metres high and eight more statues of our man Ramses in the form of the god Osiris. The lesser temple was built for wife Nefertari and dedicated to Hathor, the goddess of music, dancing and love. Its facade consisted of six ten-metre statues, four of which depict Ramses II.

Stumbled upon in 1813 by a traveller called Ludwig, who saw stone faces emerging through a sand drift, the two temples at Abu Simbel were uncovered by dredging in 1817. They were an exotic attraction for the hardiest of world travellers for almost one hundred and fifty years, until the building of the Aswan High Dam in 1960. As the dam rose, so too did the water level of the Nile and Lake Nasser. Many temples were lost forever, while others were moved and saved. In appreciation of American assistance, the entire Temple of Dendur, 80 kilometres south of Aswan, was donated to New York's Metropolitan Museum of Art.

But it was the Swedes who masterminded the most famous rescue mission of all. Answering a plea to the UN by Egypt to save Ramses' twin monuments, UNESCO accepted a Swedish proposal to cut the sandstone temples into 1036 thirty-tonne blocks, and the surrounding rock into another 110 pieces; transport the entire jigsaw puzzle 90 metres above the original level and reassemble the parts with computer assistance, inside two enormous domes of reinforced concrete—literally artificial mountains. Nothing less than the most demanding archaeological restoration project ever undertaken.

Moving urgently from a 21 May 1965 commencement point to beat the rising floodwaters, the UN spent almost five years and US$40 million of the world's money preserving the temples—without cracking or breaking a single block. At peak periods there were some 2000 people living at Abu Simbel, in a temporary town that included shops, cinemas and a swimming pool—facilities the original builders might well have appreciated. It was a triumph for modern technology but also a sobering reminder of the incredible scientific precision of the ancient Egyptians. For there was one aspect the restorers never got quite right. It is known as the Miracle of the Sun.

In the west wall of the sanctuary area of the Temple of Ramses II are four statues of gods of the temple—Ptah, Amon, Ramses II and Ra-Horakhty. Each year, at exactly 5.58 am on 21 March and 21 September, a ray of sunlight would strike into the sanctuary like an arrow, falling on the altar and then, in turn, the faces of the gods; stopping before it illuminated Ptah, who is the god of darkness. In March 1969, the saviours of the temples nervously awaited the return of the Miracle of the Sun. It came but, despite all the twentieth-century technology available for calculations, was one day out.

The gods obviously blessed me by keeping the sandstorm at bay until I had completed my tour of inspection, which ended with a walk through the inside of the false bell-jar mountain. It was the oddest of experiences, like a sudden detour through a film sound stage or the internal workings of a Disneyland ride. I'm still not sure if I'm glad I did it. A good magician does not reveal his tricks.

The sandstorm finally abated, after we wretched travellers had been bused to the only hotel in a 500-mile radius to siphon the bar dry and munch some large platters of french fries. Just as it was beginning to appear that our brief excursion into the desert was taking on Gilligan's Island dimensions, a rescue aircraft descended, was roundly cheered and managed to take off fully laden in a northward direction. Instead of an after-lunch cocktail in Aswan, I partook of a midnight kebab in Cairo. It was a hard day to be sure, but then wielding a chisel for the megalomaniacal Ramses II can't have been a picnic either. I think I came out of it best.

# TURKEY: EDGING INTO EUROPE

A surprising number of impressions of Turkey seem to have been formed solely by the film *Midnight Express*. Indeed, more than a few well-meaning friends raised well-meaning eyebrows in well-meaning despair in the days before my departure. It got so bad that I embarked with a hint of trepidation; which I shook off within a few hours of arrival. For visitors not given to strapping three kilos of hash to their abdomen in the vicinity of airports, Turkey is probably less of a police state than the Greater City of London. (However, I believe the Kurds of Eastern Turkey view the matter somewhat differently.)

I suppose there are plenty of police in Istanbul, it's just that they don't show themselves very often, at least not during the hot parts of the day. Those that are unfortunate enough to be stationed on the street to accomplish vital tasks like pointing German tourists toward Topkapi Palace seem to be overwhelmingly ignored by the citizens.

A mild form of anarchy prevails in Istanbul, at least as far as traffic is concerned. There is presently a campaign being mounted to persuade drivers to note and obey traffic lights, though nobody gives it much hope. If a hint of success is perceived, the authorities might move on to pedestrian preservation. There are zebra crossings in what was ancient Constantinople but one wonders why. The only smart way to cross a busy street is to enter into collusion with twenty other pedestrians and proceed as a block. Presented with the likelihood of sustaining substantial damage to his car, even a Turkish driver will stop, or at least swerve.

Turkey plainly belongs to the male half of its population. Despite aspirations to European status, this almost wholly Muslim

101

nation embraces social attitudes common to most of the Middle East. This became eerily apparent when I strolled through an Istanbul amusement park on a Saturday evening. The obligatory laughing, squealing and posing was all in evidence but with a bizarre twist. There was barely a female in the place. Hundreds of boisterous men and boys but nary a sister, girlfriend or wife. I thought for a moment that they might have been all busy at work at Istanbul's booming chain of McDonald's—one of the world's leading employers of metropolitan womanhood—until I recalled that the one I had passed earlier had resembled a Turkish Boys' Brigade. Even waitresses are thin on the ground. The Turks do, it would seem, lock up their daughters, at least after dark.

Turkey, let it be known, has been 'discovered'. Since the late 1980s it has been widely seen as the Greece of a decade ago—a largely inexpensive and unfailingly interesting location within easy reach of Europe.

Of course, the Turks would argue that they are *in* Europe. Although maps show only three per cent of land mass on the left of the Bosphorus (Thrace) to be officially attached to the European continent, such a toehold is considered sufficient to dismiss any Asian or Middle Eastern labels. Turkey is a NATO and OECD member, and its 55 million citizens seem to be counting down the days to full membership of the European Economic Community. If fifteen tour buses parked permanently outside the Blue Mosque is the price to be paid for such admission, then so be it.

But western? Often not so you'd notice. At a Turkish Airlines ticket office in the Sheraton/Hilton-dominated Taxim Park area— where gypsies lead giant, motley brown bears through parks for the sole purpose of good-naturedly extorting vast sums from camera-wielding tourists—I waited patiently in line while any notions of being in Europe evaporated. At one desk, three businessmen were buying seats to Teheran, the crescendo of their agitated voices rising more swiftly than my threshold of pain. The robed man in front of me was arguing about a flight to Jedda, waving around handfuls of Arabian rials. A pleasant, middle-aged female attendant was still insisting upon Turkish lira as I left.

Istanbul is not a city to which one can remain indifferent. There may be a severe shortage of luxury hotels on the level of the superb Ramada Istanbul (created by converting a city intersection and four art deco apartment buildings), but there are also more imposing edifices than in almost any other two cities put together. Even the Basilica Cistern, a poorly-marked underground water reservoir which serviced the sieged citizens of Emperor Justinian some 1500 years ago, boasts 336 giant Corinthian marble columns and a couple of colossal Medusa heads. Above ground, where the Roman, Byzantine and Ottoman empire builders actually wanted their monuments to be seen and admired, the architectural splendour seems endless.

One can walk from the Blue Mosque, down to Hagia Sophia Church and on to Topkapi Palace in a single day. Sitting proudly on the tip of the Istanbul Peninsula where the Bosphorus, Sea of Marmara and Golden Horn meet, Topkapi is the largest and oldest palace in the world. Once the domain of Sultans and their harems, viziers and potentates, it is now a 700 000 square metre museum documenting the reign of the Ottoman Empire.

The emblems and images tumble atop each other. Minarets and mosques, sultans and sandals, carpets and coffee, belly dancers and bazaars, leather and lamps. Here one can taste a little of a thousand and one Arabian nights, murder and mayhem on the Orient Express, and daring jewel raids on Topkapi Palace. Turkey, once the heart of an empire which ruled a third of the known world, can still stir the most jaded senses.

It stirred mine and satiated a few appetites in the process. I think it was the sea-bass that finally did me in. It was floating in paprika sauce and I was floating in the extravagant hospitality of a people to whom tourism is yet to become a burden. I'd taken a Sunday morning ferry up the Bosphorus from Istanbul to its final stop, the township of Sariyer. There, from the cosy, corner-window table of a stupendously well-stocked seafood restaurant, I watched Russian cruise liners gliding into the mouth of the Black Sea, returning to Odessa from warmer Mediterranean waters.

I made short work of the bass and its attendant Turkish side dishes, only slightly mindful of the feast awaiting me upon my return. That night, four hungry antipodean wayfarers sat down, in a leading Turkish restaurant, to a vast, kebab-based meal which, with liquid accompaniment, set us back a total of 25 Australian dollars. As I begged the bass to move aside and rummaged for the bicarb, I made a mental note to enquire about permanent residency status.

Leaving Istanbul requires no small degree of determination but the wrench is rewarding. Turkish Airlines provides an extensive, relatively cheap internal network using Airbuses and modern Boeings. The Aegean coastal city of Izmir—believed to be the birthplace of the Greek poet Homer—is a Silk Road staging point for visits to the ancient city of Ephesus, where the Apostle Paul wrote the epistles which survive as Ephesians in the Bible. With over 8000 kilometres of coastline (the Mediterranean, Aegean, Black and Bosphorus Seas), Turkey is a heavyweight contender in the summer holiday stakes and caters to sun lovers with hundreds of intimate coastal resort towns. On the less-visited Black Sea coast is the port of Trabzon, with its spectacular cliff-face Byzantine monastery. To the east is Mount Ararat, the possible resting place of Noah's Ark; the ancient Harran, with its curious domed dwellings, where (according to Genesis 11:31) the prophet Abraham sojourned almost four thousand years ago; the temples of Nemrut Dagi, where a minor pre-Roman potentate filled two ledges of bare mountain with massive statues of himself and assorted gods for the people of a later age to ponder upon; Van, the old Urartian capital by the immense lake of the same name and, most desirable of all, Erzurum.

There awaits, in the city of Erzurum, on the great high plateau of Eastern Anatolia, a new meaning to the phrase 'crossroads of the world'. Extend an arm and take half a turn and you can point to the borders of Armenia, Iran, Iraq and Syria. Gaze in the opposite direction and the vast sweep of the ever-strategic land bridge between Asia and Europe takes your imagination all the way to the Aegean and the Bosphorus. It is just not possible to say you have seen Turkey if you have not made your way from Istanbul eastward through the fabled Cappadocia region to the harshly beautiful plains, plateaus, mountains, lakes and forests of the great Anatolian realm.

From November to June, the daily Turkish Airlines flight from Istanbul and Ankara brings in sportsmen keen to tackle the six and a half kilometre snowfield of Mount Palandoken, listed as the world's second largest international ski resort by the International Skiing Association. In the warmer months, the flight ferries in adventurous travellers. Tired of Istanbul's intensity, they come in search of a more primitive, untouched Turkey; hoping to sift through the remnants of fallen empires.

Compared to the invaders Erzurum has had to receive and repel for centuries, this tourism trickle is easily absorbed. The city has been conquered and lost by Arabs, Armenians, Byzantines, Mongols, Persians, Romans, Russians, Saltuk and Seljuk Turks and Ottomans. From Alexander the Great to Selim the Grim, Erzurum has been on the 'must have' list of innumerable titans of terror.

And with good reason. Long a confluence of major roads and trade routes, its possession has always been deemed advantageous by the empire builders. As recently as 1882 and 1916, Russian troops were in brief control. Today, as NATO's eastern bulwark, the quarter million populated city still seems somehow . . . critical. In the elegant dining room of the 104-room Otel Oral, one can find civilian 'advisers' from England and America; quiet, middle-aged technicians on well-payed six-month assignments who have been well ingrained with the 'loose lips sink ships' philosophy. They will tell you everything about their families and their warm feelings for Turkey but absolutely nothing about their skills or employment. There are so many pregnant pauses and awkward subject changes that you want to dash back to your room and start tapping away at a political suspense novel.

No, despite its isolation, there is nothing sleepy about Erzurum; playing host as it does to both a major university and an even vaster military base. In the afternoons it is hard to determine which lines are longest—those of students gleefully escaping their yoke, or the convoys of grey and khaki weaponry.

The rich mix of students, soldiers, farmers and wealthy Iranians on shopping expeditions gives the city a surprising vitality. Although one may come expecting a deep conservatism, it's hard not to be astounded by the openness of the citizenry. Unlike Istanbul, the streets are full of young, enquiring, effusively friendly and (mostly) unveiled faces. Sometimes, it is not hard to forget just where you are.

Eastern Anatolia, like the rest of Turkey, is a giant open-air museum, with innumerable artifacts dating back to the dawn of civilisation. Hittite sculptures, Arab castles, Seljuk fortresses, Ottoman mosques, Urartu (first century) citadels, Christian murals, caravanserais and silk roads dot the landscape. From the Black Sea Mountains down through the High Mesopotamian Plain to the Toros Mountains of the south, historical and geographic riches tumble one upon another.

Yet for all its human history, which can be traced back to at least 5000 BC, the entire Eastern Anatolian region still bears the cultural mark of one relatively recent golden epoch—the Great Seljuk Turkish Empire. Seven hundred years after Constantine moved the centre of the Roman Empire from Rome to (what is now) Istanbul and commenced the Byzantine Empire, the rise of the first young Turks began. Based in Persia, the Seljuks swept across Central Asia to lay claim to most of the territory now known as Iran, Iraq and Turkey. In 1071, at the Battle of Manzikert, they seized Erzurum (then Theodosipolis) and opened up Anatolia to Turkish settlement.

As far as empires go, the Seljuks had a fairly brief run, from 1037 to just 1109. However, in that time they gave the world Omar Khayyam and evolved a distinctive culture, with fine architecture, art, design and philosophy. The legacy of those 72 eventful years is now worn proudly by Erzurum, a twentieth-century centre of learning, culture and commerce which played host to Ataturk's 1919 Erzurum Congress, where the boundaries that contain modern Turkey were determined.

Erzurum remains strangely compelling, offering myriad contrasts. The Boeing jets that descend into the city's valley each day pass over goat herders, horse carts and flat-roofed houses heaped high with crop produce. Take a morning road excursion into the Kackar Mountains to the township and lake of Tortum, through cherry and apricot orchards, and you can believe that time has stood still. This is not the Turkey of Istanbul or Ankara, but the ancient Anatolia of Central Asia.

Turkey is a rich blend of peoples, from the swarthy Mediterranean stock of the west, to the Caspian Armenians of the east, to the Iranian-extracted Kurds of the southeast. They virtually all speak Turkish but the ethnic differences are quite immense. Although the Turks are 99 per cent Muslim, it is a gentle brand of Islam, not unlike that practised in Indonesia. When not in motor vehicles, they are warm, curious and often remarkably kind. They eat, drink and make merry with an infectious voracity and are still sufficiently untouched by the ugly side of tourism to extend an almost universal hospitality.

The abundance of the country is striking. In the heart of Istanbul, on the clogged bridge spanning the Golden Horn, fishermen jammed elbow to elbow pull in silver tiddlers on an assembly-line basis. Like Argentinians, Germans and most Asians, the Turks pay significant attention to their stomachs. Dining is a serious undertaking. From one end of the country to the other, regardless of ethnic differences, they consume vast amounts of spicy, delectable doner kebab, cut from flaming spits inside almost every restaurant and small cafe. When the kebab isn't cooking, bountiful seafood is. The lifestyle is comfortable and Mediterranean, the weather temperate and the surrounds incomparable. It is not a country you visit only once.

# IN SEARCH OF THE WILD MAN OF BORNEO

Borneo, alas, is no more. It has gone the way of Ceylon, Rhodesia and the Congo. These days the mysterious and legendary home of head-hunters, hornbills and 89 species of frog is known by the Indonesian name of Kalimantan.

The wild man, if he still exists, and if he has any sense, is probably working for Union Oil and living in plush company quarters in the hills of Balikpapan, a crossroads city of some 300 000, where Kalimantan gives way to California. Fenced compounds, security guards, speed humps, country clubs and Olympic swimming pools mark Balikpapan as a most extraordinary Indonesian metropolis, where American, Australian and European voices are as common as Japanese motorcycles.

For centuries, Borneo was as remote as Japan before the Meiji restoration. Some adventurous Malay and Chinese traders bartered with primitive tribesmen in relatively safe coastal ports up until the turn of this century, when Europeans began to establish scattered settlements. Botanists and naturalists were among the first to penetrate the interior, drawn by more than a thousand varieties of bird, macaque monkeys, honey and sun bears, flying squirrels, gibbons, wild dogs and cats, elephants and gliding frogs and lizards.

Despite these forays, and the passion of adventure authors and Hollywood script writers for this jungle island, it kept its distance from civilisation until the Indonesian Republic came into being in 1945. Today, there are four Garuda jets from Jakarta every day and a five-star hotel which could easily be ranked as one of the hundred best in the world.

Herman Diener, general manager of the 220-room Hotel Benakutai, which boasts a roof helipad and a trendy health club, is one of the many Dutchmen who found a comfortable spiritual and physical home in the former Dutch East Indies once the battle for independence, which ended 350 years of colonial rule, was relegated to the history books. In many ways, he is continuing a benign civilising role which his forefathers began in the late sixteenth century.

'This hotel exists to serve the oil industry,' admits Diener. 'It could not survive from tourism. The business demand for rooms was so strong that we were forced to open in 1980, when only the first 40 rooms were ready, and build the other 180 around the guests, who didn't mind at all.' Diener, a superb photographer, possesses an unabashed love for Kalimantan and has graced his Balikpapan hotel with exquisite handicrafts, artifacts and prints of remote jungle locations to which he has trekked.

The island's wealth is concentrated in the resource-rich region of East Kalimantan. Not only is it one of the world's major oilfields, it is also responsible for 70 per cent of Indonesia's timber exports. Some one hundred foreign and domestic forestry companies are busy culling huge tracts of virgin forest, generating a real boom economy and alarming conservationists.

The western employees of the oil and timber companies appear to care little for the exotic nature of the interior, preferring to holiday in Hong Kong, Bangkok or Singapore. Few take advantage of the 161 rivers and 111 lakes in Eastern Kalimantan alone. Open to tourism for just over ten years, these waterways are the principal avenues of trade, communication and travel within a rugged island accounting for 28 per cent of the Indonesian land area but only 4 per cent of the population. Their exploration is left to the hardy tourists.

Officially described by Indonesian tourism edicts as being of 'special interest, mainly for the adventurous traveller, as modern facilities may not always be available,' Kalimantan is truly a last frontier. Surprisingly accessible, it offers all an opportunity to safely journey into something akin to Joseph Conrad's *Heart of Darkness*, little more than one air hour from Bali or Jakarta.

After flying into Balikpapan and viewing the flaming oil refinery flares by night from Pasir Ridge, amid manicured gardens and multi-million rupiah mansions, there is really only one direction to take to escape the bored American and Australian wives, and the horror of ten-gallon cowboy hats at every turn—up the mighty Mahakam River, which reaches 560 kilometres into the jungle and carries most of the region's harvested timber. One of only four rivers in the world inhabited by freshwater porpoise, the very deep Mahakam is a lifeline, a source of sustenance, and a sewer. Occasionally attaining a width of 5 kilometres, it is to the Dayak people what the Ganges is to India's Hindus, and only the fact that Kalimantan has one of the planet's lowest population densities has saved it from the putrefaction of Mother Ganges. The Mahakam seems muddy and a little sludgy but only because the equatorial climate and lush vegetation has turned most of its deltas and tributaries into swamp and marsh. Despite the logging refuse, it is essentially a clean waterway, playing host to a wondrous array of humanity. The people of Kalimantan have a great affinity with water and their majestic three-masted schooners still ply the trade route to Java.

From Balikpapan it is a three-hour car trip to the river trading towns of Samarinda (established in 1730) and Tenggarong, where a number of major Indonesian tour companies commence three, six, ten and fourteen-day river journeys—none of them cheap, but all of them unforgettable. Nights are spent either sleeping rough with a bedroll on the covered boat deck or under a mosquito net in a private room of a Dayak longhouse. Five-star luxury comfort begins and ends at Balikpapan's Hotel Benakutai.

The *Sumber Ulin* is a long, flat river taxi with open decking, but it was difficult to view it as anything other than Conrad's *Nellie*, 'a cruising yawl'. It made slow but steady time against the unpredictable current, chugging past an endless panorama of houses on stilts, make-shift jetties, orchid and mangrove coves, and children, always children, playing, washing, waving and working. More than half the population of Indonesia is under the age of twenty, a fact evident even in sparsely populated East Kalimantan. When the children weren't squealing it was monkeys, swinging through the trees in bona-fide Tarzan fashion along the river bank. Crocodiles kept a low profile; so low I spotted nary a one. Resource industry has driven the creatures well inland.

The floating village of Senoni serves as a trading post for native timber-mill workers. More than a kilometre long, the log jam carries twenty or so basic shops, selling fried bananas, Coca-Cola, and standard groceries. The river taxis berth there for refreshment stops, disgorging hundreds of hungry passengers onto the bobbing deck, then moving off swiftly. The log rafts intended for downstream sawmills edge their way along the river at a pace

*Mahakam River, East Kalimantan (Bob King)*

determined by their awesome bulk. I counted a couple of hundred logs in one raft before being distracted by an entire family living in a temporary shanty lashed to the centre. The river people live as one with their great river. Small canoes, powered by extended screw propellers, sweep up and down from house to house, village to village, carrying unimaginable goods and assorted relatives.

Fishing canoes pull alongside and offer prawns the size of small lobsters, fresh fish, and other river produce. This becomes the main course upon the tour boat, embellished with *nasi goreng, ayam goreng* (fried chicken), eggs, sambal (hot, crushed chillies) and succulent fresh fruit. At no point is one ever urged to buy anything. This is not Bali; there are no Mahakam River t-shirts or carry bags. Tourism is still a gentle intrusion and Kalimantan life, outside the oil cities, has yet to devote itself to the pursuit of the dollar. As a result it is easy to miss dishes of precious gems, superb Bugis woodcarvings, and ancient Dayak stone necklaces. All, in western vernacular, priced to clear. In far greater demand are whole red chillies which, when cut open and hung high, become an unbelievably effective insect repellent.

The Dayak people are the ultimate lure of any journey up the Mahakam. This light-skinned, fine featured race lived for centuries in complete isolation. When Asian traders landed on the Borneo coast they moved further and further inland, but when the Dutch colonisers penetrated the jungle, their primitive lifestyle was destined to change. Today the name 'Dayak' embraces over 200 individual tribes, identified as ten ethnic subgroups.

For the visitor, the first real contact with the Dayak occurs back in the river port of Tenggarong, where the sultan's palace, cemetery and grounds have been converted into a museum. Among the famous collections of Ming vases (Dayak origins are in Southern China), Cambodian and Vietnamese pottery, and assorted regal thrones, are scattered photographs of primitive Dayak headhunters, many with ears grotesquely extended to the shoulder in much the same manner as the bottom lip of some female members of the Sara tribes of Chad in North Africa.

The museum also includes some exhibits from the nearby Kuyai Game Reserve, the second biggest in Indonesia, where orangoutang, a few rhino, tree-draped pythons, civet cats, wild pigs and unlimited bird life crashes about the thick undergrowth and feeds from the wild streams.

The first major Dayak village is found 24 hours upriver from Tenggarong, on the far side of Jempang Lake, one of the biggest and (as a folklore source) important in all Kalimantan. Tanjung Isuy is a showpiece among Dayak villages. It looms as a lost city in the jungle, its grey timber waterfront dwellings giving little indication of the warmth inside.

At the main jetty, our arrival was announced and we awaited an official invitation to walk the 200 metres of clean, dirt main street to the chief's *lamin* (longhouse). Bobbing about the docks, we were invaded by children who ventured aboard in twos and threes until 43 of them were surrounding the startled but delighted white visitors. Lined up in choir formation, they consented to sing, and joyfully bellowed forth the Indonesian state song, school nursery rhymes and traditional chants. One young teenage boy seized a discarded beer can and, using one knuckle, developed an extraordinary off-beat percussion accompaniment.

The *lamin* is the core of Dayak communal life. Generally the home of several families of the same ancestral line, these longhouses can be up to 180-metres long and 18-metres wide, with up to fifty family units in residence. Raised at least three metres off the ground, they are reached by ornate (and erotic) ladders and boast wide verandahs where, once, the freshly-cut enemy heads used in ceremonies were hung. Today, families relax on these verandahs in the afternoon shade, no doubt discussing how best to spend their collective tourism income. Although they don't use cars, the occasional motorbike does rudely interrupt the serenity, and a network of lofty antennae has brought television to the village.

The path to the relatively small *lamin* of Tanjung Isuy leads past a Muslim mosque, with its inevitable battery of tin speaker horns (used to call the faithful to prayer at truly ungodly hours), and a Catholic church. Like the Torajan people of Central Sulawesi (the Celebes) who opted for Christianity over Islam because the latter forbade their intake of beloved palm wine, the animist Dayaks are tolerant of introduced religion. An average village house might well possess a portrait of Christ, a small stone Buddha and an animist altar. Anything for a quiet life, and the freedom to hunt, fish, farm and pursue the skills of weaving and embroidery which have brought the village local renown.

At the *lamin*, more than a hundred villagers, dressed in traditional garb, break into dance and song at the approach of visitors. The gateway is symbolically barred by a twisted vine, which the first visitor severs with a jewel-encrusted sword after answering *kabar baik* (we come for good reason) to the headman's demand. Once inside the compound, the visitors are danced around, adorned with garlands, refreshed with coconut milk, and sung and intoned to. The *Roik Bayu Enpat* ceremony may be well-rehearsed native theatrics but the assault on the senses is total.

Those who are not participating in the ceremony are watching it, for the entire village and its industry have stopped dead. Children have run from their classrooms and farmers from their fields. For this reason, the western-educated elders of the community speak openly about the 'fragile nature of tourism'. At present, they welcome four to eight visitors each month but this is bound to rise with the introduction of a cheaper Indonesian air pass by Garuda. Their logical answer to the disruption of village life is a move to confine tourist arrivals to the weekend.

Outside of the headman, the most important Benuaq Dayak is the *belian*, the witch doctor who administers traditional medicine and magic. He is able to discern the actions of the *Orang Gaib*, an unseen human-related being who can wreak havoc on people's lives and even steal away virile young men for immoral purposes (in reality, they probably sneak off to Balikpapan and the giant Valley of Hope brothel). In a tradition that can be traced back to the Dayak's Chinese origins, the *belian* is called upon before the erection of any new building, to ensure that no territory of the *Orang Gaib* is being infringed upon.

In March and December, the *belian* may stage extravagant magic ceremonies, if he feels so inclined. In our case, being the very end of March, he consented. That night, inside the *lamin*, spirits were summoned and potions administered. The *belian* and his junior danced and cavorted through the assembled multitude, smearing root juice on faces and lightly slapping bodies with leafy branches. At times we visitors were called upon to dance, or at least keep to the pace of the frenzied leaders, whose agility could strike envy into a Romanian gymnast's heart. The fever pitch of the ceremony was generated by a small male percussion ensemble which used drums, chimes and gongs to create an intense rhythm pattern not unlike Jamaican reggae or roots rock'n'roll. By the completion, Babaman the *belian*, not a young man by any means, was undeniably one possessed; his eyes blazing, his body glistening. The next morning when he rode with us on the river, he was a sweet and gentle old man, eager to talk (through an interpreter) of his twenty grandchildren.

Less than fifty years ago, the Dayaks lived in almost constant internal warfare, taking heads and perpetrating hideous tortures. By adopting the positive aspects of 'civilisation' and rejecting the negative, they have survived intact into the modern age as a proud and extremely admirable people. Unlike the tribes in the similar terrain of the Amazon Basin, the Dayaks have attained a relatively high standard of living and a sense of national and local unity which is becoming synonymous with most of the vast Indonesian archipelago. The wild man of Borneo may have been tamed, but he is no less rewarding to those who seek him out.

*The volume of Mahakam River visitors has grown steadily since I prepared this feature in 1985. Now they are whisked upriver in swift, air-conditioned water craft and spared the dubious delights of sleeping rough on boat decks. The income continues to contribute positively to village life; which has not been damaged to any significant extent by tourism.*

# FREEFALLING FOR FERTILITY

The fear, when there is any, can be read on the buttocks as an almost imperceptible quiver. Moving in the final, climactic stage of ascent to an exalted state of grace, the strapping Pentecost Island land diver stands gingerly at the end of a short, slender platform protruding from a vast wooden tower and surveys his land and his people, fully aware that to step down would bring no disgrace. After raising his hands to silence the swaying, chanting, whistling, stomp-dancers below, he fixes his gaze on the horizon, intones a short monologue, releases croton leaves from his belt, raises his hands in supplication and gently leans forward into thin Vanuatuan air.

As his *gol* (body), gracefully arched backwards, begins its free fall, the diver crosses his arms across his chest in a fatalistic gesture of confidence. Exhilarated and terrified in equal proportion, he plummets earthward, tethered to the thirty-metre high tower by two vines strapped to his ankles. As the vines snap taut, his platform collapses, slightly breaking a fall which, if all goes well, will enable him to scrape the slanted ground with his head and hurl himself backward, so as to land triumphantly on his feet and receive the rapture of his village.

The primitive world is disappearing. Ritualistic lifestyles are being lost to the planet at much the same rate as rainforests and clean water channels. Three days upriver in Eastern Borneo, where I once danced with a witchdoctor, formerly-feared headhunters watch Indonesian urban soap operas on television. There seems to be no point on the globe so remote that it cannot be reached by *Rambo* videos, Coca Cola, digital watches, *Thriller* cassettes, and sloganed t-shirts. The noble savage has become, more often than we would care to consider, the ignoble consumer. Burton and Livingston would be horrified.

Certainly, it is still possible to see locals stroll barefoot across hot coals, or skewer their cheeks with iron spikes, or grotesquely stretch their lips and ear lobes, or even slaughter hundreds of pigs and buffalo during bizarre funeral rituals. There are generally shows at two, four, six and eight, adjacent to the souvenir stalls and don't forget to tell your friends, now.

No, that's not fair. Tourism has not corrupted all the ancient ceremonies of the primitive realm. In fact, it's managed to save a few. At least that's what Kirk Huffman, curator of Vanuatu's National Museum, believes. He credits the profitable admission of select numbers of outsiders to the annual land diving ceremony on remote Pentecost Island with reviving and purifying an endangered quasi-religious rite.

In his opinion, 'The land dives being held now, at least on the missionised side of the island, are better than they were twenty years ago, the traditional aspects have been re-emphasised. It has a lot to do with pride. The ceremony has no counterpart elsewhere in Melanesia or even Vanuatu, and the people of Southern Pentecost now realise that they've got something that nobody else on earth has, something that can draw people from all over the world and bring much-needed money into their villages. It's a rare case of tourism actually assisting the survival of something quite precious.'

On Pentecost Island the villagers don't sell t-shirts or even replicas of their tower of entwined vines and lashed logs. Visitors are deposited on a rough grass landing strip by twenty-seater, twin-engine Otters and carted off into the jungle perched precariously around the trays of small trucks. There are no 'facilities' as such. Even at the jump site there is a single haphazardly placed log for a few lucky derrières; while the remainder of the thirty or so interlopers grab whatever possie or footing they can on the side of a steep mountain. The reception extended is more courteous than effusive though the village chief does make a point of declaring thanks for 'all your money' before the final leap.

There is no way of telling just how old the jump is. Reliable written history for the group of islands charted by Captain Cook in 1774 and known by its colonisers as the New Hebrides until 1980, starts in 1830. As human settlement of the islands preceded white arrival by up to 4000 years, the ritual could be hundreds or even a thousand years old. The participants will tell you that their fathers, grandfathers and great grandfathers jumped, but beyond that is only speculation.

However, there is an enduring legend based around a woman who repeatedly ran away from the mistreatments of her husband Tamalié, only to be caught and carted back home for more of the same on each occasion. Finally, she took refuge high in a banyan tree, tying lianas (vines) to her ankles as she reached the top. As Tamalié climbed menacingly toward his brutalised spouse, she leaped to the ground and dared him to follow her, mocking his cowardice. Seeing her miraculously fall unhurt but failing to notice the lianas, he dove to his death. As one of the scant occasions in Vanuatuan history where a man was outsmarted by a woman, the anniversary was marked with ceremonial dives by village women (an early example of sisterhood solidarity?). Somewhere along the way the men overcame their shame and took over the ceremony. Initially recognised every five years, it became an annual event related to the yam harvest. A good jump is still deemed essential for a bumper crop of the staple root vegetable.

Today, the ritual—which enables men to display their courage, strut their stuff before the village lovelies and obtain a public forum for their gripes—has been almost entirely stripped of its female component. From the moment construction of the *naghol* (tower) begins, all jumpers are forbidden to engage in sexual activity and females are strictly prohibited from the site or from areas where materials are gathered. Even on the day of the jump, they cannot come within twenty metres of the tower. Yet sexual imagery and association are inextricably intertwined with the ritual. 'There is a name for every part of the tower,' explains Kirk Huffman. 'In the case of the individual jumping platform, the pieces of wood on either side have the same name as that used for the lips of the vagina, while the piece of wood in the middle that the jumper balances his feet on, has the same name as that used for the penis. So you can imagine the depth of symbolism involved.'

Until about two years ago, the Pentecost jump was largely closed to the curious. The outside world was given a taste of the spectacle in 1955, when *National Geographic* infiltrated with a writer and photographer. In 1970, amateur anthropologist Kal Muller, on behalf of the same journal, lived in the village of Bunlap for seven months and became the first foreign devil to

*Pentecost jumping tower,*
*Vanuatu (Bob King)*

actually undertake the jump. Since then, small numbers of the truly adventurous have been admitted as passive spectators, culminating with the recent arrangement between the village elders and Tour Vanuatu to bring in groups of around 30–35 to each of the eight jumps staged in the village of Wali on the Saturdays of April and May.

My attempt to attend in 1988 was thwarted by political unrest. I almost lost the chance again in 1989 as a consequence of a dispute between the government and the chief pilot of Air Melanesia. I finally arrived for the last jump of the season, intoxicated by the occasion and the sure knowledge that no amount of clumsy New Zealand bungy jumping from bridges was any match for the ancient event that inspired the Kiwi craze. Some swift talking gave photographer Bob King rarely-granted access to the middle reaches of the tower itself, where buttock-quiver could be duly monitored. Rain threatened and fell and tourists

117

regularly slid from view as footholds in the dark clay dissolved. Even if near-naked natives were not hurling themselves through the sky and others loudly intoning songs about ancient wars and the flights of sacred hawks, the primal environment would have been worth the trek.

From my first, low vantage point I couldn't help but be reminded of my childhood visits to the bulls' pavilion at the Royal Easter Show. A veritable torrent of testicles had the female visitors gazing into their hands (and occasionally through them) for the first half hour. Dressed only in *nambas* (penis sheaths), native males of all ages pranced backwards and forwards along the flat strip of earth adjacent to the tower. Above and below them danced the grass-skirted women, plainly unsure of their temporary return to the scant dress of their forbears. It was not hard to share the embarrassment of the unmarried women who shyly clutched bundles of foliage to their chests throughout the day.

A steep climb from Wali village revealed the *naghol*—an extraordinary tapering complex emerging from the mountainside like a prehistoric beast. Even before the first jump, I shivered inwardly at the thought of anyone even climbing this irregular jungle edifice with its straggling anchor vines attached to the hill behind. The closer I got, the more imposing this steel-free skyscraper became. Not a single nail nor piece of wire had been used to secure seven kilometres of creeper vines to the hundreds of tree trunks or branches assembled around a *koro* (standing tree). Over an intensive ten-day construction period (during which much kava is imbibed) the jumpers, including a number of newly circumcised youths seeking acceptance into the men's community through their first jump, had diligently prepared the tower to accept the presence of the *armat*—the spirit of the cruel and clumsy Tamalié. They had slept under the structure at night to ward off the destructive 'Poison Man', the most malevolent spirit of all.

Divided into twelve levels, each corresponding to a part of the human anatomy, the *naghol* can accommodate 53 jumping platforms, starting with relatively short drops for the initiates. But while the tower is a communal effort, the actual platforms, the *sigols*, are the sole responsibility of each diver, who can then not claim to have been sabotaged by an evil, spirit-summoning grudge bearer if a tragedy occurs. Which they do. Each diver expects to lose some ankle skin but, when lianas break, projectile bodies can go hurtling into the bush or tumbling down mountain sides with catastrophic results.

The most common injury is not a broken neck but a broken collarbone. The head is instinctively pulled in on impact and the collarbone takes the punishment, even though the angled soil is carefully cleared, turned and softened to a depth of twenty centimetres. Some European doctors have said that the G-forces at the end of a jump are enough to tear limbs out of sockets, yet this doesn't happen. In fact, village doctors claim the activity to be a useful form of frontier chiropracting and prescribe it for aching joints. Kirk Huffman would be loathe to follow such medical advice. 'I've seen videos of jumps where lianas have snapped and divers have been spun around so much that they're almost screwed into the ground. The real danger, if you jump too far out and swing back at a dangerous angle, is being torn apart like a chicken's wishbone.'

There is one quite famous fatality on record. It occurred in the presence of Queen Elizabeth and Prince Phillip at Bunlap village early in 1974, and stirred great bitterness between the missionised and non-missionised sides of the island. The royals arrived out of season and the animist elders cautioned against staging a special jump. Their warnings were ignored in the official rush to impress the monarch. John Tabi stepped in at the last moment and used another man's platform. His immature lianas proved not to have sufficient spring and he was speared into the ground, reportedly just at the moment when Liz had turned to Phil to ask about the corgis. He died before he could be flown to hospital, becoming the jump's only known death.

This tragedy served to enhance the authority and control of the four non-missionised villages on the southeast side of the island, which insist on the observance of an extensive catalogue of taboos and still conduct closed jumps. It was these villages which kept the tradition alive when misguided Christian zealots forbade their mystified flocks to raise towers in the manner of their forefathers. Although inter-clan warfare ceased back in the 1920s, there is still a degree of tension between the two sides of the island, as exemplified by a 1978 incident where non-missionised villagers raided a Catholic mission station, shot cattle and burned houses. Arrested by mainland police and taken to court, the raiders were released by a judge who claimed their actions were justified by the 'great pressure' which they were under.

Up on the first stages of my tower, boys about five to eight years of age were coming to grips with their own great pressure. Some young larrikins were hurling themselves into the void almost before the lianas could be tied, while others hesitated so long that a surreptitious prod in the rear from dad was needed to decide their fate. In one case, even that proved ineffectual and the quaking lad took the long walk back along his *sigol*, more embarrassed than shamed. Officially there are no practice sessions, though in the months preceding the jump, some fathers wade out to a large rock off a small landing beach with their young sons and hold them by the ankles as they practice diving, while young girls stand on shore chanting the traditional songs.

Once mastered, the dive is almost paradisiacal. The jumpers talk of suspending their senses and entering an alternate realm of being. Anatol, a 28-year-old offshore-educated speaker of French, English and his village dialect, was the penultimate performer at the final 1989 jump, leaping from the 'right shoulder' of the *naghol*. A twenty-year veteran of the rite, he has worked his way up from level to level and is now poised to take the ultimate honour of tumbling from the 'forehead' on a *naghol* that will be named after him. A gentle smile revealed his eagerness. 'Maybe next year,' he murmured.

When Anatol does accept the honour of his village, he will be expected to execute not just a jump but *the* jump. Well defined, ritualistic drama is integral to the spectacle. The participants play to their own audience—villagers and tourists alike. The man who hurtles down the full drop (approximately 30 metres) is seen to hold the future of the yam crop and island prosperity if not in his hands then by his ankles. If he lands with suitable style he will be rushed by whooping peers, who will slash his lianas and hoist him aloft, as a true Pentecost hero. Outside of injury, the only thing likely to spoil Anatol's day will be the dreaded dislocation of his penis sheath. For the first half of my day at the jump, I interpreted the instant clutching of genitals upon impact as a reaction to pain rather than the expression of modesty that it actually is. In the non-missionised areas it is still a dark taboo for a woman to sight an uncircumcised adult glans.

So many shared and disputed taboos come to bear on the Pentecost jump that it is hard to imagine how it has survived intact for so long. While most of the men evoked spirits from the tower, at least two crossed themselves (and, incidentally, fell poorly). 'For the people of Southern Pentecost, the creating god is a being called *Barakolkol* who did his thing at the beginning of time and sat back and retired,' explains Huffman. 'What really affects the lives of the people today are certain types of natural spirits and the spirits of dead ancestors. Most of the ceremonies and rituals are to establish forms of contact with these ancestors, so that they will smile upon their descendants.'

Like New Guinea and Borneo, this tiny (61 kilometres long) island just three hours by air from Australia, the birthplace of Vanuatuan prime minister Father Walter Lini, is seething with mythology and mysticism beyond the understanding of most mortals. Even by Vanuatun standards, the place is . . . uh, weird. Kirk Huffman, the 41-year-old American-born Cambridge-educated naturalist-in-residence swears it is 'the most complex place on earth,' by virtue of the fact that 'the language and culture here is three times greater than Papua New Guinea. Some 145 000 people speak 105 different languages and we don't know how many dialects. There are some complete languages spoken by only 50 people. The land dive can only be performed by people who speak the language known as Sa'a, and there are only about 1200–1300 of them left. On the other side of the river they speak Apma and have an entirely different culture.'

The survival of the Pentecost jump as a ritual open to outsiders is far from guaranteed. While it has become a replacement display of manly courage in the absence of local warfare, and some villagers believe that the event gains prestige in direct proportion to the size of its audience, there is a general concern sweeping across all of Vanuatu that ceremonies staged for outsiders and not done strictly to tradition are losing power and angering spirits. 'That's one of the reasons why there are not so many groups dancing for tourists in Port Vila these days,' says Huffman. 'There is a feeling amongst the chiefs that they shouldn't prostitute their customs for tourist dollars. That isn't such a bad thing though. At least we won't end up with bungy jumping on Pentecost!'

# SAMURAI SLEAZE

*Penthouse* and *Playboy* are freely available on the bookstalls of any major Japanese hotel. There are no pages removed or text blacked-out, as is often the case with western magazines in such Asian nations as Indonesia and Malaysia.

However, there is a notable difference. All pubic hair has been carefully, individually removed by what would appear to be sandpaper. You see, the display of pubic hair, in print or in public, is against Japanese law.

Such restrictions need not concern the proprietor of a popular bookstall at busy Tokyo Central railway station. For he openly displays a wide range of quite legal magazines that can only be described as mild kiddie porn. They feature naked pre-pubescents who, of course, do not have any pubic hair.

For an introduction to the social mores of Japan that's hard to go past, but if you actually board the subway trains at Tokyo Central, you may find the system astounding for reasons other than frequency, punctuality and capacity. To stand in a carriage during rush hour and survey the reading material of the seated commuters is an essential step in coming to grips with a morality which sits uneasily with most westerners.

The prosperous, middle-aged Nipponese businessman in his immaculate Brooks Brothers suit with his alligator-skin briefcase will either be reading a corporate dossier or a comic book. And not just any comic book. Printed in the mega-millions, the thick, lurid, mass-appeal publications preferred by Japanese of all ages are jammed with the sort of violent sex that is generally sold from under the counters of seedy 'adult' shops in most nations.

Full of exploding breasts, forced anal rape and assorted carnal carnage, they betray the social base of what appears on the surface to be the most civilised nation on earth. These comic books are not clutched sheepishly to chests or hidden inside daily newspapers. They are consumed openly, almost proudly, and then left on the seat for anybody, adult or child, to pick up.

The Japanese call their comics *Manga* and each year 1.2 billion are sold in magazine and book form—around 27 for every household. Many have squared glued backs with up to 350 pages containing as many as fifteen serialised stories. In fact, Japan now uses more paper for its comics than it does for its toilet paper.

The scatological reference is not accidental. Like sado–masochism, excrement is not uncommon as subject matter in both adult and children's *Manga*. The prince of comics, *Shōnen Jump*, which can sell over three million copies per week (about the same as *Newsweek*), achieved its supremacy in 1970 when a serial titled *Toiretto Hakase* (Professor Toilet) made its debut. According to *Manga* expert Frederik L. Schodt, it starred a scientist who worked in a toilet-shaped laboratory and who, in the first episode, in the company of his assistant, cured a beautiful girl of constipation by shrinking to microscopic size, entering her digestive system through her mouth and attacking the problem in her rectum with shovels. A carelessly lit cigarette triggered an explosion which saw them both 'blown' to freedom.

In *The Great Railway Bazaar*, Paul Theroux relates observing a young girl engrossed in a comic book on a train journey to Aomori. When she laid it down to visit the toilet (no scatological reference intended!) he glanced through it and was, as he put it '. . . instructed and cautioned. The comic strips showed decapitations, cannibalism, people bristling with arrows like Saint Sebastian, people in flames, shrieking armies of marauders dismembering villagers, limbless people with dripping stumps and, in general, mayhem. Between the bloody stories there were short comic ones and three of these depended for their effects on farting . . . I dropped the comic, the girl returned to her seat and, so help me God, serenely returned to the distressing comic.'

That Japan is a male-dominated society virtually goes without saying. That the dominant males have a proven appetite for brutal, deviant and illicit sex perhaps needs to be said. 'We have a great time there but the Japanese are very weird people,' believes Michael Hutchence, lead singer of INXS, a band with a strong Nippon following. 'They have the sickest sense of morality.

The kids there buy join-the-dots S&M on the streets! You can't really create an enormous stir in Japan. You do it through the glossy rock magazines, that's about all. You have to fight against heavy government restrictions on foreign music. They have this sort of KGB for pop which says that 95 per cent is going to be Japanese and it's going to be sixteen-year-old girls in ponytails singing coy little love songs and being drooled over by the male masses, who are all pretty sick.'

As affronting as these manifestations of Japanese morality may be to supposedly 'liberated' westerners, they need to be balanced against one undeniable reality: Japan is possibly the safest and most honest nation on earth. A tourist (and very likely a local) could walk unmolested through the darkest streets of Tokyo at midnight with 10 000 yen notes pinned from cuff to collar. Leave your camera on a subway and you need only patiently await the carriage's passage around the loop to retrieve it. If it isn't there, then another tourist has stolen it. Certainly few Japanese would endure the shame of being seen to remove another's property without permission.

In a country where vending machines remain intact and ever-operable on most street corners around the clock, and attempts to explain vandalism to those who have never travelled abroad are politely but obviously received as fantasy; where gangsters go about their business like so many Rotarians, rarely touching the lives of those outside their private underworld; where the rape and violent assault of innocents is almost unheard of—one question continually arises. Just whose morality produces the better society?

While we simmer in the juices of our suppressed obsessions, the Japanese are getting their rocks off without undue embarrassment to themselves or inconvenience to others. Most Japanese cartoon and children's television shows are so extreme that they are unable to be shown in Australia or America—yet Nippon youth do not generally mug strangers, sell their bodies in laneways or collapse in public toilets with syringes hanging from their arms. Instead, they appear healthy, happy, industrious and polite to a fault. Even actual teen rebellion is pretty tame stuff. A Japanese punk is a kid who buys a Mickey Mouse t-shirt and carefully tears it . . . a little bit.

Westerners have been in a bind about Japanese morality for centuries. In 1863, Sir Rutherford Alcock, the first British minister resident in Tokyo, was perturbed by 'the utter confusion of the sexes in the public bath houses, making that correct which we in the west deem so shocking and improper'. But, as Pearl S. Buck once observed: 'If there is one single truth about Asia, it is that, while each country is totally different from every other country, Japan is the most different of them all'.

It is the extreme virtues coexisting harmoniously with the extreme vices which provides the greatest paradox for outsiders. The writings of J.D. Bisignani, a leading American Nipponphile, clear the confusion a little. 'In essence, the Japanese believe that human beings have two souls: one is sublime, timeless and changeless and binds us spiritually to a higher reality; the other is earthbound, rowdy, bawdy and pleasure seeking. Both, they believe, have their proper places and should be appropriately cultivated. What sets the Japanese man apart from the western man is his frontal approach, naivety and lack of hypocritical hang-ups. As long as a husband puts his family first, Japanese wives will turn a blind (but perhaps sad) eye to episodes of infidelity and even encourage their husbands to indulge.'

And indulge they do. To the extent of taking more prostitutes than any other male race. If you travel to Japan in search of cherry blossom trees and tea houses, don't be too surprised if you have to search for them between the topless and bottomless bars or coffee shops, 'bath house' brothels, strip joints, pornography emporiums with a strong line in scatology and bondage, and tens of thousands of vast, glittering Pachinko parlours (a mild form of gambling, rather like a mini-pinball game, which appears to have an almost narcotic hold on millions of Japanese of every social class). Like the hundreds of business-suited drunks who roll about the subways on Friday evenings, sexually adventurous Japanese men carry no stigma and bear no shame. Indeed, their peccadillos are accepted as fair compensation for a ceaseless contribution to the Nippon postwar industrial miracle, one that often forces the abandonment of the sort of home life which we hold sacred.

Of course, Japanese women enjoy no such latitude. 'A Japanese man who does have a sexual liaison is not considered immoral but merely succumbing to his earthly soul,' says Bisignani. 'A woman's allegiance and first loyalty belongs to her family. If caught being unfaithful, she upsets the social order and is damned more for a breach in social decorum than for immorality. A prevalent interpretation of Confucianism even goes so far as to state that a man's sexual desire for his own wife is immoral. These baser feelings should only be for mistresses and bar hostesses where they belong, not for the exalted bearer of his children.'

If visitors find it strange that there is no apparent contradiction between erotic and religious love, it may be because there is not, in any western sense, 'religion' in Japan. Certainly they are an inspiringly spiritual people and not the heathens that early explorers insisted, but the three major faiths—Shintoism, Buddhism and Confucianism—seem more codes of ethics and behaviour than active-worship lifestyles.

This absence of the firm Christian principles upon which the New World was founded has prompted most foreign criticism. Comte de Beauvoir may have been sufficiently enchanted by mixed bathing in 1872 to write 'In Japan, one lives in full daylight; modesty or rather immodesty is not known; it is the innocence of the earthly paradise'. But a century and a half earlier, Kaempfer's *History of Japan* formulated the far harsher view that 'The Japanese have a sharply contrasted character: on the one hand they are modest, patient, courteous, hard-working and clean as well as artistic and ingenious, while on the other hand they are proud, ambitious, cruel and uncharitable as well as passionate and revengeful'.

Those who deal with the Japanese invariably find that the overwhelming ritualistic generosity and politeness deftly obscures an often amoral and distinctly un-Christian approach toward business principles and an almost complete lack of concern for the welfare of any people outside their own enchanted kingdom. The concept of foreign aid is still relatively alien to the Japanese, who impart the unmistakeable impression that they view the rest of humankind as slightly inferior. The Germans thought they were the master race; the Japanese know they are.

The Japanese today are still all the things Kaempfer listed and, as the traditional past meshes with the technological future, the dichotomy is ever widening. It was as recently as 1979 that a foreign correspondent with the *Far East Economic Review* re-presented a timeless observation. 'An outside observer may find more than a touch of the unreal in the reality that is Japan,' he wrote. 'What at first appears to be straightforward at a second glance quickly takes on aspects of the absurd.'

# THE GOOD LIFE
# GUARANTEED

'Tell me,' she enquired, somewhere between the soup and fish, 'do you still have your Aboriginal problem?'

'Problem?'

'Yes, do you still have any or have you been able to get rid of them by now?'

Although I'd been waiting, almost hoping, to stumble upon a classic hard-line white supremacist for two weeks, she so caught me by surprise that I couldn't recall ever having been so incapable of coherent reply. With my silence obviously read as some sort of complicity she blithely continued, while black waiters hovered about and her husband buried his face in a napkin. 'The Tasmanians had the right idea, but they didn't go far enough. Now the only chance Australia has is sterilisation or very strict birth control. If you do that you should be able to get rid of most of them in a generation.'

Sitting across the dining table of an up-market safari lodge near Harare, demure in her pastel frock, this softly-spoken woman in her early fifties was presenting a blueprint for genocide, and didn't much care who heard her. I'm sure I tried to patiently explain that, despite our appalling record of treatment, most of us were more than pleased, perhaps a little proud, to share our vast continent with one of the oldest surviving races on the planet. After all, I mildly chastened her, it was human beings she was referring to. 'Not really,' she murmured between sips.

The wife of an Irish pharmacist, she had been born in Rhodesia of British parents and, for reasons known only to herself, chose to remain in the new Zimbabwe after 1980 independence, when the greater majority of her like-minded compatriots were flooding south to the white empire of South Africa. As such she had become a real anachronism—a white Zimbabwean still clinging openly to notions of inherent superiority.

Near the end of his days, arch-colonialist Cecil Rhodes boasted: 'They don't change the names of countries, do they? I give myself a thousand years.' In fact, it took less than a hundred years for Rhodesia to pass into the history books. Predictably, the demise of the white state which virtually abolished black land ownership in 1930 and soon after prohibited blacks from entering the skilled labour force was long, bloody and overwhelmingly futile.

Before the brutal seven-year war of independence, there were well over a quarter of a million whites running Rhodesia. Today, not many more than 80 000 remain; although border caravan parks are full of 'returnees', white families who panicked and fled in fear of violent retributions and are now not so much trying to reclaim abandoned businesses and homes as just find a way to return to the only place they can really call home.

Of course, most of the country's old masters will never return and Zimbabwe is well rid of them. They are known less than fondly as the 'Wenwe Club', after the favourite pastime of holding court in the white clubs of Johannesburg, Durban and Cape Town with never-changing tales of 'When we were in Salisbury . . . 'or 'When we were running Rhodesia . . .' Gradually the tag is changing and many of those in self-imposed exile are now being referred to as 'Sowetos' ('So, where to now?').

Of the five frontline states, Zimbabwe easily qualifies as the greatest embarrassment and irritation to South Africa, representing all that Pretoria insists is impossible. Blacks and whites work together productively and peaceably in a mostly-efficient black governed nation, one of the most stable on the African continent. Despite isolated instances of appalling border-area atrocities, often the work of the barbarous South African-backed MNR (Mozambique National Resistance) guerillas (and just as often related to simmering inter-tribal bitterness), there is no real sense of menace or intimidation. Even being the only white face on a quiet street in the late evening stirs no real anxiety. It's just not that sort of place.

The lack of open friction is astonishing, given that eight years ago every able-bodied white male was in uniform, defending Rhodesia. That they now work (and occasionally relax) side by side, and seem to have forged deep friendships with men they were recently trying to kill is some manner of modern miracle. At one game reserve, the white chief guide's two principal black assistants were former freedom fighters he had actually fired upon during one mountain campaign. 'It was something that both sides felt they had to do,' he reasoned, 'but it wasn't like Ireland where they seem to feed off the strife, year after year, almost enjoying it. Here, the hatred departed as soon as we laid down our arms. When the uncompromising Afrikaner-types, who were all as thick as two planks anyway, upped and left, there wasn't much left to fight about.'

For all his independence-war ruthlessness, honed by ten years behind bars, Robert Mugabe proved to be a near-model African statesman, astute enough to realise that white expertise and civil structure was worth hanging on to after the curfews, exclusions and entrenched disadvantages were jettisoned. Indeed it's hard to find a white, even in secret conversation, convincingly opposed to the man. 'If we call a black a dirty kaffir,' explained a female shop owner, 'we can get thrown into jail. But, by the same token, if a black called me a bloody stupid white, he can be arrested too, for the same offence. I think Mugabe tries hard to be fair.'

Eight years after the fall of Rhodesia, Zimbabwe's character is still unmistakeably British. The wide, jacaranda-smothered streets of Harare, give or take the token Samora Machel Avenue and Julius Nyerere Way, might well be in the English midlands. There is Shepperton Road, Stanley Avenue, Rotten Row, Raleigh Street, Cecil Square, Sans Souci Road, as well as the plush suburbs of Avondale, Highlands, Borrowdale, Mt Pleasant, and Alexander Park.

Along Orange Grove Road are million-dollar mansions (with attendant red Mercedes coupés) that would not be out of place in Toorak, Rose Bay or Red Hill. The 'right' areas of Harare and the secondary city of Bulawayo bespeak good wages and cheap labour. Despite periodic supermarket shelf shortages—sugar one month, salt the next—the good life in this part of the world is still very much a good life.

A still-vocal Ian Smith doesn't seem to think so but Andre, a 27-year-old white boilermaker raising a family in Masvingo, is one of the many young Zimbabwean whites who view the old firebrand's ramblings as an embarrassment. 'Almost everything he told us about life under black rule was a lie. We're still recovering from a war that needn't have been fought. We weren't murdered, our homes weren't seized. Blacks were always told

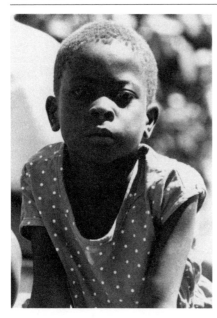

*Zimbabwean child, near Mutare*
*(Bob King)*

they couldn't do anything properly so they held back and didn't try. But once they were given a chance to handle their own affairs, they came through. No, the good life didn't disappear, it's still here, no matter what they call the country.'

Revolutionaries tore down the Cecil Rhodes statue in Harare, but his grave in the Matopos region is still a perfectly-tended monument. On paper, Zimbabwe is a Marxist state and certainly its television concerns itself greatly with the selfless deeds of Comrade this and Comrade that, and the newspapers serve up the odd flattering profile of Che Guevera and Fidel Castro. But behind the lip service to the Grim Trinity (Marx, Engels and Lenin), Zimbabwe is about as Marxist as New Zealand. The straightforward capitalist economy, with the white-run tobacco industry at its core, is more concerned with the Dow Jones Index than the state of collective farming in the Ukraine. Luxury consumer goods may be horrendously expensive but they are also reasonably plentiful and there are no queues.

Mugabe's political juggling act has served to preserve his small core of disproportionately influential whites. 'Nobody else will have us!' thundered a young Harare businessman. 'A white in South Africa, no matter how bigoted he may be, can emigrate to places like Australia without much trouble. But if we want to live in Australia, we find we're not wanted because we're 'communists' and thus undesirable. Communists! Bloody hell. Being labelled an imperialist was a damn sight better than that.'

Even those who have no interest in permanent departure are blighted by what seems to be viewed as Mugabe's most draconian edict; one which turns even the most prosperous citizens into embarrassed parasites on the rare occasions that they travel abroad. It's all to do with the currency, which is as fervently policed as the dwindling rhino herds. The possession of foreign banknotes by nationals is a jailable offence and even use of the local variety is tightly controlled.

Adult Zimbabweans, who are forbidden the use of credit cards, are annually permitted to take Z$480 out of the country (a little more than a month's average earnings), after the purchase of tickets. This can be accrued for three years, giving a maximum travel booty of Z$1440 (approximately A$1150) which might cover a couple of weeks in a reasonable hotel in London, Sydney and New York, but barely seven days in Tokyo. So, managing director or labourer, Zimbabweans are forced to go on the scrounge. 'The only way you can do it is to have friends overseas who will let you sleep on their couch, borrow their car and eat their food,' says Bill Annandale, the owner of a chain of record stores. 'You can't buy souvenirs or take your hosts to dinner or anything like that. It makes you feel so awful that you want to stay home.'

Traditionally, the way to assuage a troubled conscience was to invite foreign friends to Zimbabwe and lay it on thick for them. Shout them to Victoria Falls, Lake Kariba, Hwange Game Park and other sumptuous spots, and pick up all the bills. That worked fine until another churlish government decree, late in 1987, demanded that all hotel tariffs be paid in foreign currency, something that a local just can't do. The end result is that the world is unlikely to experience waves of Zimbabwean tourists for some time yet.

However, the flow is not impeded in the opposite direction. While Kenya has long courted American tourists besotted by *Out of Africa*, Zimbabwe has turned its attentions to Britain, Europe and, increasingly, Australia. Qantas' introduction of a weekly 747 service to Harare, with direct connections to London, has helped change Africa's image as a dark and distant location, and put some of the world's best-managed wildlife herds within relatively easy reach.

'Mixing with people from other cultures is the only way we

can grow up,' contends Temba Hove, a black 35-year-old owner of a modest Harare video production studio who left Rhodesia as a teenager to see the world and eventually study in Australia. Temba came home after independence ('because I was curious') and hasn't budged since. He still finds it difficult to fully express his range of emotions. 'We all believed that Rhodesia was forever. Most of us didn't even try to imagine what it would be like to assume control of our own lives. Up until 1977 any land could be declared "white" by the government and the owners turned into squatters overnight.

'When I left there was a curfew and all blacks had to be out of the city by 7.30. I lived with that, I was used to it, I didn't question it. When I arrived in Sydney I was so apprehensive. I would think "My God, am I really allowed to go into this cinema?"; and after I discovered I could, I found myself just walking into town late at night, not really wanting to be there but just enjoying the feeling.

'I suppose the exhilaration of independence was so many little things contributing to an overall feeling that finally you were a man running your own affairs. It was being able to walk down Baker Street at 11.30 at night without being challenged by a policeman. It was being able to sit in a restaurant and order a meal rather than standing in a long takeaway queue by the back window. It was being able to walk into exclusive white stores like Barbours and ignore the "Right of Admission Refused" signs.'

It was in a Hertz office, from an effusive bundle of black charm called Esther, that I had first learned of Barbour's admission policy. When I raised it with the genocide advocate at the safari lodge she insisted that my informant was 'a malicious liar' and that the department store had always been 'full of blacks'. The sad thing was, she seemed to believe it herself.

For young, intelligent blacks like Temba Hove, the 'little things' have not been quite enough. 'Mugabe was seen as the extreme of the extreme and even a lot of blacks expected him to come into Harare and shoot the first white he saw. But it was quite the contrary. In fact, the standard of living for whites hasn't really been touched at all. The money hasn't changed hands, it's still in white pockets. The cost of food for ordinary people is about the same as in Australia, though most people here earn only a third of the wages. Farming is very much controlled by whites and they still own most of the best land. That side of independence is still knocking on the door.'

This realisation seems to have taken root among those of more violent persuasion than Hove. It was the October eviction of black Matabele squatters from a farm 30 kilometres from the uncommonly peaceful and elegant city of Bulawayo which initiated the slaughter of sixteen white Pentecostals, the worst single instance of internal violence against whites in eight years of independence. A month before, the country's first car bomb since the war exploded in a predominantly-white Harare shopping centre car park. The ancient rivalry between the predominant Shonas (Harare and the north) and minority Matabeles (Bulawayo and the south) is the root cause of the internal friction; something, for a change, which can't be blamed entirely upon South Africa.

The belief that South Africa systematically destabilises the frontline states is so ingrained that it is almost part of the constitution. In the past year alone, the MNR was held responsible for the loss of 100 000 lives and the destruction of almost 500 schools within Mozambique (2058 in the past five years), as well as for the recent axe murdering of thirteen Zimbabwean villagers near the far southern city of Chiredzi. Volunteer doctors from Australia, Canada and America have filed sickening reports of violence against children which recall the horrors of Pol Pot's brief reign. Francisco Madeira, Mozambique's ambassador to Zimbabwe, claims that 85 000 children a year are dying at the hands of bandits. 'The MNR is an arm of the South African defence force,' insists an unswayable Hove. 'They want to bring countries like Mozambique and Zimbabwe to their knees, so they can turn and say to the world "look, the blacks can't run their own lives".'

Whatever the extent of Pretoria's machinations, Zimbabwe is the best ad for black rule that Africa has. Few of its current problems are unsolvable and there is none of that dank resigned air of defeat and despondency which afflicts much of the third world. Simply, it works, with a numbers balance between whites and blacks not too dissimilar to the one which white South Africa says would destroy all it has established.

*Five years on, this remains a reasonably accurate personal observation of Zimbabwe. Of course, there have been changes. The British street names recently got the chop and, with South Africa trying to return itself to world favour, border destabilisation is far less of a problem. With Qantas now also servicing Johannesburg direct, Harare is no longer such a Southern African pivot point.*

133

# DON'T CRY FOR ARGENTINA

The Saturday matinee queue in fashionable Avenue Corientes snakes two blocks from what is, at least temporarily, the most popular cinema in Buenos Aires. The theatre district of the aggressively stylish Argentinian capital offers a wide range of Hollywood fare, from *Jewel Of The Nile* to the inescapable *Rambo*. But the prime drawcard is *The Official Story*, the Argentine drama–documentary which took out the Best Foreign Film award at the Oscars in April. The queues are just as long all over the vast South American nation—from the elegant Bariloche ski resort in the Andes to the isolated and exceptionally uninteresting Patagonian centre of Rio Gallegos—as a diverse array of citizens exercises a freedom unimaginable five years ago.

In the major cities of the world, film buffs are watching *The Official Story* with morbid but detached fascination. In Argentina, a significant number of those patiently awaiting a cinema seat are fervently hoping to discover a reason, an explanation or even a clue concerning the 8000 or so *desaparecidos*—the disappeared.

It is hardly possible to encounter an educated Buenos Aires resident who does not claim to have a relative, friend or friend-of-a-friend who was snatched off the streets by General Leopoldo Galtieri's official thugs during the dark years of military government, which came to an end with the election of Radical Party leader Raul Alfonsin in October 1983. There is a disarming openness about discussion of the atrocities committed and the possibility of a return to military rule. 'If they take power again,' contends one veteran government employee, with almost chilling matter-of-factness, 'there will be the most terrible massacre.'

'But this time we will know what is happening and how to resist,' claims Carlos, a wealthy 41-year-old Buenos Aires factory owner. 'Before, we let it happen because we did not want to know. It was like believing you have a terrible disease but being too scared to go to the doctor.'

The near universal 'we were lied to, we were misled' lines are most readily forthcoming when conversation turns to the Falklands War. Intelligent Argentinians seem honestly embarrassed by not so much the loss as the debacle itself. Real tears are shed for the poorly-trained, ill-equipped adolescent boys sacrificed in the icy South Atlantic waters to a true march of folly. Yet, there has been no softening of the universal attitude toward legitimate ownership of the desolate sub-Arctic rocks. The global map printed in the Aerolineas Argentinas in-flight magazine shows 'Is. Malvinas (Arg.)' in bold type. Then just to make sure the point is not lost, there are a number of huge signs erected around the country, by roadsides and in airports, boldly proclaiming *Los Malvinas Son Argentinas*—The Falklands are Argentina's. It only takes a week in the country to find oneself agreeing with the seeming logic of the contention.

If there is any substantial, lingering anti-British feeling then it is to be found among areas of most poverty and in remote southern towns used as staging areas during the conflict. Few British tourists now venture into the country, but those who do encounter little animosity. With a twelve-year prison sentence just handed out to General Galtieri for his culpability, the Argentinians are more than entitled to name a few streets Heroes of The Malvinas Avenue in honour of the poor lambs led to the slaughter.

Tales of insanity and excess during the final years of the reign of the generals abound. A teacher in Mendoza told me how the population was beseeched to donate food and even jewellery to the war effort, and how one woman who gave up a much-loved family heirloom in a spirit of patriotic concern was horrified, a few months later, to observe it strung around the neck of a local general's wife. A shopkeeper in Salta chuckled over the regime's film censorship policy. Violent shoot-em-ups were passed freely, but the Jane Fonda film *Coming Home* was banned because it was unthinkable that war should be opposed by men in uniform and impossible that a soldier's wife would even contemplate adultery.

The Falklands War, like oppressive military rule, may have seemed a reasonable idea in the beginning, but it soured when it interfered with the one thing dearest to Argentinians' hearts—

their lifestyle. Within hours of my arrival in Buenos Aires, a resident was explaining, almost proudly, his country's prevailing philosophy of life. The foreign debt may be $50 billion, inflation may be rampant, low-level wages may be increasingly inadequate but, he boasted, 'as long as we have a full belly, we don't worry about anything else!'

To an outsider, there appears to be scant few truly empty bellies in Buenos Aires, the third largest city (ten million inhabitants) in Latin America and second largest Spanish-speaking metropolis on earth. At midnight, most nights of the week, it can be difficult to find a table in any one of the city's 6000 restaurants. The locals eat, drink and make merry with a hitherto unwitnessed gusto. And what they eat, almost without exception, is meat and more meat. Argentina has 54 million cows and eight to twelve million are slaughtered annually for consumption.

The most heavily patronised eateries are the *parillas*—hearty, friendly barbecue barns where whole carcasses of cows, sheep and goats (known locally as the delicacy *chivitos*) roast on giant steel skewers around a roaring open fire. At Las Nazarenas, adjacent to the Buenos Aires Sheraton, I paid around A$7 for a rump steak which came in at a little under a kilo—cooked! It arrived at my table hanging so far over the edge of the plate that it soiled the tablecloth. I consumed a little over half before abandoning the task as unachievable and earning a scornful glance from the waiter.

By all the health standards that the western world hold sacred, the Argies are going about it all the wrong way. They eat huge amounts of red meat late at night, then go to sleep on it. They also consume voluminous amounts of wine, rich pastries and most anything else put in front of them. Yet the national incidence of heart disease, high cholesterol and obesity is apparently no higher than elsewhere.

The answer, one soon begins to suspect, is that these people were to the manor born, even if the manor is currently in desperate need of major structural repair. The uninitiated's preconception of Argentina as a part of the South American mosaic of dust, flies, poverty and insurrection does not survive for very long. The country sees itself, and is seen by its neighbours, as a European nation a long way from home. To travel to Argentina is to experience the Continent encapsulated. There are moments you feel you are in France, or Italy, or Switzerland, or Spain; but rarely South America. This is colonialism taken to completion—almost

*Curious Buenos Aires bedfellows—Pierre Cardin and the Communist Party (Bob King)*

no indigenous Indians have survived with their bloodlines intact and, unlike the Brazilian melting pot of Rio de Janeiro, a black face in a crowd causes heads to turn. Even the macho national emblem, the great gaucho cowboy, is a dying breed.

Along the busy Florida shopping mall, the elegant, sophisticated citizens of Buenos Aires stroll about in their tailored leather coats, stopping occasionally to listen to what may be the best street buskers in the world—a man who plays complete Beethoven symphonies on a piano accordion with such passion and fire that you expect a beam of light to return him to heaven; ensembles of young Chilean refugees with pan pipes and acoustic guitars; and surging Latin steel drum bands who could raise the dead. The mood is one of prosperity and contentment—if only that damn $50 billion debt would disappear, life could really be as the Argentinians imagine it.

Strolling about the parks, plazas, boulevards, Rodin statues and street cafes of the city, it is not hard to imagine how extraordinary a place it must have been before the problems began. The Nazis who fled devastated Europe for Argentina in 1945 must surely have had the last laugh on the world. Older citizens invoke the past often—'back at the beginning of the century when we were rich' prefaces many a wistful reminiscence. In fact, Argentina's tumble into the financial abyss is remarkably recent. The country grew fat on agricultural exports to the allies during World War II, while remaining distant from the conflagration. In the vast pampas lands, where rich topsoil can be over two metres deep, it is said that if you poke your finger in the ground for more than five minutes it will begin to sprout. Down south there are vast oil and gas resources; all over there are mineral deposits. The only thing that would appear to be lacking is a certain spirit.

Argentina, like Australia, was widely touted as a major global force-in-embryo at the turn of the century. Both possessed great natural wealth administered by small, white populations under no immediate threat. In varying degrees, both countries have failed to bear the fruits of their promise. The root of Argentina's problems is chronic political instability. Radicals, socialists, conservatives and the military have kicked power about like a soccer ball for so long nobody is quite sure what political system the country is supposed to have. Regimes have lasted one day, nine months, two years, a decade; and the people have learned to accommodate the prevailing mood. At the moment it is unfettered freedom, and the unmistakeable signs of a sudden release from bondage are plentiful. It seems that every building and monument in Buenos Aires is disfigured with gaudy graffiti, which appeared within days of Alfonsin's election. The conservatives complain bitterly about the spread of crime and pornography which accompanied the fall of the military.

Raul Alfonsin appears, by any criteria, to be a decent, honest leader attempting major political and social reforms in the face of enormous economic problems. The relative stability and moderation he has been able to introduce, if it can be maintained, may well commence a recovery that will enable the high-living Argentinians to pay for their collective extravagance. However, some suggest that the influence of history rules against it.

In *Passage Through Eldorado*, Jonathan Kandell draws a comparison between Argentina and the United States, another nation colonised by Europeans who systematically destroyed the indigenous population. He contends that many immigrants to the new world of the northern hemisphere, such as the Irish, came to escape famine or persecution and were eager to work hard to find a better life, even if it meant developing a wild interior. On the other hand, the Spanish and Portuguese first came to the lower hemisphere to plunder: 'The people who flocked to the Iberian colonies did not want homesteads anyway. They despised manual labour for, like Cortes, they had not come to "scratch the land like a peasant". Many were minor gentry who dreamed of Indian servants and leisure in the colonies . . . these immigrants settled almost entirely in the cities. Pioneering was discouraged and, in any case, there were no volunteers.'

What has emerged from this heritage is a proud but undeniably pleasant people who consider themselves wholly superior to all other inhabitants of their continent. Travel writer Michael Shichor claims that there may be something in the old joke that, if you buy an Argentinian at the price he is worth and then sell him at the price he thinks he's worth, you will have made the deal of a lifetime. But while outsiders laugh, these hardy white South Americans are living life to its fullest. On a Saturday, there is not a park, a tennis court, football field or waterway that is not thronged with thousands upon thousands of incredibly active, sickeningly healthy people, engaging in seemingly limitless pleasurable pursuits.

After three years of democracy, many Argentinians feel they are returning to the international community. Tourism is expanding rapidly and no country in South America is better equipped to handle it. Some seven million Argentinians holiday within their own country each year and the tourist infrastructure is superb. The country offers glaciers and waterfalls, elite alpine resorts, fine architecture, painted deserts, national parks and wildlife, as well as gourmet food and quality clothing. Certainly there is little to dispute in Buenos Aires' claim to be the 'Paris of South America'—if only for the 200-metres wide Avenida 9 de Julio, a worthy rival for the Champs Elysées.

*I visited Argentina in 1986. Alfonsin inevitably fell out of favour with a people who prefer a little more panache and vitality from their leaders. Carlos Menem, with his Ferrari and his flamboyance, managed to surprise even those who voted for him by largely conquering the scourge of inflation. The army still appears to be confined to barracks.*

# THE OPENING OF A
# FORBIDDEN CITY

It is in the inescapable company of media implanted memories that one visits Hanoi in the era of *doi moi* ('renovation'). Memories like Boxing Day 1972, when waves of B52 aircraft relentlessly bombed the gracious, ancient city, then the capital of North Vietnam. By the time the lethal rain ceased on 30 December, 26 planes had been downed and more than 1600 civilians killed.

Inevitably, you arrive almost expecting to see gutted buildings and shattered suburbs and leave doubting that anything had ever actually disturbed the elegant, colonial ambience of one of the most aesthetically impressive cities in Asia. Writer John Pilger probably confessed on behalf of us all when he said, 'I used to see Vietnam as a war rather than a country'.

If you ask nicely, your guide might take you down a tiny laneway to the Ngoc Ha village square where lies the tail of a B52 reputed to have been brought down by local militia on that terrifying Boxing Day. He may even take you—though only if you express interest—to Bach Mai Hospital where a sombre monument marks the bomb strike which levelled the building on that same day. You can also spend a morning walking through the Military Museum, with its collection of intact MIG jet fighters and the very tank (no. 843) which smashed down the gates of Saigon's Presidential Palace on 30 April 1975. You can be directed to the remnants of the under-street bomb shelters. But that, by and large, will be it. 'Vietnam wants to forget the past,' declared General Secretary Linh to foreign reporters in 1988.

The portion of Vietnam's 67 million population under the age of twenty seems to have done so already. If it wasn't for visitors' infernal questions, they'd probably never have cause to speak about it. In Hanoi, with its wide, tamarind-tree-lined streets busy with nothing but bicycles, and its series of pagoda-dotted lakes, thoughts of hostility seem terribly incongruous. You don't encounter bitterness in the Vietnamese, they've got too much else to occupy them. The veterans of almost any invading army seem to come and go as they please. Walk down by the walls of the ominous 'Hanoi Hilton' prison on Hoa Lo Street, where some American flyers were incarcerated for more than eight years, and you may well encounter visiting, gift-laden Yankee veterans, making some sort of peace with their past.

The 'Hanoi Hilton', like almost every other significant building in the city of three million, is painted in a muted shade of yellow. This, apart from the architecture itself, is the most enduring legacy of the French, who bombarded Danang in 1858 and ruled the country with a series of admiral governors until their humiliating defeat at Dien Bien Phu in 1954. Notwithstanding that a canny Marseilles merchant may once have had a few hundred thousand gallons of yellow paint that he cleverly unloaded on Indo-China, this pastel toning remains one of the most evocative aspects of the city. In the neighbourhoods built entirely by French contractors, the yellow is offset by green window shutters and cream stucco facades.

The gentle grace is enhanced by the relative quiet. There are so few cars in Vietnam that you can walk down the shaded, leafy streets of Hanoi with nothing to disturb your reflection beyond the swish of bicycles or the trundle of dilapidated trolley cars. At Ho Chi Minh's Tomb, an obedient duplicate of the Lenin mausoleum in Moscow, long lines of out-of-towners file past the granite edifice in subdued mode. Precious little attention is paid to a large statue of Lenin, the emblem of a failed ideology. Twice, as I was driven by it, my Hanoi hosts mumbled something along the lines of a disdainful 'he'll be coming down soon'.

Unused tramlines still run through the Old Quarter, the soul of a city which has been the capital of Vietnam since the Ly Dynasty in 1010. In the fifteenth century this 'city with 36 guilds and streets' was the heart of King Le Thai To's empire. Then it was a labyrinth of crowded lanes with such evocative names as Silk Street, Broiled Fish Street, Sail Street and Medicine Street. Today, it is Hanoi's busiest quarter, replete with produce and flower sellers and traders of myriad goods and services, from haircutting and manicuring to fortune telling and genealogy. One old man does a thriving trade in large Vietnamese flags and a rapidly decreasing trade in hammer and sickle emblems.

With only its architecture, gardens, colonial ambience and six hundred pagodas, Hanoi would be an appealing city. With its water, it is truly seductive. Few cities outside of Venice are draped so gracefully around waterways. The very name Hanoi is extracted from the term 'the city inside a bend of the Red River', and from the moment you cross the Thang Long or Long Bien bridges on your way in from the airport, the atmosphere is decidedly aquatic. The city is surrounded by the Hong, To Lich and Kim Nguu Rivers, and shaped by a scattering of lakes, ranging from large ponds to the vast, sea-like West Lake, on which the large Thang Loi Hotel has been built.

Hanoi lives around its lakes, laying on waterside cafes, paddleboats, storybook foot-bridges, street entrepreneurs and a string of annual water-based festivals. The heart of the activity is the Restored Sword Lake, with its Turtle Pagoda and reflections of willows and flame trees. As the legend goes, in 1418 AD, warrior Le Loi beseeched the heavens for assistance in defeating Chinese invaders. The golden tortoise of the lake answered the pleas with a magic sword that dispensed lightning from its blade. The warrior drove back the hordes and, soon after, was boating on the lake when the tortoise leapt out of the water and reclaimed his weapon. Many are the parallels between this legend and that of King Arthur's Excalibur and the Lady of the Lake.

Water is also at the centre of the greatest attraction outside of Hanoi. Five hours drive north, over two car ferries, within 80 kilometres of the Chinese border, is daunting Ha Long Bay, Vietnam's equivalent to the Pyramids, Grand Canyon or Cappadocia. Here is the remains of a prehistoric world; thousands of irregular pinnacle mountains shoot up out of the water, covered in foliage and sometimes riddled with caves. You can sail in and out of these bizarrely sculptured rock formations for hours or days in an eerie, undisturbed atmosphere.

If it were within the borders of almost any other country in Asia, Ha Long Bay would have a deep path worn to its precincts. As it is, the few outsiders who make their way the 165 rugged kilometres north from Hanoi, tend to feel like Apollo moon shot stowaways. To emerge blinking into the sunlight within sight of any of the 1500 square kilometres of this transcendent realm is to feel set apart from the remainder of humanity.

'A fence of mighty stone pillars, each one separate, starting sheer up out of the sea to the height of cathedral towers,' is how Crosbie Garstin, an explorer early this century, described this unique aquatic terrain. 'Islands take on human profiles,' he gushed, 'others look like crouching frogs, sugar loaves and ships under sail. They are prehistoric monoliths and church spires. It is as though the architectural giants of the world, grown senile and eaten with age and weather, had been dumped down here to crumble quietly away.' Of the Cavern of the Marvels, he himself marvelled, 'Stalactites hung from the ceiling to the floor, strings of them, glistening white, a yawning mouth with strings of nougat'.

There are an estimated 3000 islets, pinnacle mountains and jutting limestone and dolomite rock formations in Ha Long Bay. The odd outcrops found along the coast of Thailand, though better known, don't even merit serious comparison. Long a part of Vietnamese mythology, this vast field of bizarrely eroded and sculptured monoliths—comprised of organic sea and plant matter compressed by water and gnawed by miniscule tide-level molluscs over thousands of years—features prominently in the tales of battle that are so much a part of Vietnamese history. In the thirteenth century, General Tran Hung Dao hid in these caves the stakes he would plant in the bed of the Bach Dang River to cut off the retreat of the Mongol invaders. Vietnamese naval ships also took advantage of the large, hidden caves—some capable of holding up to 3000 people—to lie in ambush for Chinese warships.

There's every chance some of the battle galleons are still there, complete with a full complement of skeletons, rusted swords still held aloft. So plentiful are the caverns, grottos and tunnels that they are still being discovered. The familiar ones have grand names and fanciful legends—the Grotto of Wonders, Father and Son Rock, the Fighting Cocks, Customs House Cave, Surprise Grotto, the Unicorn, and the winding, two mile long Hang Hanh Tunnel. Many of the islets, covered in stunted and twisted vegetation, have tiny, perfectly-formed beaches; others have openings so high they can only be reached by pelicans and sea swallows. The yellow-haired macaque monkeys on one particular island provide a valuable vaccine, which is used internationally.

The Maiden Grotto took its name from a complicated legend involving Nang He, the beautiful daughter of a fisherman who was starved to death in a grotto by the order of a rich boat owner whose bed she refused to share. At her burial site, a rock was later discovered in her shape (which was, by all reports, rather pleasing). Close to the shore of Ha Long Bay stands the Island of Poems, rising 1000 feet sheer from the sea, where, centuries ago, poets and scholars spent their days in meditation and quiet discussion.

Described as the coming to life of a classic Chinese ink painting, Ha Long Bay has, of course, an attendant legend to explain away its splendour. Ha Long means 'where the dragon descends into the sea' and ancient tales abound of fishermen sighting dragons— symbols of great power—in the area. It was, as the stories go, an extremely magnificent dragon which plunged into the bay from his mountainous home, twisting and turning as he went, his mighty tail carving out huge crevices on his way to the sea. As explanations go, it's as reasonable as anything else you're likely to come up with as you gaze upon the maze.

Like India's Simla during the days of the Raj, Ha Long Bay became a popular retreat during the French colonial era a century ago. Officers, senior merchants and titled families maintained villas and retreated there from the tropical south, partaking of the herbal medicines made from the yellow aniseed common to the area. It was here, in June 1948, that Emperor Bao Dai tried to reach agreement with the country's Gallic colonisers, by signing the Accord of Ha Long.

Even today, the remnants of the French era still take their holidays in the many hotels along the Bai Chay Road, which runs parallel to the main beach across from the bay. In peak season, on a balmy evening, the beach is packed with families laying out ample spreads of food, hiring bathing costumes, and generally frolicking in a studiously dignified manner. In the hotel dining rooms the animated family conversations are just as likely to be in French as Vietnamese.

Of Ha Long Bay's five main hotels, the most impressive is the Ha Long Bay Hotel, a converted colonial hospital, complete with huge rooms, spacious balconies, window shutters, trundling ceiling fans and a mood unchanged since the turn of the century. Painted in pale yellow shades, like the public buildings of Hanoi, it is as gracious a hotel as the north of Vietnam has to offer.

At the moment, there's really no way around the arduous (though interesting) road journey required to reach this cosmic wonderland. There is a ferry from the port city of Haiphong (possibly the most bombed city on earth) to Cat Ba Island, where you can transfer to a bay cruise, but most visitors are taken directly to their Ha Long hotel for the pause that refreshes before being taken out onto the bay for two, four, six or indefinite hour excursions. It is advisable to devote more than a flying day to a visit, for it is said that you can spend a full week on the water and still not sight every wonder.

As hypnotic as Ha Long Bay may be, every visitor must return to Hanoi; inevitably changed by the experience and determined to despatch friends to this extraordinary part of the world. The aquatic commonality serves to preserve the trance, as does the relatively sombre tone of the city.

The people of the once strongly Catholic Hanoi differ significantly from the residents of the racy, vibrant Saigon. Hanoi folk, though just as strong and unyielding in their demeanour as all other Vietnamese, are far more reserved, cautious and conservative. A few decades under Eastern Bloc influence does tend to do that to you. During the war, Saigon knew bars, brothels and rock 'n' roll, while Hanoi marched to a different drummer altogether. 'Uncle Ho' remains the spiritual light of the north, while the south tends to look more readily outwards for its future. The DMZ may no longer appear on maps but there is still a tangible line running through the middle of this populous sliver of fertile coastal land.

Effectively isolated by war and power politics since before World War II, Hanoi is like a rare specimen preserved in aspic. Tattered and tarnished on one hand and noble and pure on the other, it stands as a hidden outpost of a redundant age. For the past fifteen years its charms have been the domain of well-behaved Russian factory workers on 100 per cent subsidised eastern holidays. Now, tired of roubles and desirous of dollars, the Vietnamese have opted to accommodate curious capitalists. The richest rewards will go to those fleet of foot and eye who absorb the atmosphere before 'development' takes its inevitable toll.

# KARIBA!

The manager of Barclay's Bank in the Zimbabwe resort town of Kariba is concerned by the increasing number of unauthorised evening withdrawals. The telexes to London don't seem to bring much relief; head office doesn't know how to stop hungry elephants crashing through the bank's mango trees either.

Although Kariba is sited at the very peak of a large hill, the pesky pachyderms manage to wreak havoc there most nights. When they finish leaning on the bank's ever-weakening walls, they are wont to deposit themselves in the backyard swimming pools of various alarmed residents. It is said that the ultimate revenge on an enemy in this part of the world is to stash a bag of oranges under his car, thus ensuring that it turns turtle by morning.

Kariba, the pretty 30-year-old town which burst into life as a construction camp for dam workers, is the main staging area for journeys onto and around spectacular Lake Kariba, one of Africa's greatest wildlife sanctuaries. Kariba is to Zimbabwe what Bariloche is to Argentina, the Bay of Islands to Java or Phuket to Thailand. The lake is an aquatic playground, a restful retreat, a national treasure. That it happens to be teeming with almost every exotic African animal (apart from the giraffe) is the plus that sets it apart from other water wonderlands.

Before 1960 there was no lake at Kariba, just the swiftly flowing Zambezi River, fresh from its dramatic plunge down the awesome Victoria Falls. Then, on May 16, 1960, Queen Elizabeth concluded ten years of labour by flicking the switch to start the giant generators attached to the 128-metre high Kariba Dam wall. By 1961 a giant inland sea had formed, stretching back 290 kilometres from the wall and spanning 42 kilometres at its widest point. One writer described it as 'melting constantly from azure to aquamarine to amethyst and, at sunset, becoming a vast sheen of molten copper'.

This engineering marvel was not hailed by all. The native BaTonga people called on Nyaminyami, the River God, to curse the man-made abomination. However, their ire decreased in direct proportion to the increase in their sardine fishing income. The wildlife also recovered from its abrupt displacement. The world's attention was captured by Operation Noah, a mercy boat- and air-lift, helmed by game ranger Rupert Fothergill, of some 5000 beasts (representing 35 mammal species alone) from isolated high ground to the shores of the Matusadona National Park.

Initially shaken, the relocated animals—elephants, zebras, antelope, hippopotamuses, lions, leopards, rhinoceros, crocodiles, warthogs, buffalo, gnu, and hundreds more—thrived on the succulent grasses which the new lake provided. Elephants, buffalo and large cats, normally averse to deep water, could be seen swimming between islands and shores, following ancient game trails with an age-old instinct. Birds flew in from all over Africa and even Europe to perch on the tops of the petrified trees which still protruded from the lake's average 18-metre depth. Introduced fish, such as bream, chesa, sardine, vundu and tiger fish (up to 15 kilograms), bred by the (literal) millions.

Suddenly, Lake Kariba was one of the most desirable travel destinations on the African continent, drawing animal admirers, fishermen, naturalists, photographers and lovers of a good time. Up went the hotels, the safari lodges, the marinas and even a casino—all with good taste and a concern for the environment. The Club-Meders stuck to Caribbea Bay while the more discerning visitors sought out and gave international reputations to the prestigious, game-drenched lodges—Bumi Hills, Spurwing Island, Tiger Bay, Fothergill Island, Zambezi Resort and Water Wilderness among them.

But for the truly astute African adventurer, there came to be only one realistic way to experience Lake Kariba, and that was by boat. At present there are at least ten reputable companies chartering crafts out of Kariba. These range from 15-foot fishing boats to 55-foot luxury cruisers. Most are self-piloted, with all facilities and provisions included.

There is no question that some of the best game viewing in Africa can be achieved from a floating position. My most memorable African experience was on Lake Kariba, bobbing in a power boat with its engine killed just five metres from three young, but huge, bull elephants—an unthinkable proximity on land. These proud pachyderms, who had swum over to one of the lake's many tiny islands, were trying to impress and intimidate us by snorting and squealing, stamping their feet and flapping their ears wildly. It was quite a floor show, culminating with the surprise appearance of a surly hippopotamus, who had wandered onto the scene to see what all the fuss was about. Upon his arrival, our guide wisely powered up the outboard.

At Bumi Hills Safari Lodge, overlooking the lake, I was regularly entertained by spider monkeys hurling themselves between trees. An early morning game drive down to the lake shore brought me close to a family of zebras who dominated my total attention for more than an hour with their ceaseless playful skylarking. From inside a Landrover—which the Kariba wildlife has come to recognise as just another beast—I observed buffalo, antelope and all manner of birdlife at close range, as if I was a part of the natural panorama myself. Breathtaking is simply too mild a word for the experience; or for the next day's light aircraft flight from Bumi Hills to Fothergill Island (undertaken after we had driven up and down the grass landing strip to frighten away any lurking animals) which swept extremely low over hundreds-strong elephant herds.

From Lake Kariba, the mighty Zambezi is well worth exploring. Upstream is the imposing Victoria Falls, while downstream is possibly Zimbabwe's finest game park, Mana Pools. Part of the vast Middle Zambezi wilderness area on the Zambian border, this is a wildlife park *par excellence*, a region of long cool alluvial woodlands interspersed with tiny glades and sun-dappled herds of impalas grazing among dense groves of Natal mahoganies. There are some 12 000 elephants in the park, as well as varied antelope, baboons, hyenas, black rhino, leopards, lions, cheetahs and buffalo (herds of up to 2000 are not uncommon in September/October).

While Kenya receives most of the international attention and American visitors, it is Zimbabwe (and particularly the Lake Kariba area) which affords visitors the greatest opportunities to view astonishing wildlife in uncrowded, virtually untouched domains. Zimbabwe's preservation and utilisation of natural resources has provided a model for Africa and a glimmer of hope for future generations who would otherwise stand a good chance of never seeing wildlife in its natural state.

# TURTLE'S TEAR FACTOR

'Wherever I am in the world I call home regularly to check the tear factor,' explained eccentric American, Richard Evanson. 'If it's down I get on the first plane.' Home, for 53-year-old Evanson, is Turtle Island, his own sublimely beautiful 500-acre tropical enclave in the Fijian Yasawa group. The 'tear factor' is the number of salty drops which splash Turtle's dock during the moving farewell ceremony to which departing visitors are subjected prior to boarding a Turtle Airways seaplane bound for Nadi Harbour.

An awful lot of people cry when they leave Turtle, they really do. Not just gooey secretaries who've never been abroad before, but successful businessmen and captains of industry. After a week in Evanson's seductive, deftly (almost scientifically) managed resort, it takes the inner resolve of a prize fighter to depart without some display of emotion.

Turtle, the sole location for both *Blue Lagoon* movies (Jean Simmons, 1949 and Brooke Shields, 1980) is an expensive up-market retreat which attracts the likes of Rupert Murdoch, John Cleese, Ringo Starr and Barbara Bach, and the Duke of Roxburge. Listed by *Harpers & Queen* magazine as one of the '300 Best Hotels In The World', it accommodates a maximum of twelve couples at any one time, carefully indulging their personal tastes in food, beverages and recreation.

Express a desire for a day at the beach on Turtle and you find yourself being ferried to one of the island's fourteen perfect white-sand coves by boat or horseback, complete with a hamper full of champagne and lobster, and the implied assurance that you and your partner will not be disturbed by any other form of human life until your stipulated hour of return. Toss a warm smile in the direction of the breakfast staff and get ready to devour an indescribably fine quail-egg and crab omelette. Request a sturdy mount and watch the wild goats scatter as you gallop along the sand. Opt to get married there and become the centrepiece of a display of traditional pageantry the Coldstream Guards would have trouble matching.

At night, as you sit under the stars on the beach and polish off various Indian curries or superb seafood hotpots by hurricane lamplight, and excitedly swap rich anecdotes with intelligent, well-travelled fellow guests—friends for life within an hour, them all—you begin to understand the tear factor and wonder how you'll fare when the staff come down to the dock and serenade you back to turgid civilisation.

'It took me a long time to realise just what I was doing right that had such an effect on people,' confided Evanson, who bears a resemblance to Gregory Peck. 'I had the strange situation of not really knowing why I was so successful. When I started, my roofs leaked, I served wine like battery acid, you got chicken at every meal and if you dropped your fork someone wiped it on their shirt and gave it back to you. Yet 90 per cent of the guests were leaving reluctantly, saying "something's happened to me here, I feel really good". I knew I had something but I didn't know what it was and my dilemma was that I was too scared to change anything for fear I would screw up the formula.'

Finally, the secret unfolded. 'I kept wondering why all these guests who'd been to Fiji five or six times were saying that our staff were warmer and more caring. Then I realised that I'd found a way of taking advantage of Fijian customs and traditions in a way that other resorts were not. You see, in Fijian tradition, a visitor is practically the most important event of their lives. Everything is dropped, possessions are shared and the visitor receives all your attention. At every other hotel the guest turnover is so high that the staff can't ever really extend themselves fully. But on Turtle, with so few guests and a generally longer stay, the staff are able to develop quality relationships with the guests and involve them in their unique culture.'

The first time I took my place at the long dining table on the sand, beneath a shimmering Pacific sky, I turned to face the All American Girl—tressed blonde hair, sparkling blue eyes, perfect skin, glistening tombstone teeth and designer clothes that your average designer couldn't afford. Beside her was the All American

Boy. He was called Bud or Chuck or Randy or something like that, and was football coach at UCLA. They were newly spliced and you could almost catch cupid's arrows. When I told sweet Deidra that I thought she was very lucky to be honeymooning at the world-famous Turtle Island Lodge, she gushed 'Yes it was wonderful of Burt'. Burt who? 'Burt Reynolds, he paid for it.' Okay, I'll be the mug. Why? 'Well, he's marrying mommy soon.' And he was too. You see, my fellow diner just happened to be the daughter of actress Loni Anderson. These days, Burt is officially her stepdaddy.

There is never a paucity of interesting guests on Turtle but even if you arrive during an accountant's convention there would still be Evanson himself, who tells stories as enchantingly and as effortlessly as your favourite uncle. Tales rich in self-effacing humour and priceless anecdote which remind you that the very fabric of Asia and the Pacific is interwoven with salty, rakish dreamers and romantics from Europe and the New World; adventurers who drifted east in search of fortune and freedom. They rarely found the first but were unwilling to forfeit the second, so they stayed. In this frantic age it may seem that those great characters who inspired writers from Maugham to Mitchener have disappeared and the world is poorer for their passing. Not entirely. In *Asian Portraits*, wanderer Harold Stephens contends: 'In other times things moved more slowly so these people stood out. On a six-week sea voyage you got to know everybody on board. Today you may be sitting next to the most amazing character on a jet plane but barely have the chance to exchange a few words.'

Richard Evanson, with whom you can exchange as many words as you wish, purchased Turtle Island, one of only twenty of the 600 or so Fijian islands that are privately owned, fifteen years ago for just half a million American dollars, and recently turned down an offer of US$22 million cash from German industrialists, the Krupp family. A former street-corner paper-seller with a degree from the Harvard Business School, Richard worked on the Minuteman missile project for Boeing and eventually sold his cable television business to CBS for US$8 million. Then the bubble burst. His marriage to Kayla Clapp, daughter of multi-millionaire industrialist Norton Clapp, ended in divorce and he found himself shelling out $100 000 to assorted shrinks.

So he fled to the Pacific to find a new focus for his life. 'My fast lane was very fast,' he recalls. 'I was into anything that

*Richard Evanson, Turtle
Island (Bob King)*

provided a fast thrill, even skydiving. It was a wild, dissolute and
purposeless life and I was a hopeless, overweight alcoholic. Then
it all changed by accident. I was into a romance that was becoming real tense so I went to the airport and caught the first plane
out of the country. It happened to be going to Tahiti. So I spent
a few weeks there and called in at Fiji on the way home for five
days.'

Evanson found his new focus and a great deal more, on his
tropical island. Then he decided to spread the joy around. 'I
expend a lot of energy trying to determine what's happening to
my guests, how they feel inside, and how I can make them feel
more welcome, more relaxed. I decided in 1980 that I wanted to
share my dream and my fantasies. I run the show, I don't have
to take orders from anyone. This place couldn't be run by a
corporation because they have to do what's in the best interests
of their shareholders to get maximum return on investments. I'm
not interested in the profit motive. I only want a return on my
feelings for this land and its ecology. I pour every cent I make
into helping nature improve on its performance. I've planted
250 000 trees since I've been here. I've bred rare birdlife and
discovered how to collect and preserve my water. That's my
reward.'

Unfortunately, Evanson's noble vision is often tainted by mis-
understandings of his strict rules of admission, which can cer-

tainly seem draconian on cold paper. Apart from a minimum stay of five days, he stipulates mixed, English-speaking couples only, with children allowed only in two specified periods. All of which makes perfect sense when he offers his reasons.

Essentially, Evanson sees his resort as not so much the ultimate escape as the ultimate dinner party, where like-minded people can come together in a relaxed, conducive atmosphere to exchange their feelings about life, the universe and everything. 'What are the steps you would take in planning a dinner party?' he challenges. 'You are going to select guests you think are going to enjoy each other's company. I can't be sure of that but I try to improve the chances of it happening. First, I tend to market Turtle in America and Australia because there's a kind of love affair between the two countries at the moment. I don't have guests who can't speak English because they would feel isolated and that would make everyone else uncomfortable. And I have a minimum stay because I don't want people popping in and out of here who *you* don't know.

'I don't have singles because I don't want some guy on the make and all the other males worrying about maybe losing their own partners. I even said no to Robert Redford for that reason when he wanted to come on his own—even though my female staff nearly strung me up for it! If a couple says they want dinner on the beach or the dock or anywhere else, that's fine, we'll arrange the most romantic meal they've ever had. But we won't do it for two couples because little cliques start to form and the special mood that exists breaks down. Certainly I respect privacy and you can be on your own as much as you want in the daytime, but in the evening we come together to share our experiences of the day, and that is the richest experience of all. It wouldn't work if people were hidden away in little batches. I'm even thinking of having cards left in the bures saying: "If you want to entertain in your room, please invite us all. Because I wouldn't want to be the one left out, would you?" '

It seems nobody wants to be left out on Turtle, not even its most famous clients. After a few days on the island, Ringo Starr took to walking down onto the dock to warmly welcome incoming guests he didn't know from Adam, while Rupert Murdoch apparently helped serve dinner one evening. 'The great thing about Turtle is that, in a way, it's almost classless,' says Evanson. 'At dinner, we can have a film star seated next to a clerk and they get along famously. Normal social barriers just disappear. Everyone wants to be involved in the events of the island, particularly our turtle release ceremonies.

'Over the past four years we have released 170 turtles back to the sea. The local people catch them while fishing or diving and bring them to us. We've never eaten one but we do pay $30–$50 each for them and use them as an excuse for a picnic or party. First we get out our engraving machine and carve the names of the guests on the turtle's shell, then we climb into a big boat and go out to sea and release it. Of the 170 we've let go, only three have ever been caught again, and in each case the names and dates could be read clearly. In these situations everyone wins—the turtles live, the villagers get some money and the guests feel good for having helped preserve something wonderful.'

As a father of four (including a six-year-old half-Fijian son, Charles), Evanson appeared mortally wounded when I even laughingly accused him of being anti-child. 'In the early days I had children all year round and, personally, I loved it,' he insisted. 'The problem was, the Fijians love kids so much that they spent all their time with them and began neglecting the adults. Also, our guests tend to fantasise about a tranquil, untouched, unspoiled, romantic island paradise and, for some of them, children don't fit into that picture. So now we have two periods a year, which coincide with American and Australian school vacations, when guests can come with their families.'

Subtle overtones of romance and carefully cultivated memories are Turtle's stock in trade. When prospective guests express an interest in the island, they are sent a one-hour VHS video presentation which includes footage from American TV chat shows (on which Richard is a popular face), and scenes from the more recent *Blue Lagoon* film. If they decide to book, they are asked to bring their tape along and surrender it upon arrival. Then, during the misty departure ceremony they are handed it back complete with at least 30 minutes of unobtrusively-captured footage of the highlights of their stay—dining, horse-riding, conversing, playing volleyball, et al. No invasion of privacy of course, just a cute and worthwhile memento.

The unique touches are often small but they coalesce into a remarkable ambience. One by one, Evanson has stripped away irritants, one of them being money. Guests might as well put their folding greens in the office safe upon arrival because there's absolutely no use for them. The hefty tariff includes absolutely everything from arrival to departure, even a bar fridge full of champagne for those who wish it. Take a trip to the shell market on a nearby island, walk away with whatever you like and the boatman will simply jot down your purchases, so you can take care of them by credit card at check-out time.

The rules turn some people away, to be sure. But Richard Evanson doesn't really care. After all, he reasons, Turtle is his home and he can share it with whom he pleases. 'I don't want jet-setters, trendies, plastic people, nit picking anti-social grouches or obnoxious drunks here,' he reels off in a sort of well-practised liturgy. 'On the other hand, if you're nice, friendly and you truly, as a human being, like other human beings, please come and have the experience of your life. I'm not going to change the character of my product, ever. I won't be tempted to put in more rooms or fill in my mangrove swamp or invite the cruise liners to stop by.'

For all his earnest efforts to achieve a complementary guest mix, Richard occasionally has a few of the planet's least-impressive inhabitants slip through his shark net. 'Two or three of them stand out in my mind, and one turned out to be a great lesson to me,' he admits. 'He must have had a real insecurity problem because he was incredibly insulting to the staff. Now usually that doesn't last long because the Fijians won't rise to it. They just come back with love and respect and after a couple of times most people can't stand up to that. But this guy could.

'On his last day I said at my morning staff meeting, "I'm not going down to the dock to see this asshole off and I wouldn't blame any of you guys if you didn't either". But Daniel, my senior Fijian and a former school teacher, said "No boss, that wouldn't be right. Just because he's that way, it doesn't mean we have to do the same." So they went down to the seaplane after lunch and sang their hearts out to that guy. And he just broke down crying, like a baby. His lady wrote to us a few months later and said that it had changed his life. Now that's really the tear factor in action!'

*Turtle Island, which now accepts fourteen couples at any one time, has since been visited by the likes of actor Rob Lowe and rock stars Eddie Van Halen and Axl Rose, all with their partners of the moment (Van Halen's being actress wife, Valerie Bertinelli). It has easily survived a rash of imitators and stands unchallenged as the premier luxury Pacific retreat. Richard Evanson has fathered children with three Fijian women, one of whom is his new wife.*

# PARADISE IS DOING NOTHING ATOLL

Somehow the small, shrivelled rasher didn't seem worth the effort. Not mine, theirs. The Muslim kitchen staff had ritually washed themselves seven times so that my eggs could be garnished with bacon. This peacemaking with Allah, I was to discover, is but one of the cultural compromises which has enabled tourism in the Maldives to burgeon since the scattered Indian Ocean archipelago nation opened the tourism door fifteen years ago.

Alcohol is another matter again. Even though liquor permits enable tourists to consume most known fire-waters with impunity, few of the 182 000 citizens of the all-Islamic Maldives—the smallest independent nation in Asia—are prepared to serve it to them, at least with any skill or enthusiasm. That task is more often undertaken by Sri Lankan Tamils or other 'non-believers'.

For Carmine Travaglione, an effusive 39-year-old Perth builder who transformed a childhood passion for *Robinson Crusoe* and *Boys' Own Annual* stories into a profitable fleshed-out fantasy, cultural compromises are all in a day's work. His fiefdom is Ihuru, a perfect, oval-shaped desert island that could easily have emerged from Daniel Defoe's fertile mind. Here, through patience and inherent geniality, he has been able to successfully ingratiate himself with a rigidly conservative people taught from birth to suppress a wide range of emotions.

Although the unyielding and impassive stares from the dark brown eyes of the Sunni Dhivehin people seem to suggest a cold harshness, a fifteen century relationship to the sea (fishermen account for more than half the workforce) has produced a serene,

156

practical people who reflect their environment. A West German tourist who murdered his girlfriend and was given the harshest penalty the republic has to resort to—banishment to an uninhabited island in an outer atoll—vigorously resisted attempts by his consul to transfer him to a home gaol.

The Maldives has a form of racial separation by natural accident which would have left South Africa's white masters drooling. Of the 1190 islands straddling the equator like the spray from a cartographer's pen, a little over two hundred are inhabited by Maldivians. Of the not inconsiderable remainder, 54 have been given over to foreign or local operators as tourist 'resorts'—a grand word for flyspeck coral outcrops no more than two metres above sea level which can, like Ihuru, be circumnavigated on foot in six minutes.

By grand design or fortuitous circumstances, most of the 100 000 annual visitors rarely intrude upon Maldivian family life, which is carried on well away from prying eyes. Unlike Bali, where embarrassed tourists often stumble upon the morning or evening ablutions of an obviously irritated Hindu population whenever they leave the hotel zones, the Maldives remain all but untouched by a tourism boom which brings in well over US$30 million each year. When Singapore Airlines' jumbos disgorge passengers upon the slender isle of Hulule, occupied entirely by a modern airport, they are immediately taken to any one of the 54 resort islands by speedboat or native dhonis. Apart from a visit to the crowded capital island of Malé (one is sufficient), with its 13 000 bicycles, native contact is confined to the able-bodied males who are prepared to leave their families for months on end and travel for up to three days by slow chugging dhonis from islands up to 400 kilometres away.

'They are very set in their ways, with a lot of rules and regulations,' explains Carmine, who joins with his local staff in the observance of the fasting month of Ramadan. 'But it is their discipline which enables them to live on a tiny island like this for up to a year without seeing their families and with just four days off each month in Malé. There are very few fights or disputes. When you get to know them they're a delight, a nice race.'

Of course, empathy comes easier when the loneliness is common to all. Carmine eagerly awaits each school holidays, when his wife and two pre-teenage children fly up from Perth for a few intense weeks. For the first year of his residency, the Travaglione family lived together in tropical splendour, with Alisa and Benjamin schooled by correspondence. 'Their education wasn't suffering and, like me, they loved every second of living in paradise. But I felt they were missing out on relationships with people their own age, so I sent them back home,' he explains with more than a tinge of regret. Since then, he has tended to celebrate the presence of his few Australian guests with unbridled enthusiasm, offering his every comfort in return for some cosy after-dinner chats with news of home. These often take place at the end of his jetty, while giant stingrays and gentle six-foot sharks glide beneath dangled feet, and the shimmering night skies look as if God has knocked the top off a bottle of milk and sent it splashing.

As one of the few Australian operators, Carmine treats his leasehold and his employees with admirable respect, proving a contrast to a number of European-run resorts where jet-set trendies apply suntan cream with one hand and lob empty cans into the ocean with the other. Ihuru's nearest neighbour has an attractive local name but, being owned by an Italian cigarette company and used for the filming of its television commercials, is commonly known as Marati Time Island. When the resort's proprietor recently offered an edition of customised t-shirts at a cool A$60 apiece, he took in a quarter of a million dollars in three months.

By another pleasing contrast, the tiny t-shirt shop on Ihuru manages to screen vivid tropical fish motifs onto sturdy garments for less than $5. That sits well with patrons who eagerly tuck into Sri Lankan curries, fiery Maldivian omelettes, tiny sugar bananas and myriad fish dishes in an open, yet cosy dining room with a sand floor. With probably the most physically attractive island in the North Malé Atoll, Carmine could easily pave, tile and polish everything in sight and draw the mega spenders, but he just doesn't have the heart for it.

'I've tried to preserve the character and beauty of my island by limiting construction to 37 simple, comfortable bures (huts) but, unfortunately, a lot of resorts seem to believe that, as long as they've got one palm tree in the place and nice blue water all around, they can build concrete boxes to put people in, like Singapore hotels. I think they lose sight of why people come here in the first place. It certainly isn't for five-star comforts or wild night-life.' Neither is it for shopping or exotic artifacts. The attraction appears to be rather singular—fish and their surroundings.

After consuming my shrivelled rasher, I donned a mask and snorkel, ventured just twenty metres from the front door of my bure and was instantly absorbed into a spectacular marine panorama straight out of a Jacques Cousteau film. A school of a hundred or so brilliant red and silver fish darted by to the left, while chunks of what I first imagined to be coral changed shape and colour to my right, and a remarkably large and lazy green fish floated over to peer into my mask. With over 40 metres of clear visibility, I glided over plunging chasms and eventually emerged from the water babbling like the schoolboy who fell through the skylight of the girls' change room on sports day; to the bemused grins of old hands who now scuba dive to mighty depths but can clearly remember their own first venture beneath the calm surface.

Carmine grinned the broadest. After all, he snorkels around his island twice before breakfast each and every day, often playing tag with sharks. That's one of the perks of the job which keeps the son of a timber cutter and railwayman away from his previous hard toil of building giant drainage systems in Western Australia. 'I did some research into the Maldives after hearing about them from a friend,' he recounts. 'Some eighteen months, nineteen islands and $45 000 later, I ended up with Ihuru. It wasn't ever intended that I come up here as manager, I was just the main investor. But after seven months of operation and a $100 000 loss, I was forced to take over. I stayed for about four and a half months and went home, but after another six months I had to return to Ihuru. I've been here permanently since December 1985. I consider myself pretty fortunate. I know it sounds silly but over the years you try to make the fairytales in your mind a reality.'

Carmine remains enchanted by the Maldivians, some of the ablest seafarers in the world, and some of the craftiest businessmen. 'Dealing with the government here is never easy,' he reveals resignedly. 'These people have been traders for centuries so they can be very shifty. You have to keep a fairly low profile. There isn't the same recourse to legal avenues as we're accustomed to. But there are so many things about them I love that I can put up with all that.'

There is one incident in Maldivian history which tickles Carmine and all those who learn of it. When an elderly Sultan, the 93rd, took office in 1943, the reins of power were effectively assumed by Prime Minister Muhammed Amin Didi, a health fanatic who immediately introduced a complete ban on smoking. Although there were food shortages and other internal problems wracking the nation, it was the smoking ban which incurred the wrath of thousands and led to him being attacked and arrested upon return from an overseas holiday in 1953, the year he had been declared the first president of the republic.

Today, adult Maldivians proudly suck on their *bidi*, a cheap cigarette of heavy, imported tobacco rolled in newspaper, the consumption of which undoubtedly contributes to an appalling average lifespan of 52 years. With low supplies of fresh water and almost no natural resources beyond fish, the Maldivians have to import virtually everything. But apparently they don't bother with vegetables, because the common diet—of rice, sugar and fish—is responsible for fatal intestinal problems. Fortunately, membership of the United Nations since 1966 and subsequent access to the World Health Organisation is gradually improving the living standard of a people whose annual per capita income is around $200.

Still, what they lack in health, they can claim in fierce pride. Like the nuggety Thais, the Maldivians can claim to have never been colonised or occupied . . . almost. The Portuguese were in control, at the invitation of a rogue sultan, for fourteen years from 1559, and invading Malabars occupied for four months in 1753. Apart from that, the world has let the Maldivians be and they, for the most part, have gone unnoticed. In fact, their major contribution would appear to be a single word in the English language. The word 'atoll' is derived from the Dhivehi word *atholhu*.

The Maldivians know all about atolls, they have 26 of them. They also know about spouses. The country has the highest divorce rate in the United Nations, with eighty per cent of citizens having severed the knot at least once. With divorce, on the male's part, being an uttered 'I divorce thee,' it is not uncommon to encounter locals who have been married up to twenty times, though often to the same mate. One prominent Malé dignitary can claim almost ninety instances of wedlock. No mean achievement in his allotted two score and twelve!

Longevity doesn't feature strongly in any avenue of Maldivian existence, particularly tourism operation. Carmine Travaglione's personal paradise in the Indian Ocean may be abruptly terminated in two years time, if the authorities choose to reallocate his lease to a local operator. If that unfortunate eventuality does occur, he may be forced to dust off his builder's tools and make do with Perth's nearby Rottnest Island on weekends. Although it's a scenario he doesn't like to ponder for very long, there *are* contingency plans. 'Well, I have noticed this lovely little island over in another atoll,' he mumbles, as the waiter brings another round of frosted fruit shakes.

*Carmine Travaglione's lease on Ihuru was not renewed and the island now has local operators.*

*Global warming and the subsequent rising of sea levels continues to threaten the very existence of the Maldives. It is, in fact, possible that the country will not exist in twenty years time.*

*Maldivian dhoni (Bob King)*

# TASTING THE SPICE ISLANDS

There are history lessons to be learned on the Indonesian island of Ambon which seem to have escaped western schoolbooks. The physically striking Amboinese, devout Christians in the heart of an Islamic nation, view Australians more as brothers than neighbours. Many believe that the 999 islands in the Moluccas group—better known as the fabled Spice Islands—were once part of the Australian land mass. How else, they ask, does one explain the presence of wallaby on the islands, or the origin of the Moluccan word *ostralia*, which translates roughly as 'Have you seen it?'

Hardy Moluccan mariners may indeed have visited the northern coastline of Ostralia to trade with Aborigines well in advance of white settlement of the Great Southern Land. But today, contact seems largely confined to the annual Darwin to Ambon Yacht Race; a mini Sydney to Hobart which sees some 25 boats race across the Timor Sea for five days every August, battling for an honour which has yet to reach the status of the America's Cup.

Few Australian yachtsmen, or even the World War II veterans who pay homage at the superbly maintained Allied War Cemetery, are aware that the lush, gentle island of Ambon was once a pivot of global power, a possession so precious to European nations that it can be reasonably claimed that Christopher Columbus was in search of the Moluccan Islands when he accidentally discovered the American continent.

Trading in spices—pepper, cinnamon, cloves, nutmeg and mace—was active in Asia from the first centuries of the Christian era, and documents from the T'ang Dynasty in China make reference to the name *Miliku*. The first mention of cloves in

European history is found in the records of seventh-century Greece. By the end of the Middle Ages, the value of spices, which made their way to the old world by way of long and arduous trade routes from the ports of China and India, had surpassed that of jewels and cloth. It was known that all these priceless condiments originated from the mysterious Spice Islands but it was not until cartographer Fra Maura published his map of the world in 1440 that the race to find and control the islands could begin.

The Portuguese opened the first trading centre in 1511, stretching the parameters of their *feitoria, fortaleza e ingreja* (gold, glory and gospel) crusade to embrace spices, which they hauled away from the island of Ternate in staggering quantities. The Spanish came and went, and it was not until 1579 that the English and Dutch entered the picture. The Portuguese, miffed by the interlopers, descended upon them with a 27-ship armada. After a number of early defeats, Holland threw its own flotilla into the fray and by 1605 the Portuguese fort on Ambon had been sacked and almost 350 years of uninterrupted Dutch rule of the East Indies (later Indonesia) commenced.

The bitter struggle for the monopoly of the spice trade contributed to the decline of great powers and the rise of lesser empires. It was also a direct cause of colonialism in most of the Asian region. Ironically, under Dutch rule, the Moluccas gradually lost their coveted status, as smuggled seeds took root in Zanzibar and India. Even other islands in the East Indies, such as the Celebes, began to produce vast crops of clove and nutmeg. In time, the islands which had helped build the great cities of Venice, Lisbon and Amsterdam were forgotten backwaters, left mostly undiscovered and undeveloped to this day.

As if to add insult to injury, this unique transition zone between Asian and Australian flora and fauna endured ferocious bombing attacks during World War II. Allied forces battled the tenacious Japanese through the rugged islands, almost to the exclusion of other regions of Indonesia. From this conflict arose the legend of Dolan, an Australian private who led the Nippon invaders on a merry chase, so infuriating them that when he was finally shot from the rear, the locals were forbidden to bury his corpse. Today, his grave is a shrine.

Of all the people under the Indonesian umbrella, the Moluccan Islanders (of which the Amboinese are the most prominent) appear to have been the most concerned about the furtherance of their unique cultural, social and political identity. Certainly, the current generation of this handsome, fiercely proud people is unashamedly Indonesian and there is as much flag waving and singing of the national song in Ambon City as there is in Jakarta, Surabaya or Medan. But some of the older people will quietly recall the ill-fated Republic of South Moluccas, which was crushed by national troops in 1950, just two years after the Dutch had been driven out. Minor guerilla activity continued until 1968, by which time Ambon City had been bombed on three occasions. Today the remnants of an impotent Moluccan Islands government in exile can be found in Holland, avowing loyalty to the Dutch monarchy in much the same way as aged Nazis in South America light candles on Hitler's birthday.

Just how this magnificent group of islands will handle the ravages of increased western tourism is uncertain. The residents and the government openly welcome the revenue, without seeming to understand the implications of Club Meds and high-rise holiday hotels being dotted over one of the world's last surviving paradises. At present, the available hotel accommodation is basic but comfortable and the Ambon airport, 36 kilometres from the city, closes at five sharp every afternoon.

Ambon City, with more churches than Adelaide, is rather like Singapore before Mr Lee tore down every building erected before the war. The named, paved streets, are wide and clean, traversed by bicycle becaks and expensive western cars purchased with revenues from oil, nickel and timber harvested on the vast nearby island of Ceram. Ambon, by comparison and despite its position of leadership in the Moluccan group, is an incredibly tiny 14 by 30 miles. Although it is centred in Indonesia's 'Ring of Fire', which has seen 70 serious eruptions since European settlement, the island has no active volcanos.

For visitors arriving by air from Bali, the first surprise is Ambon Bay, a Sydney or Rio de Janeiro harbour in microcosm. The second is the absence of rice paddies, mangy dogs or any signs of poverty. Instead, one encounters sago forests and spice groves; shrill, almost deliriously happy children; tastefully dressed and uncommonly attractive citizens; modern, western style housing (even the odd tennis court); and a seemingly endless panorama of vivid, colourful Christian murals. Just why some of these people question their place in Indonesia becomes immediately apparent. Although their dominance has been lost, the islands still cultivate spices. The fragrance of cloves and nutmeg permeates the air at all times. Village craftsmen stitch clove twigs into stick-figure men and large intricate mounted ships. Others pound the trunks of spiky sago palms to extract the sludgy pulp which forms the staple Moluccan diet, while the leaves are woven into baskets.

When the bottom fell out of the spice market, many Moluccans turned to the sea for their livelihood. Surrounded by coral reefs and deep seas, the islands have long attracted marine biologists. But now tourists are seeking out the much-touted Sea Gardens. While not quite in the league of the Great Barrier Reef, they do have the advantage of being considerably less patronised. At Namalatu Beach, near the village of Latuhalat, a few small coins buy the services of an outrigger canoe with rower, and a serene glide across blue, coral waters.

At another end of Ambon Island, near the overgrown Pulau Pombu island concentration camp, built by the Japanese in 1943, the remote Honimua Beach offers surroundings straight out of *Robinson Crusoe*. While the visitor frolics on the white powder sand or in the warm, lapping waters, obliging young boys climb palm trees to gather coconuts, which are sliced and served for the immediate refreshment of those emerging from the water. No wonder the Dutch didn't want to give the place up!

The only intrusion upon this storybook scenario is likely to be a merry busload of wizened war veterans thrashing through the undergrowth in search of any one of four prisoner of war camps. On alternate days, the former Japanese guards drop by to pay their respects as well. These nostalgia package tours for old soldiers are thinning out each year, like the front ranks of an Anzac Day march. Within a decade, the depressing camp sites will have been reclaimed by the jungle and remembered only by historians.

It requires the better part of a morning to journey to Port Hurnala on the far side of Ambon, where noisy and crowded ferry boats leave for Ceram and other outlying settlements. There is something unmistakeably Pacific about the palm-lined coast, draped with fishing boats and peopled by bronzed natives with broad smiles. All roads in this area lead to the famed village of Waai, home of the holy eels and a number of relatively sacred carp, which dwell in an underwater cave beneath a mountain spring. Villagers willingly flick the water surface to draw the beasts from their hole, enticing them with a supply of eggs. The eels take them raw, while the carp are more partial to those soft boiled. If you ask village elders just why the eels are holy, they will very likely offer the entirely reasonable response: 'If they were not holy, the people would have eaten them by now'. Of course.

The northern side of Ambon boasts most of the forty fortress ruins on the island. The most impressive is Fort Rotterdam at Hila, built in 1597, sixteen years after the Portuguese fort at nearby Hitu had been destroyed and its residents driven to Ambon Bay, where they established Kota Laha in 1575. Renamed Fort Victoria when it fell to the Dutch thirty years later, this settlement evolved into Ambon City, which now has a population of a quarter million.

High in the hills of this sacked, bombed and always beloved city is Dusun Wisata ('land to visit'), a retreat sought out by academics, eccentrics and smart cookies from all over the world. Operated by Lieke Mahakena, a ship captain's wife with a perfect command of English, this seven-room homestay is a veritable Garden of Eden. Much like an exclusive country club, it sits in 22 acres of perfectly manicured orchid gardens and spice groves. Visiting dignitaries are invited to plant trees, and more than a few Aussie gums are in evidence. By a far boundary, at the foot of a hill, local women sing loudly as they wash in a stream and feed the deer which many Amboinese families keep as domestic pets.

At the moment, many Amboinese believe that their Australian brothers all live in Darwin ('Surely that is your major city?' enquired one) or are all in their twilight years, weighted down by campaign medals. The tourist stampede to this hidden empire, coveted by western civilisation since the fifteenth century, is inevitable. In Ambon City, three becak pedallers will not allow you to take their photograph together. Not because they want money but because they believe the combination is profoundly unlucky. In ten years time, they'll probably hold out for the cash.

# VICTORIA: NORTHERN AUSTRALIA'S FORSAKEN SETTLEMENT

In the annals of grand colonial failures, the ambitious but disastrous Port Essington settlement, on the Cobourg Peninsula, not far from today's city of Darwin, ranks as one of the most noble. Conceived by the architects of the British empire as a gateway city to rival Sydney, Victoria was to be a bulwark against Dutch and French expansionism in the southern East Indies. Instead, it became synonymous with isolation, despair, sickness and death.

Almost one hundred and fifty years after the brave but bedraggled band of Royal Marines, who had toiled for eleven years to introduce the structure of European civilisation to a fiercely inhospitable environment, abandoned their cursed community, the bush has reclaimed most of their garrison. The few contemporary visitors who seek out Victoria find a scattering of crumbled brick buildings and their foundations, in an eerie atmosphere of serenity. Even the indigenous Madjunbalmi Aborigines give the site a wide berth.

One can only stand among the ruins and try to imagine the night in April 1839, when a visiting team of French naturalists were entertained at Victoria's Government House with Chateau Margaux claret and fine French brandy. The 'considerable village', then but a year old, proudly boasted a church, hospital, a collection of military buildings, and a number of civilian settlers' cottages, each flanked by healthy gardens. Later that year, during a terrible cyclone which destroyed or severely damaged most of the tiny community's achievements, Government House was lifted off its stone piers and deposited three metres away. It was the portent of tragedies to come.

Centuries, perhaps tens of centuries before the arrival of the British, the Cobourg Peninsula was inhabited by Aborigines, one of the oldest races on earth. They had close links with the seafaring Bugis, Malays from what would become known as Makassar on the southwestern side of the Celebes (now the Indonesian island of Sulawesi). Bugis traders would sail their large prahus on the northwest trade winds past the Peninsula to the Gulf of Carpentaria, where they would fish for trepang (a sea-slug also known as bêche-de-mer), cure it on the beaches of the great southern land and return home on the southeast trade winds. The trepang, considered a great delicacy in Asia, would then be traded with the Chinese for silks, teas and other exotic goods.

It was in 1823 that East Indies trader William Barns suggested to the British Colonial Office that a settlement be established on the north coast of New Holland (Australia) to facilitate Asian trade and provide a refuge from pirates. There were, he pointed out, only two major European settlements along the entire length of the East Indian Archipelago—the British city of Singapore at the western end and Dutch Batavia (now Jakarta) in the middle. The admiralty supported the move, less out of concern for fostering trade than its fear of Dutch and French expansionism.

So, in 1818, Captain Phillip Parker King explored and named the Cobourg Peninsula and Port Essington and, less than ten years later, two ill-fated settlements—Ford Dundas and Fort Wellington—were established. Eleven years after these two experiments were abandoned, the British became serious about northern settlement and began construction of what would be an all-purpose military garrison, a trading post and, in time, a great city. All hopes were on Victoria.

Initial enthusiasm for the awesome task was enormous. Marines and civilians settled with their families, prepared for the long haul ahead. A stone jetty was built and supplies for the settlement came from Sydney, Calcutta, Timor, Java and Kissa. Early difficulties—such as surveyor Captain King's incorrect assumption that the region had an adequate fresh water supply—were almost cheerfully surmounted. But by the seventh year, the settlers were drained of life and spirit, and progress had ceased. Expectations of trade were never met, essential supplies arrived infrequently, the tropical climate and isolation proved both oppressive and depressive, and sickness ran rampant. Dysentery, diarrhoea, malaria, influenza and scurvy were commonplace. At times, half the garrison would be desperately ill with fever and the remainder confined to light duties. Malaria eventually claimed a full quarter of the settlers.

*The remains of the 'new Sydney', Cobourg Peninsula, northern Australia (Bob King)*

News of what has been described by historian Peter Spillett as 'an all-pervading sense of futility and despondency' was conveyed to London, where the viability of the outpost was questioned. The Colonial Office, having been advised by the major shipping companies that Victoria lay out of the path of proposed trade routes and they were not interested in it as a refuelling stop, had no interest in prolonging the agony of the weary inhabitants. The Lord's Commissioners of the Admiralty, who had once had five warships stationed at Victoria, had long revised their theory that the withdrawal of the Royal Marines would repudiate British sovereignty and invite foreign powers to take possession, so they, equally, saw no pressing reason to continue.

The orders for total abandonment finally reached Victoria on 13 November 1849, on Her Majesty's warship *Meander*. They were received with mixed emotions. Since the despairing communications had been sent, conditions had stabilised and many believed that it was possible for the community to survive and even prosper. However, with the messages taking up to a year to reach

London, it was not possible to convey this mild optimism without being seen to be ignoring orders. By the end of the year, Victoria settlement was nothing more than a series of lonely buildings, already overgrown by bush. Of the 149 brave souls who had attempted to carve order out of wilderness, 43 lost their lives.

After Victoria Settlement was abandoned, the area was still visited by the traditional Aboriginal owners, Macassan trepang fishermen, pearlers, salt-gatherers, buffalo shooters and timber cutters. But after the 1869 settlement of Darwin and its swift growth, the inhospitable Cobourg Peninsula was essentially forgotten. Today, few Australians are aware of the failed city that could have been the capital of Australia's Northern Territory.

There is access only from the sea for those who come to examine the remnants of Victoria. After a light plane flight from Darwin to Smith Point in the Gurig National Park and Cobourg Marine Park, it is a three to four hour boat journey from the Black Point Ranger Station down Port Essington to the location of the old jetty and Adam Head. There, with the aid of a guide or a compass, it is possible to locate the ruins, which have been preserved and partially restored by the Northern Territory Conservation Commission.

Protected by its own remoteness, the Cobourg Peninsula is one of the most pristine examples of tropical coastal wilderness in the world. With the recent opening of the impressive $8.5 million Seven Spirit Bay wilderness habitat—a perfectly integrated 48 capacity hotel built with the approval and involvement of the four clans who constitute the tribal ownership—reaching Victoria settlement is now considerably easier. The hotel takes small parties aboard its Cobourg Runner to and from the settlement, in the company of informed, sympathetic and extremely capable guides. In a region of great beauty where saltwater crocodiles and deadly box jellyfish tend to discourage most aquatic frolicking, the journey brings visitors within safe proximity of the extraordinary natural environment.

On Adam Head, within the frail ruins laying in brown brick heaps before you, it is tempting to think of yourself as the first visitor in a century and a half. As in Tierra del Fuego, the highlands of Nepal, or the Arctic Circle, there is nothing to dispel the illusion.

# A TWENTY-SECOND-CENTURY PREVIEW

The urinal sort of, ah, locked on to me. It registered my presence before its pristine porcelain surface and flushed (rather than blushed) as I stepped away. The nearby wash basin, similarly bereft of handles, buttons or plungers, also gushed forth liquidly as soon as it sensed my proximity. In a society where every delight and necessity could once be accomplished by the touch of a button, even the touch component has been removed. No doubt body-heat sensors are being developed as I write.

All this took place in the toilet of the private bar in Tokyo's Seiyo Ginza Hotel; up in my room the technology was even more dazzling. It wasn't just the remote-control drapes, the twin video players, or lighting possibly designed by Ellis D. Fogg or the Grateful Dead. No, it was the bathroom, which could have been an exhibit at a space-age trade fair. The television-on-a-swivel with a remote control in the shape of a powder-puff compact placed just near the toilet seat was a useful diversion, though I had encountered it before. I think I'd also previously come across heated mirrors and a switch which filled the room with steam within ten minutes.

What I hadn't been expecting was a device to defeat the bane of every traveller's existence—showers which either scald or snap-freeze. I've hurled myself in shock and pain from many a glass cubicle after failing to finetune the two taps before the needles of spray struck my defenceless flesh. The Seiyo Ginza had it all solved, in the form of a graduated visual display thermostat. Just set the dial to 40 degrees and step under the nozzle with complete confidence.

*Hi-tech cabaret busking in the Japanese city of Sendai (Bob King)*

Japan is one giant theme park and the theme is Japan. The country has one foot in the sixteenth century and the other in the twenty-second. The gadgetry, the sheer electronic wizardry can be truly overwhelming. Basically, the country *works*, like a Swiss (no, make that Japanese) watch. With almost childlike glee, Nipponese inventors seem to have met every practical need of the population (to say nothing of a great many wonderfully impractical needs), though not always with gee-whiz hooziwhatzits.

It doesn't take microchips to put the braille indentations I found on the feeder paths from Sendai railway station, nor the magnifying glass dangling beside pristine telephone books in public booths. But it does take a certain kind of population to keep them there. In a country where vandalism is absolutely inconceivable, it is possible to have banks of functioning vending machines operating around the clock in darkened laneways of major cities. Vending machines which contain cans of beer, bottles of whisky, packets of batteries, cans of hot coffee or cold melon juice, *manga* (comics) and all manner of foodstuffs.

The ubiquitous vending machines turn up everywhere, with the most astonishing variety lined up in vast banks in subway and railway stations to dispense tickets. Unless setting off on a particularly long and convoluted journey, a Japanese citizen would not line up to buy a ticket from a person behind a window unless the Emperor issued an edict. Coins and notes are fed into slots at a breathtaking pace—no change too difficult, no note too large. The volume is daunting, the efficiency almost beyond belief.

Tokyo commuters use weekly train tickets just like the poor wretches in Australia. They carry them in wallets in back pockets, in handbags, and at the bottom of shopping bags. These days, some of them also leave them there as they proceed through barricades. Sensor beams not only find and read the tickets wherever they are carried, they actually deduct value from them!

It is within the Japanese railway system that the full scope of advanced consumer technology becomes evident. It was in a rail carriage that I found out about the assassination of Rajiv Gandhi. I wasn't looking over the shoulder of a newspaper reader, but gazing up at a digital display screen which provided reasonably up-to-date news headlines. On the *Shinkansen* ('bullet' train) these same screens advise such details as the name of the next stop and the distance to it, along with the temperature, weather summary and cheery greetings. On the express train from Narita Airport to Tokyo, there is an illuminated route map with an incremental red display line which pinpoints the train's exact position in the Japanese countryside. That there is also a public telephone, vending machines and, in one car, a hot and cold self-serve bar, hardly seems worth mentioning.

Not that the human touch has been entirely eradicated. Most trains have women pushing trolleys laden with elaborate lunch boxes and other goodies along the aisleways at regular intervals. When you select and pay for your can of coke, chocolate bar or pack of dried seaweed, she will pull a portable bar-code reader from her smock pocket and zap it across your purchase before you've had time to mutter *domo arigato* in her direction.

If it saves time, they invent it. If it breaks down, they fix it. If it amuses them, they play with it. They build monorails to soar over crowded city streets and wire escalators so that they only function when somebody walks onto them. Junkies and malcontents don't destroy that which serves them and the politics of envy seems to be blessedly absent. Until you dig a bit deeper into social mores, it all gives off a utopian aura.

# LIVING FOR DEATH IN TORAJALAND

It could fairly be said that the people of Torajaland live for death. High in the rugged central mountains of the swastika-shaped island of Sulawesi (formerly the Celebes), one of the few truly primitive funeral rituals to survive the twentieth century has become a compelling, if slightly macabre drawcard for travellers of a certain tenacity.

It is a bone-crushing, nine-hour, 330 kilometre road journey, over some of the foulest roads in creation, from the Sulawesi capital of Ujung Pandang (formerly Makassar) to the ancient villages of Makale, Rantepaeo, Kete and Palawa in the high, lush, isolated Tana Toraja region. Known traditionally as the Land of Heavenly Kings, the place where animists believe their forefathers descended from heaven some twenty generations ago, this remote kingdom of rarefied air and vivid green textures is the second most visited area of Indonesia after Bali—despite the arduous passage and the availability of only a small number of bungalows and basic hotel rooms.

Torajans treat the passing of their loved ones with an unsettling combination of solemnity and celebration. The Torajan Feast of the Dead ritual is an elaborate, strangely moving spectacle, possibly unchanged since ages uncharted, which unites the inhabitants of an almost cosmic world in weeks, months and even years of extraordinary behaviour.

According to the tenets of Aluk Todolo, the ancient Torajan religion which survived the coming of both Christianity and Islam, death frees the soul to join its ancestors in the eternal afterlife, far beyond the southern horizon. If all the proper rites are conducted, earthly goods can accompany their owners to their afterlife so they may continue their existence in the same manner as in their beloved Toraja. (Who *was* that fool who said you can't take it with you?)

This view of death has given Torajans a common purpose. A lifetime of wealth is spent on staging a lavish ceremony which, in the case of important citizens, can require the sacrificial slaughter of up to two hundred buffalo and a thousand pigs. Before the arrival of the spoilsport Dutch colonisers, fresh human heads were employed in the ritual. Villagers suspected of witchcraft had their hands thrust into steaming pitch. If their fingers burned they were found guilty of sorcery and sold to a nearby village for beheading. Today, the large number of human skulls scattered all over Torajaland attest to this grisly practice.

Because a person's worth and standing is determined by his funeral, as many as 10 000 people are likely to attend a major week-long ceremony. The most popular aspect, with both residents and tourists, is the slaughter of buffalo by master swordsmen. As each mighty beast falls, children rush forward with bamboo tubes to collect the warm blood gushing from the severed jugular vein.

The cost can be enormous. When Chief Datutiki passed away, well over $150 000 was spent assuring his prosperous passage to the hereafter. Many of the sacrificed buffalo were the rare white-spotted variety, each worth around $3500. For a remote native civilisation, this level of expenditure is quite astonishing, and younger academics are beginning to question the wisdom of it all.

A body may be kept in state for up to two years, while relatives, friends and dignitaries from all over Sulawesi, Indonesia and the world are summoned. Offerings to the dead are carefully monitored and any skinflints become social outcasts liable to receive meagre offerings upon their own demise. Such a prospect is too terrible to even contemplate so gifts are generous in the extreme, particularly as they must be strictly reciprocated by other family members.

The formal funeral is the only 'death' that Torajans recognise. Anyone pronounced medically dead is considered to be just 'a sick one' or 'one with a headache' and his relations with the living will remain unchanged. He will be served food and drink three times a day, washed regularly and dressed in finery. The corpse will be kept in the house while funeral arrangements are being

*Torajaland resident (Bob King)*

made. Today, formaldehyde and modern embalming techniques render this practice relatively hygienic though such wasn't always the case.

The degree of funeral rituals is dictated by the dead person's caste, and high-caste funerals may extend beyond the standard seven days to two entire weeks, punctuated by banquets, kick boxing, cockfights and the vast consumption of potent palm wine. Because 45 per cent of Torajans are nominally Christian (Catholic or Protestant) services somehow find their way into the ancient activities.

Once the high-caste corpse has been officially declared dead, the coffin is carried in procession to a *liang*, a grave or small cave hewn from a sheer rock face and reached only by expert climbers. These elaborate graves, which were believed to be safe from thieves, can take between three and seven years to carve out of the steep cliffsides. (Those most commonly viewed by visitors are Lemo and Londa, near Rantepao.)

Unfortunately, thieves have not been deterred by the severe logistics. European art dealers offer staggering prices for the carved wooden effigies which are placed on a gallery outside the stone graves. This led, in the late 1970s, to the spectacular theft, by international master criminals, of more than a dozen of the prized artifacts. The deep distress suffered by the Torajans almost caused the closure of the area to tourism.

Which would have been a great shame because the nature of Torajan tourism has been far more constructive than destructive. There are no signs of the traditional balance of life being altered; perhaps because those who seek out the area are more interested in ancient culture than surfing beaches. There are no Kuta curs to be found along the tiny village trails, although Torajans do have their own form of consciousness alteration. One gets the distinct impression that a great many adult residents, ever-equipped with long bamboo tubes of palm wine slung over their shoulders, seem to be in a permanent state of mild intoxication. Whacked in the wilds.

Whatever their indulgence level, their hospitality is warm and it is not unknown for the tourist to be invited to stay in a *tongkonoan*, a large, ornate rice-barn house pointing to the north. As legend has it, this particular style of architecture came about when the Torajan people first arrived in Sulawesi from the southern province of China. They pulled their magnificent boats up onto land and overturned them to provide temporary living quarters. The carved bows were faced north to remind them of their former homeland and thus a building tradition was born.

Although the shuddering ride up into Torajaland has the virtue of a stop at the east coast port of Pare Pare, where one of the world's finest spiced seafood meals can be devoured, many visitors are now choosing to fly, at least one way, on a 16-seater Merpati propeller plane which uses a grass landing strip and is likely to return you to the relative comforts of Ujung Pandang.

After days of close proximity to expiry and its trappings, in the company of sedate, other-worldly people, it comes as almost a relief to swoop down over a soccer field and watch hundreds of boisterous Indonesian children suspend their games to allow you to land in front of the goal posts. As the plane's rear ramp is lowered, hundreds of laughing, shrieking kids surround and almost carry you aloft like a rare prize they have seized from the skies. It is a rare exhilaration, for if ever you needed to be reminded of the surging vitality of life it is after you have spent time with those who live for death.

# FIVE OVENS—NO
# WAITING

The first thing that hits you is the smell. A pungent, sweetish, almost nauseating odour that even seems to infiltrate the weave of fabrics. A day later and thousands of miles away, it will still be with you, as an odious reminder of your visit to Spring Hill. It is the odour of burned flesh.

It breaks no new ground to say that attitudes toward death are remarkably different in Asia. In India, Hindus burn corpses on pyres by the side of Mother Ganges and hurl the remains into the putrid river. On Spring Hill, as befitting the ultra-tech island state of Singapore, there is something of the laundromat or car wash about the Buddhist crematorium which doubles as a macabre tourist attraction.

In the hands of an advertising agency, Spring Hill would no doubt proudly offer 'Five Ovens—No Waiting!' This is the McDonald's of the funeral industry; a streamlined, inexpensive and largely emotionless disposal centre where relatives can suck on Cokes from a convenient machine while their loved ones are processed through the first available channel. It is, in contrast to the expensive, formalised funeral ceremonies of the western world, a culture shock in the true sense of the term.

The Chinese crematorium–temple complex atop Spring Hill, just ten minutes from downtown Singapore, is an open-sided, high-roofed aircraft hangar-styled structure. Up one end are the five numbered ovens; down the other are the tables where relatives painstakingly pick through the ashes and bones of their dear departed with chopsticks, so as to reassemble the remains in natural order (head up, feet down) for internment and storage in ornate yellow urns. Out the back is a huge sacred tortoise pond; a fetid home to thousands of algae-encrusted snappers who provide the only diversion to the nearby bake-off.

In the centre of the 'hangar' is a pool of on-duty monks, straining with serenity as they await calls to officiate at the brief, functional ceremonies in which mourners, bearing modest offerings of fruit and foodstuffs, participate before and after the ovens claim the corpses. There are no long black veils here. Shorts, t-shirts and sandals seem far more common. It's almost as if everyone is just calling in on the way to the beach or golf course (getting rid of the cadaver in the car boot could well mean more room for the five-irons and putters).

While those sifting and sorting through grandma's ashes will sometimes gently wave away an intrusive camera, there is no hostility toward curious western onlookers, who are, in the main, simply ignored. Neither is there any weeping, wailing or gnashing of teeth on display. Each funeral is carried out with a minimum of fuss, effort and overt emotion. A quiet dignity prevails and few voices are raised.

Yet for all the matter-of-factness about the building's purpose, a palpable discomfort creeps through those who are unfamiliar with the passive Buddhist attitude toward the life cycle. It is extraordinarily difficult not to relate the spectacle on offer to western Christian notions of life, death and the hereafter. As fascinating as the experience may be, one inevitably feels like an intruder. Beset with clammy skin, confused emotions and a real physical unease, departure, back down the hill to bustling Singapore, may come considerably sooner than anticipated.

# MOUNT BROMO DAWN

For even the most adventurous traveller, there is a certain trepidation about climbing atop a sturdy steed at the base of an active volcano at around 3 am and being led along a rocky path in pitch blackness, with only the distant plunk of stones hitting water to alert one to the sheer drop to the right . . . or is it left . . . side?

Now, adventure knows its limits. I may be an honorary Dayak (Borneo) tribesman, empowered to exorcise the average suburban home, and I may have once lost all feeling in a number of extremities while investigating a beaver dam in the Tierra del Fuego National Park, but my self-preservation instinct is as strong as the odour of an ancient Armenian armpit.

My hosts, however, were wonderfully persuasive, pointing out that the young handlers had never lost a paying customer and that the horse ride to the rim of steaming Mount Bromo is fast becoming one of the most popular tourist excursions in Indonesia. It may not exactly be the legendary Krakatoa, East of Java, but then most of its present-day conquerors do fall a little short of the Sir Edmund Hillary or Doctor Livingston physical profile.

The volcano is partly reached by road from Indonesia's second largest city, the sadly squalid Surabaya, which some may recall as the starting point of German flier Hans Bertram's *Flight Into Hell*. Collected from my luxurious hotel around midnight by a large, swift bus which weaved its way through the seething humanity (even at that time of night!) of the eastern corner of the monstrously crowded (90 million inhabitants) island of Java for three hours, I was deposited in the tiny mountain village of Ngadisari. The climatic change, from the steaming humidity of

Surabaya to the sharply cool air of the Tengger mountain range, was dramatic. If I'd forgotten my blanket I would have been in trouble.

Some 30–50 saddled horses met the buses and the great climb to the rim began. The first leg, along a dark, steep, narrow, cobbled mountain path was the most harrowing, as men and mounts developed a sense of each other. My beast proved comfortingly docile; my photographer was rather less fortunate.

It was only three kilometres to the small guest house at Cemaralawang, where we wide-eyed riders gorged ourselves on scalding hot chocolate, awaiting the call to remount for the final leg; planned carefully to land us on the crater rim just in time to witness the spectacular sight of the sun's ball of fire creeping over the mist blanket in a blaze of rich colour.

The tiny outpost accommodated a diverse array of humanity, surprisingly dominated by young European women. More than a few Dutch, the dreaded colonialists of the prewar years whose civilising expertise proved to be kindly remembered and often missed, return to places like Bromo to establish a link to their past or that of their parents. The warm camaraderie in the small hut was unforced, as each rider managed to overcome language barriers sufficiently to impart the tender state of their individual derrières. My photographer, whose relationship with horses is as strong as Thatcher's with flying picketers, seemed to be walking decidedly bow-legged.

Leaving Cemaralawang, the horses descended rapidly into the stark, barren and decidedly eerie Sand Sea, the floor of the Tengger caldera. For an hour we plodded across a lunar landscape which could well serve as a location for a post-nuclear holocaust film epic. As light filtered through the clouds, the bare terrain was splashed by grotesque shadows, suggesting all manner of prehistoric life forms. If old Tyrannosaurus Rex himself had stepped out from behind a contour in the earth there would barely have been a ripple of surprise. It was truly another world.

The Tenngerese—the 300 000 or so inhabitants of the 40 villages above 1500 metres in the Tengger Range—have many of the characteristics of the Sherpas of Nepal. Capable and quiet, they instill a sense of security in the often disorientated but always enthralled visitors in their charge. Bromo is a holy volcano, each year playing host to the spectacular Kesada Festival which draws many thousands of devout worshippers. The God Dewa Kusuma is believed to reside in the smouldering depths, ready to receive sacrifices thrown down into the terrestrial fires of the mountain's bowels. Fortunately, for some time now, none of the offerings have been human.

The horses were reined in at the holding area by the foot of a long, steep, stone staircase. This proved to be the end of the trail for the elderly and overweight members of our party, who baulked at the prospect of the strenuous climb to the top or who harboured a fear of sudden eruption, which last occurred in 1930. Others were wary of the narrow rim, with nary a fence or hand-hold, on which climbers must stand when they leave the last stone step and almost tumble into a black void.

As many as a hundred foreigners and scores of teenage Javanese 'picnickers' and lovers awaited the sunrise, eyeing carefully the bursting jets of steam and inhaling the sulphur stench. There was almost an air of Black Mass, until shafts of sunlight began sweeping away the macabre aura. Blessed with a clear morning, we could see the sun rising over the island of Bali, from our elevation of almost 2200 metres. To the south, the clouded peak of Mount Semeru, Java's tallest volcano (3676 metres), loomed.

In the cold light of morning I think we all felt a little sheepish at having been so alarmed by the silvery grass hills and rugged landforms. Although I still expected a rocket to land any moment, there was nothing really menacing about the Sand Sea, which possessed its own strange beauty. The ride back was brisk and comfortable, for all but my photographer, whose unfortunate buttocks were festooned with large red saddle weals.

The entire journey took less than twelve hours and I was back in my hotel well in time for lunch and a well-deserved sleep. I may not have peeked into Dante's Inferno but I was armed with sufficient exotic experiences to ensure that my back-home yarns sounded as if I had.

# ON OKINAWA

The healing and prayer meeting of the Third Mobile Alabama Baptist Church convenes every Sunday at ten. Not in Mobile but in the sprawl of Naha City on Okinawa. The church is wedged between a pachinko parlour and a karaoke bar and is largely frequented by black American servicemen; some of the 50 000 soldiers who are still stationed on the Japanese island some 47 years after an 82-day naval and aerial bombardment marked the first time in recorded history that the 'Land of the Gods' had been invaded and conquered by foreigners.

Their presence is initially evident on the roads in the form of reckless driving and extreme discourtesy absolutely unknown elsewhere in Japan. Soldiers of any origin are rarely desirable diplomats and the good parents of Okinawa are still locking up their daughters half a century after the unimaginable happened. 'They are wild boys,' giggled a girl from the tourist office when I asked about their behaviour. She wouldn't admit to having dated a soldier but eagerly told me, in trembling tones, of her many friends who had peered into the jaws of the beast and survived, sometimes with virtue intact.

Okinawa is where Japan's precious homogeneity goes off the rails, and the encamped Americans are just a part of that which has caused Okinawans to be viewed as second-class citizens by other Japanese for centuries. Like the Amboinese of Indonesia, they are a unique people absorbed not quite seamlessly into a large and powerful nation. Certainly they are Japanese—and have been since the seventeenth century—but with some Pacific permeations not altogether unexpected on an archipelago of 65 palm-fringed sub-tropical islands almost opposite Taipei and closer to Korea, China, Hong Kong and the Philippines than to Tokyo.

Slightly swarthy, with wavy hair and a larger build, they speak their own dialect, not readily understood by mainlanders, and possess a casuality at odds with the stressed intensity of their northern cousins (and live longer as a result). Far less guarded among outsiders than most Japanese—a consequence of interesting mixed bloodlines from ancient trading with the Philippines, Indonesia and China—the Okinawans were less inclined to shut out the world during periods of Japanese isolationism.

Getting away with the infractions to national policy often came down to a case of out of sight, out of mind. To a large degree, it still is. Unsettled a little by the overt individuality of the million or so inhabitants of the Okinawa prefecture, Japan proper has tended to place them in its peripheral vision. Not so much an embarrassment or even an irritation; more the loud guest at the dinner party who used the wrong spoon for the soup and just laughed when it was quietly pointed out to him. All of which doesn't bother the Okinawans unduly.

I made it a point of asking a range of breezy citizens how they would first rank themselves—as Japanese or as Okinawans. Almost unanimously they opted for the latter, albeit after some minor mental conflict. There is a strong general awareness of Okinawan origins, of the fourteenth-century Ryuku Kingdom with its Sho Dynasty, and a fierce pride in the traditional fine arts, a rich array of stridently distinctive performing arts and a unique pork-dominated cuisine (with snake garnishings) which have emerged from more than five hundred years of interaction with Southeast Asia, Micronesia, the Pacific and, more recently, America.

Delicate, heavily symbolic traditional dance is beloved throughout Japan but nowhere is it performed with more dramatic flair or tinged with more subtle sensuality than in Okinawa, where it can be accompanied by the *sanshin*, a three-stringed, snakeskin covered instrument believed to be the prototype of the longer-necked Japanese *samisen*. Music and dance seem to constantly reverberate around the islands. The annual Eisa Festival sees 200 000 people view and participate in a drum-driven form of mass ceremonial street dancing. Every summer the main athletic park hosts the Peaceful Love Rock Festival and young fans of Okinawan rock—Japan's most interesting strain of contemporary music—converge from all over the country. The tone-deaf members of the community seem to gravitate toward the martial arts; Okinawa has the largest number of karate participants in Japan and its champions are internationally renowned.

Inevitably, mainland Japan's curiosity about its exotic southern territory has overcome its unease with nonconformity. After decades of automatically flying to Hawaii, Guam, Tahiti and Australia to lie under palm trees and eat seafood, Japanese holiday-makers and honeymooners are finally discovering their own tropical realm. Tokyo subway stations are plastered with posters and banners touting the recreational charms of Okinawa, and the island's tourism bodies have produced some of the most lavish come-hither literature outside of the art catalogues of major western auction houses.

All to considerable effect—classless 747s from Tokyo and Osaka descend daily, jammed to the gunwhales with close on 500 passengers, intent upon peering at the seabed through the portholes of a strange submarine, sucking on some local sugarcane, lounging around the pools of scores of luxury hotels and the beaches of outlying islands, watching a mongoose and cobra fight to the death, and snapping up bargains in laquerware, pottery, glassware and dyed textiles. At least that is what is on the itinerary. There is also a hidden agenda not covered in the glossy booklets.

In a country that has more peace memorials than railway stations, where not a shot has been fired in anger (apart from water cannons at lively student demonstrations) since 1945, Okinawa offers a titillating taste of warfare for those so inclined. The theme of downtown Naha is militarism—American to boot. There is shop after shop after shop stuffed full of Yankee army surplus goods and mass-produced war trinkets. Fancy a mortar shell for your front garden? A brace of hand grenades to liven up New Year's Eve? A case of cartridges to prop up a pot plant? A flak jacket or ammunition belt for chic disco wear? A bayonet to reach the most remote back itches? A khaki helmet to deflect kamikaze coconuts? It's all there, along with a cornucopia of American pop culture emblems, such as baseball caps, letterman sweaters and football uniforms.

The American military presence is constant, though not just in the form of bad drivers and churches a long way from home. I came close to death from choking when I commenced consumption of an American chilli dog at a roadside fast-food truck just as the sky blackened, the air churned and my eardrums were near rent by the sudden approach of a lethal jet fighter, which materialised out of the ozone like Batman over Gotham City and attempted to give me a crude haircut as it dropped down on a runway a few metres away.

Although the Chinese, who dominated the islands in the fourteenth century, called Okinawa *shurei no kuni* (the nation that keeps the peace), its name is now synonymous with warfare. After island-hopping through the Pacific, inching back the Japanese juggernaut at a fearsome human cost, American forces unleashed devastating war upon the islands on Easter Sunday in 1945. Five divisions of marines with air and sea support engaged a cornered, fanatically determined Japanese army which had turned ancient tombs into gun emplacements and riddled caves and sea walls with labyrinthine tunnels.

The civilian population suffered terribly as the hand-to-hand combat and bombing onslaught became more ferocious. Those who did not choose suicide after hearing terrifying propaganda which painted the young American soldiers as sadistic murderers and rapists had to face flamethrowers, grenades and relentless firepower. Nothing was spared in this first battle for Japanese territory. When a 246-metre long battleship, the *Yamato*, was despatched from Tokuyama naval base to repel the invasion, no less than 350 US aircraft were sent to sink it off Nagasaki just one day into its journey.

By the time the American flag was raised on 22 June, the death toll exceeded a quarter of a million, including Japanese commanders General Ushijima and General Cho who observed the *bushido* ritual and committed *seppuku* (self disembowelment). The United States appropriated Okinawa, rebuilt the cities and occupied the islands formally until 1972, when they were returned to Japanese sovereignty (and the arduous task of converting right-hand drivers to left-hand drivers began). For the powerless Okinawans it was just another episode in a long history of seemingly inevitable outside control.

The tenacity with which Japan has attempted to wrest control of the northern Kurile Islands from Russia does not bode well for any independent stirrings in the hearts of proud Okinawans. But with membership of the Japanese nation comes advantages of prosperity shared by only one other group of Pacific area islands, Hawaii. From the main Okinawa Island down to Yonaguni Island (from where, on a clear day, you can see Taiwan and be bothered by the world's largest moth), the levels of transport, housing, tourism facilities and nature preservation on the Ryuku Islands are rarely less than impressive.

The Ryukyus, washed by the Black Warm Current from the Philippines, are broken into three main groups, with the Miyako Islands to the southwest offering the greatest array of aesthetic delights. Replete with coral reefs, deserted beaches, thick jungle foliage and primeval forest, rare animals (the Irimote wildcat), rich birdlife and floral diversity, ancient tombs, folkcrafts and an almost lethal local sake, these tranquil (though occasionally typhoon-raked) dots upon the blue are perhaps Japan's least-publicised treasures. The well-visited Miyako Island itself, which, like the city of Kyoto, was spared destruction during the war, has the best-preserved examples of traditional Okinawan architec-ture—houses built low with sturdy tiled roofs and surrounded by coral to withstand fierce winds.

For the moment, most Okinawan visitors remain on the main island, which boasts one of the busiest festival calendars outside of Bali—at least one major event every month. The Naha Oh Tsunahiki tug-of-war in October, the Naha Dragon Boat Race in May, and the Naha Marathon in December draw the sort of teeming crowds one would expect in Tokyo. On the days when the streets are not riotous with merriment, tourists leave metro-politan Naha for the forty minute drive to Okinawa City, a 1974 amalgamation of Koza city and Misato village (built on the site of the eleventh century Goeku foreign trading village). The attrac-tion, particularly for hordes of GIs, is the neon-flooded Goya Street, with its bars, clubs and assorted pleasures of the flesh.

If Okinawa was its own political entity it would at least be visited by those westerners keen to add another country to their travel list. But as a part of Japan it is inevitably relegated, by reasons of distance and ignorance, to the very end of a need-to-see roster that is top-heavy with Tokyo, Osaka, Kyoto, Nagoya, Sapporo, Hiroshima and Nagasaki. To think of Okinawa as Japan is as short-sighted as thinking of Alaska as America or even Tahiti as France. This coalition of cultures stands both proud and apart.

# THE TROGLODYTE REALM OF CAPPADOCIA

The locals call it Cappa*dokya*, visitors prefer Cappa*dowshia*. It looks more bizarre than any lunar landscape foisted upon us by Hollywood 'Golden Turkey' award contenders and is the second most visited area in Turkey after the ancient city of Istanbul. I can't recall any location more strangely captivating, any natural phenomena so unsettling. I'm not sure if it currently ranks as one of the wonders of everybody else's world but it's certainly one of the wonders of mine.

Cappadocia is kilometre upon kilometre, valley upon valley of surrealistic volcanic formations—fretted ravines, 'fairy chimneys', erratically sculpted rock pinnacles and cones, underground cities, rock-hewn churches and monk cells; all bathed in changing tones of warm red and gold, cool green and grey. A breath-stopping troglodyte realm beyond even the imagination of a Disney or Spielberg.

It wasn't always Cappadocia. The name, which pops up in the Bible a few times, arrived with Roman invaders in 17 AD. Which is just a bit past last week in the overall Turkish scheme of things. After all, just a couple of hours' drive away is the town of Catal Hoyuk, believed to be the world's oldest known human settlement, kicking off around 7500 BC.

Sitting squarely in the middle of the Anatolian Plateau, the land bridge between Europe and Asia, Cappadocia has seen scores of conquering and retreating armies dashing eastward and westward across its soil, stopping occasionally for the odd bout of raping and pillaging. At least a dozen civilisations have risen and fallen in the lees of the region's stark valleys, and the land is stained with the blood of soldiers and saints, princes and prophets, crusading Christians and marauding Muslims (and vice versa).

And as the soldiers of fortune from almost ten thousand years of turbulent history passed through this affronting terrain, each one would almost certainly have dismounted and marvelled at the sheer improbability of it all. Hittite, Roman, Persian, Macedonian, Christian, Byzantine, Seljuk, Mongol or Ottoman, he would have gazed at the splendour around him with fear-tinged awe; as do the agog visitors who come in the closing years of the twentieth century AD.

History surrounds and almost suffocates you in Turkey. Along with Israel, Egypt and Greece, it is the cradle of human civilisation and stone-hearted be the man who can touch so tangible a manifestation of the past and not be brought to dwell upon his origins. The spirit of millennia past, of trade routes and battle trails, of flourishing arts and culture, of devout faith and barbarism, is all-pervading.

Cappadocia's dramatically unique terrain came about as a consequence of the violent eruption of two volcanoes—Erciyes Daği and Melendiz Daği—which layered the region in the hot volcanic ash that became known as 'tuff'. In time, this ash hardened as a softish, porous stone, which was moulded and shaped by natural forces of erosion into ethereal shapes. Hard rock caught in the ash served to protect pinnacles of tuff from erosion, resulting in huge boulders balancing precariously atop slender columns.

By the time man came on the scene, the terrain was ready to be easily carved and hollowed, with primitive tools, for habitation or storage. Stone, Copper and Bronze Age man found the substance malleable and, when mixed with dung, exceptionally fertile. So, protected and nourished, he survived all onslaughts. In fact, the native Anatolians were so loath to give up their unique world, even when faced with the regular toing and froing of marauders, that they carved out about ten elaborate, 8–10 level underground cities and rolled stonewheels across the entrances when the blood started flowing (lest it be their own).

Although Christians would eventually cut chapels, churches and monasteries out of rock faces, then decorate them with fine frescoes, the tone and form of human adaption was well established before their arrival. Four thousand years before Christ, the valleys of Cappadocia began to be dotted with doors, windows and turrets. All available land was cultivated and herds were grazed by these early Anatolian cave-dwellers. Yet every intrusion by man was absorbed so that it blended unobtrusively with the hand of nature. Six thousand years later, apart from a few hotels dug into rock, a long stream of tourist buses, and even a Rock Palace Disco Bar, not a lot has changed.

The Cappadocia region forms a rough triangle, several hundred kilometres around. The entire area is scattered with mysterious formations and first-hand history, but most visitors head straight for the spectacular Goreme Valley where the most dramatic examples of eroded and adapted tuff are to be found. The main entry point is the city of Nevsehir (population 60 000), the provincial capital. From there it is just 15–25 kilometres to most of the major sites—the Goreme and Zelve Valleys, the edifices of Uchisar and Ortahisar, the Kaymakli and Derinkuyu underground cities, the 'fairy chimneys' of Urgup, the White Valley, and the Goreme Open Air Museum in the Elnazar Valley with its rock-hewn churches and monasteries.

Most visitors come down from the Turkish capital of Ankara (formerly Angora, famous for its goat hair) by bus or hired car. The four hour trip is comfortable if not terribly engaging. Each small Cappadocian town offers cheap and plentiful accommodation but the most attractive and practical place to base oneself is the village of Urgup, with its cobbled streets and eerily alien atmosphere. The volcanic soil of the area is responsible for the vibrant belt of green which surrounds the town. Wine, grains, fruits and honey are all in plentiful supply.

With a rental car, a good map and at least two days, you can take yourself on a trip through a Turkish Twilight Zone, poking in and around the valleys and peaks. Time seems to evaporate as you wander about the cave houses, precipices, caravanserais, museums and churches. And in every village and beside every spectacular stone formation are the polite Cappadocian traders, offering inexpensive Byzantine dolls, Arabian lamps (that you are sorely tempted to rub, over a chanted incantation), pure silver jewellery, pottery, onyx, brass carvings, antiques, carved tuff 'fairy chimney' replicas, goat herders' shoulder bags, and the region's famous handwoven carpets.

I bought one fine rug from a tiny house straight out of Aesop's Fables, just near the entrance to the Kaymakli underground city. It came with a proudly recited original poem from the former sea captain who sold it to me (but only after painstakingly explaining the history of the design and natural origins of every colour).

Unless you have a full week, there is not much chance of

sighting everything of worth in Cappadocia. The best you can do is to travel fast and efficiently, trying to take in the major attractions, always keeping an eye on the light. Every formation photographs differently as the day moves on and the angle and quantity of light changes. What can be dull at midday can be dazzling at 4 pm.

The most affronting exhibit in this entire realm is Uchisar, a towering free-standing rock in the shape of a medieval fortress, pockmarked with the openings of caves, cells and storerooms, plonked right in the middle of a small township. For reference, try to imagine one of the Olgas rolled into downtown Dubbo.

Over by the Goreme Valley is the Open Air Museum, a circular complex of seven churches and a monastery, reached by a walking track and, occasionally, tunnels and ladders. Most of the churches boast outstanding frescoes from the tenth and eleventh centuries, giving some indication of the size of the Christian communities which flourished in Central Turkey at that time. Unfortunately, in between being discovered and then protected as tourist drawcards, many of these wall paintings were seriously damaged by mindless vandals. It is doubtful that they can ever be properly restored.

Just over a ridge a few kilometres away is the tiny town of Zelve, a former monastic retreat based in two canyons. The dead-end road to this sleepy burg is notable for its access to fields of absurd, phallic rock pinnacles, which have been known to extract more than a few embarrassed giggles from the matrons on the tour buses.

The underground cities, where tens of thousands of hardy Anatolians existed for decades, emerging only to tend their fields when the all-clear was given, are astonishing. By a combination of strolling and crouch-crawling one can descend through rooms, chambers and cells until complete disorientation sets in. Although every passage is electrically-lit and handrails are provided, an almost indescribable rush of relief accompanies your re-emergence into the crisp Cappadocian air.

Conversely, there is a palpable feeling of regret and loss as you depart Cappadocia. A realisation that, no matter where you travel throughout the remainder of your days, you will never again find yourself in an environment remotely like this supernatural landscape. If the moon was like this, the first passenger shuttle would have left years ago.

# THE HIDDEN MACAU

A day trip to Macau on the jetfoil from Hong Kong is one means of adding another country to your tally, but it is most certainly not the way to fully appreciate one of the most engaging cross-pollinated cultures in Asia. In a day you can obtain but a hint of the Portuguese enclave's unique flavours; in three you can begin to appreciate why it commands such loyalty from those who find it far more satisfying than its intense and crowded neighbour sixty kilometres away on the other side of the Pearl River estuary.

In almost every regard there is more to Macau than meets the eye. More space, more exotic food, more accommodation, more history, more industry, more festivities, more surprises, more real charm. Macau may only have a total area of 16 square kilometres, but there are some 70 kilometres of driveable roads leading to almost twenty major hotels, seven casinos and innumerable churches, gardens, forts, inns, temples, parks, monuments, museums, gates, lighthouses and restaurants.

Many cities like to believe they have a rich and evident history, but few preserve their past as vigorously as Macau, where strict development and renovation controls mean that the sort of old buildings which, in other Asian centres, can only be seen in books of sepia-toned photographs, stand proudly and still perform the functions for which they were built. Just one example is the eighteenth-century Leal Senado (Loyal Senate) which still houses the Municipal Council.

The cobblestones and flagstones which still pave so many Macau streets were brought to the busy and pivotal trading entrepot three hundred years ago as ballast in ships which carried tea, silks, porcelain, silver, spices and other treasures between China and Japan and from those great empires to the rest of the world. When the heavy-laden ships left for Europe and the New World (the tea which caused the Boston Tea Party came from Macau), the stones were discarded on the harbour shores.

It was almost five hundred years ago that Portuguese explorer Jorge Alvares first set foot in Southern China, and more than four hundred and fifty years ago that Macau was established to consolidate the scattered Portuguese Pearl River trading posts which had been set up in his footsteps. By 1604, the Dutch considered the port so important that they attempted to invade and vanquish. They attempted again in 1607, 1622 and 1627 and were repulsed each time.

The Portuguese not only held on tightly to Macau, they fashioned it into one of the most important outlying Iberian settlements after Brazil, lavishing upon it grand architecture and a pivotal spiritual responsibility. The first Christian to set foot in China was a Portuguese priest, and Macau—even though it was known to every sailor in the world for its mulatto ladies of pleasure on The Street of Happiness—served as the gateway for Christianity to China and Japan and the headquarters of the Catholic Church in Asia. Today, its most famous landmark, the imposing facade of St Paul's, once described as a 'sermon in stone', stands on the site of a fifteenth-century Jesuit church.

Just as enduring a legacy is the spectacularly well-evolved cuisine which has no comparison in Asia. When the Portuguese came they brought not only their own recipes but ingredients and dishes from India, Malaya, Timor, Africa and South America which blended with the foods of China to create a rich, exotic Macanese style. To eat out in Macau is to eat remarkably well— spicy and peppery African chicken from Mozambique, bacalhau cod from Portugal, sumptuous feijoadas stew from Brazil, sizzling, piquant Pearl River prawns, fragrant green Macau soups of considerable substance, and a rich diversity of Chinese food— Chiu Chow, Shanghaiese, Cantonese, Szechuan, Hunan and more. To boot, there are also Italian, Vietnamese, Burmese, Filipino, Korean, Thai and Japanese restaurants of commendable quality.

There is no shortage of places to partake of this fine fare but the most satisfying procedure is to hire a Macau Moke and head off from the city area over the bridge to the islands of Taipa and Coloane, where an entirely different Macau presents itself: one of sandy beaches, shady lanes, intriguing side streets, pine forests, ponds and farming communities. Although Taipa now has a Hyatt Regency Hotel and a racetrack and will soon have an international airport attached to it, and Coloane is about to feel the impact of a large Westin Resort hotel with equally large golf course, these islands are still very much frozen in time.

Once a hide-out for pirates and bandits, the European-toned villages of Taipa and Coloane islands preserve a languid, family-based, self-sustaining life that seems centuries rather than minutes removed from the mainland. In the community squares residents and visitors sit, talk, eat, ride bicycles, play dominoes or mah-jong and even watch television under rows of old banyan trees near cream-coloured public buildings. The tiny restaurants are unpretentious but uniformly excellent, the company never less than robust.

Coloane has a seafood praia and shops selling all known fish by-products. Hong Kong Chinese come over for the day to buy dried fish, fresh fish, fish paste, shark's fin and rare sauces. The main village is home to fishing junks which moor in the stream separating Coloane from the Chinese island opposite. Indeed, it is for the construction of junks that Coloane is renowned throughout Asia.

Visitors are free, at their own risk, to wander through the extensive junk-building yards where the graceful and eminently functional seafaring craft are made (from huge trunks culled from rainforest trees in Malaysia and Borneo) with almost no modern tools, to a centuries old tradition. It costs about half a million Australian dollars to commission one of the larger junks with one to three engines, which are built in fifteen days by quiet, dedicated craftsmen and then, after being outfitted with sophisticated navigational equipment, sailed off to Japan, Vietnam, Malaysia or the Philippines where they will remain in use for at least fifty years.

Master crafts are important in Macau, where the ambience of the enclave is its most enticing aspect. That which is worthwhile is preserved, be it the manufacture of high quality fireworks (banned in Hong Kong), or ancient fortresses and citadels. And when the Macanese restore they do it in impeccable style.

Take the Pousada de Sao Tiago on the main waterfront drive, which began life—back when William Shakespeare was in good health and writing plays in England—as the Fortaleza da Barra, a fort and chapel which helped repel the armadas of covetous European nations. The remains of that noble structure now form

*Taipa village serenity, kindly brought to you by . . . (Bob King)*

the core of a five-star hotel and restaurant which regularly wins major awards and plaudits. With cannons, walls, stone passage-ways and even the chapel still in place, it has become an emblem of the Macau way of doing things. In most other places, the bulldozers would have toppled the walls as soon as the land valuation was at hand.

Although it seems an odd thing to say about an enclave that is almost five full centuries old, Macau's time may well have come. Its economy is booming and its mood confident. Macau doesn't bustle and it doesn't build towering glass and steel sky-scrapers and it doesn't fill its streets with more cars than there are spaces for them. It is casual, elegant and wonderfully patient and it seems to place human values ahead of corporate ones. It doesn't argue with the Chinese because, more than anyone else, it has learned from them—learned to take the long view of matters, learned to appreciate and employ fine and traditional arts.

Six million people a year go to Macau and it's a fair bet that most of them go back—to shop, to eat, to gamble, to see the Grand Prix and, perhaps most important of all, to absorb the atmosphere of the oldest, and very likely the last, piece of Europe in the East.

# BLUES, BLUEGRASS AND BOURBON

My cab driver began apologising before we'd left the precincts of Nashville Airport. Her dung-splattered rubber boots had set my nose twitching and she'd spotted my grimace in her rear-view mirror. I didn't catch the opening of her explanation-cum-apology but one recurring phrase registered on that early, decidedly frosty Tennessee morning. She had been, it seems, 'slaaaaarpin' the haaaargs' before beginning her shift.

I didn't really need her to 'run that by me again' three times to understand that she had been slopping the hogs, but I was so enchanted by her delivery that I thought I might as well let her educate an out-of-towner. The enchantment must have been mutual for, at a downtown traffic light, she spun around and spurted, 'Gollllly, y'all sure do have a furrny aaaaccent!'

I let it pass. Most Americans, in an endearing way, believe themselves to be the centre of the universe and if an upstanding Nashville citizen wanted to view me as an exotic curiosity, well . . . it was her turf. Anyway, we were closing in on Music Row and I didn't need any other diversions.

You don't have to love music to feel at home in Tennessee and Kentucky but it certainly helps. Rather like a fondness for ice in Antarctica. Country, blues and bluegrass music is an integral component of the states' cultural, social, historical and economic life. It touches almost every aspect of activity inside the encircling ring of the Appalachian Mountains.

Indeed, a certain admiration is due to these wily southerners, particularly the residents of Nashville. Even forty years ago, country music was disdained by haughty northerners as the music of hillbillies and hicks, an embarrassment embraced by poor white trash. Undaunted by the denigration, Nashville dubbed itself 'Music City USA' and, one by one, the major record companies opened offices and built recording studios. What was a healthy million-dollar industry eventually began turning over billions, and the very name Nashville became internationally synonymous with country music.

Now, in the fine tradition of American enterprise, the city capitalises on that reputation in ways diverse and inventive. Visitors arrive keen to visit the Country Music Hall of Fame and Museum, the Grand Ol' Opry and Opryland themepark, and the famed Ryman Auditorium, which housed the Grand Ol' Opry (on air since 1925 without a single Saturday night missed) from 1943 to 1974, then find themselves offered an array of associated attractions that could well keep them in Nashville and nearby Hendersonville for a month.

Why there's Marty Robbins' Memorial Showcase, House of Cash Inc. (as in Johnny), Hank Williams Snr/Jnr Museum, (Conway) Twitty City, Kitty Wells' Country Junction, the Jim Reeves Museum, Ray Acuff and Minnie Pearl's Museum, Barbara Mandrell Country, Music Village USA, Country Wax Museum and Mall, Recording Studios of America, Music Valley Wax Museum of the Stars, the annual Country Music Fan Fair (every June) and, of course, Music Row, where the serious business of country music is carried on.

Memphis is a wee bit more subtle in its exploitation . . . well, except where all things Elvis are concerned. Over 650 000 visitors a year take the guided tour through Graceland on Elvis Presley Boulevard, then bend their credit cards inside the many adjacent souvenir emporiums. Graceland has recently been augmented by Graceland Plaza, where one can tour the King's customised jet, *The Lisa Marie*, and peruse the Elvis Presley Automobile Collection, where pink Cadillacs abound.

Unfortunately, so do Elvis fans. Going there once is fine—Paul Simon did just that, and the experience generated one of his best songs—but virtually living on the street outside, as a great many overweight, illiterate, white southerners seem to do, is another thing again. Like their late King, these particular devotees (who may well be able to tolerate, even appreciate, the crimson, lime and tiger-skin colour scheme inside the house) appear to eat burned bacon, mashed potato and gravy three times a day out of one side of their mouths while mumbling the words to *Don't Cry*

*Daddy* out of the other side, as they lovingly fondle souvenir mugs and teddy bears. It's quite a circus.

*Graceland, Elvis Presley Boulevard, Memphis, Tennessee*

If you get Graceland out of your system early, you can investigate the Memphis that actually shaped the young Presley and those other southern music icons who also recorded at the legendary Sun Studio on Union Avenue—Jerry Lee Lewis, Carl Perkins, Roy Orbison, Johnny Cash and blues greats B.B. King, Howling Wolf and Junior Parker. Memphis, on a bend in the mighty Mississippi, where 60 per cent of the nation's cotton crop is traded, is the legendary home of the blues. It was on Beale Street that W.C. Handy first heard raw delta blues and shaped it into a form with mass appeal. It was in the foyer of the Peabody Hotel, still redolent with the mournful wailing of riverboat blues purveyors, that farmboy guitarists and shouters were recorded for posterity.

In Kentucky, champion thoroughbred horses and bourbon whiskey are undeniably primary emblems but bluegrass music, as popularised by state hero Bill Monroe in the 1940s, has touched almost as many people as the Kentucky Derby and Jim Beam. There is, however, little formal exploitation of this mountain blend of banjo, fiddle and guitar. Instead, it is the more sedate Stephen Foster who is deified, even though he only wrote *My Kentucky Home* during a visit to his cousin's mansion. In today's Kentucky, with a million acres of carefully managed 'great outdoors', the 235-acre My Old Kentucky Home State Park ranks with the Daniel Boone National Forest as the most-visited of 44 state parks. In summer, fifty of the balladeer's songs are featured in an evening musical drama.

Yet for all this preponderance of music attractions, it needs to be said that one could be a tone-deaf renouncer of rhythm and still have joy unbounded in the states of Tennessee and Kentucky. Admittedly, it would be far easier in the latter but, despite appearances to the contrary, Tennessee does occasionally march to the beat of a different drummer.

Memphis has a particularly rich texture, as befitting a major river city. Just completed is the National Civil Rights Museum, on the site of the Lorraine Motel where Martin Luther King was assassinated in 1968; and the Great American Pyramid, a 32-storey sports and entertainment complex. Out on Mud Island is a 52-acre river park, with the Mississippi River Museum and the actual *Memphis Belle* B-17 bomber which survived 25 missions against Nazi Germany and has recently been immortalised by film-maker, David Puttnam.

Perhaps as a deliberate defence against its predominant image as a brassy, schemes 'n' dreams city, Nashville is replete with a surprising number of museums and exhibits which display fine arts, African sculpture, Indian crafts, Civil War artifacts, tobacco art and history, Christian stained glass and exotic wildlife. Outside the city, in the Western Plains and the heartland, is the wide southern experience, from antebellum mansions to rustic log cabins to pristine frontier land. In fact, the state's Great Smoky Mountains is the most popular national park in America.

Every time I go to Tennessee I promise I'll spend more time amid the natural splendour but, you see, there's this hot little blues and jazz combo down on Beale Street in Memphis that plays this wonderful . . .

# PRANCER, DANCER, RUDOLPH AND A MAN CALLED CLAUS

The Finns would certainly never be demanding about it but, just the same, they would like the world outside their borders to note a change of address. Santa Claus, contrary to common perception, does not reside at or near the North Pole. It seems that he moved to Finnish Lapland around the same time Mickey Mouse departed smoggy Anaheim for the sunnier climes of Orlando.

Thoughtfully, the jolly red gent left a forwarding address: Rovaniemi SF-96930, Arctic Circle, Finland. Which is just as well, given that he receives—and answers—almost a million letters a year, from children in some fifty countries. Even those addressed to the North Pole manage to find their way into the Finnish postal system in time for a reply before the tinsel is taken down for another year.

The scale of the operation is underlined by the fact that Santa has his own post office and postmark, and receives a substantial stamp allowance from the government, along with fifty helpers. In fact, the internal Finnair service which bears visitors from Helsinki into the Arctic Circle city of Rovaniemi sports his visage prominently on the aircraft fuselages and tailfins, leaving no doubt at all that the upper half of Finland, at least in December, is Santa Claus Land.

It is, of course, a great deal more. The immense allure of this part of the Arctic Circle was drawing visitors well before Santa's relocation. This is the glossiest and most seductive travel brochure come to life. Snow-covered from October, it is one of the world's premier winter wonderlands; an accessible, enveloping realm of fells and cliffs, reindeer and sled-dogs, shimmering ice crystals and snow-laden pine trees, and myriad winter sports carried on in the blue-tinged winter night which occupies all but a few hours of each day.

Rovaniemi, the confluence of the Polar Road and the Arctic Ocean Road, with a prehistory of 8000 years, is perhaps best known as the training ground for the very best Olympic downhill skiers, who hone their skills on the severe slopes of Ounasvaara, which rises from the banks of the Kemijoki River.

But it was not for the world's most adventurous and visually edifying skiing that I landed myself in Rovaniemi a few days into a new year. I came at the behest of the eternal child inside us all; I came to give life to a dream of longstanding. I wanted to meet Santa and discuss affairs of state.

My obsession with all things pertaining to Christmas manifests itself in bizarre forms. Chief among them is a vast collection of seasonal recordings—hundreds upon hundreds of cheery ditties graced with bells, chimes and innumerable 'ho ho hos'. Around my house on Christmas Eve can be heard the lilting tones of *Santa And The Purple People Eater* by Sheb Wooley, *Santa Claus Go Straight To The Ghetto* by James Brown (who, of late, certainly hasn't been a good little boy!), *Sock It To Me Santa* by Bob Seger, *'Zat You Santa Claus?* by Louis Armstrong, *I Was A Teenage Reindeer* by Jim Backus, *A Surfer's Christmas List* by the Surfaris, *Put The Loot In The Boot Santa* by Mae West, *Santa Claus And His Old Lady* by Cheech & Chong, *Santa Doesn't Cop Out On Dope* by Martin Mull and *A Christmas Boogie* by Canned Heat with Alvin and the Chipmunks. Why, I have seasonal recordings by Bruce Springsteen, Joan Jett, the Blues Magoos, Spinal Tap, Enya, Prince, the Monkees, Jethro Tull, the Singing Dogs and Slim Pickens, and that's just the tip of the snowdrift.

(Beneath the tip is the song *(I Want A) Rockin' Christmas* by Ol' 55, which spent seven weeks at number one in Melbourne in 1976. Sporting the immortal refrain 'Listen to me Santa, won't you bring my lover to me, wrapped up in ribbons and dropped down my chim-in-ey,' it happens to bear a lyricist credit by one G.A. Baker.)

My expedition began in the midst of Rovaniemi, the heart of what has been termed 'the most civilised wilderness in the world,' at a snowmobile base. Here I donned plastic thermal overalls, moonboots, heavy gloves, a balaclava and hood and headed north along the surface of the frozen Kemijoki. If I was about to revisit my childhood, I couldn't have wanted a better preparatory playground. With this vast, wide river virtually to myself I left a joyful wake of doughnuts, zigzags and snow crest crash-throughs, stopping only to drill a hole in the thick ice cover for a spot of fruitless fishing. The north of the country may have a relatively small proportion of the 187 888 lakes that leave the Finnish map looking like a rotting parchment, but the national obsession for fishing is still very much alive and well.

A detour from the Kemijoki an hour after leaving base deposited my party in a Lapp reindeer farm; the sort of impossibly perfect visual panorama that used to be painted on the lids of chocolate boxes and biscuit tins. There are only 2500 real Lapps (the aboriginal Sámi people) in this part of the world, well outnumbered by 200 000 reindeer. Yet their almost regal air and the predominantly red traditional costumes which many of them wear to this day give them a prominence beyond their numerical strength. Largely unwilling to recognise the political borders which divide the land in which they have herded and roamed for more than two thousand years, their spiritual home extends across the tops of Sweden, Norway, Finland and Russia.

A Lapp's relationship with his reindeer herd is not dissimilar to a Bedouin tribesman's bond to his camels. The noble beast provides warmth, labour, nourishment and transport, and is integral to the survival of the Sámi people. Indeed, when I arrived at the stable compound just off the Kemijoki, the finest specimens were arrayed for maximum emotional and aesthetic effect. They were all on hand—Prancer, Dancer and Rudolph, Dasher, Donner and Blitzen, the whole team. The fulfilment of my dream was so near I could almost touch it. Surreptitiously, I checked their hooves for signs of scuffed roof tiles.

After a round of welcoming rituals, we were off dashing through the snow. Not so much in a one-horse open sleigh as a humble three-reindeer sled sans handgrips. Perched precariously in the centre of a reindeer hide-covered wood pallet, I clung to any fingerhold I could find as I was hurled through a total white-out world at a dizzying, exhilarating velocity. Back at the farm a genial, considerate Lapp grandmother, who could have been Mrs Claus, was thoughtfully preparing me a dish of sautéed reindeer with crushed cloudberries. On my return I hesitated but a moment before this unexpected repast; tracking down Santa would require a full stomach, even if it was full of the very beasts who had borne me so majestically.

Nailing down old Saint Nick is often more a matter of good fortune than forward planning. The cottage industry that helped

*Delivering a Santa wish list in
person (David McGonigal)*

him become a household name is now a veritable empire spread
over the vastness of the top half of the fifth largest nation in
Europe. There are seven locations where he may be encountered.
The least likely is his private domain on the trackless wilderness
of Korvatunturi Fell, where he has been known for centuries as
the good-natured elf who rescued the lost and made well hurt
and sick forest creatures. Here, the grand old man of Christmas
recharges his spirit in private.

Visitors in search of an audience tend to head for Santa Claus'
Village, ten kilometres from Rovaniemi, a complex of sixteen
individual enterprises dealing in handicrafts, jewellery, wooden
toys, leather goods, reindeer meat and souvenirs, and including
a children's playground and the Hundred Elf House. If he is not
to be found there, a trek may need to be made south to the city
of Ranua, the home of Santa Claus' Wildlife Park, the world's
northernmost zoo. Vast and spacious, the park has 200 animals
representing fifty different species, as well as a rock park with
geological specimens displaying the natural riches of the arctic
zone. Sited next door is Santa Claus' Toy Animal Workshop in
the granite Murr Murr Castle, where his helpers use thirty of the

real animals as models for ceramic statuettes and cloth and wooden toys.

With the aid of modern technology, the Murr Murr Castle Elf is in direct contact with Santa's home on Korvatunturu Fell by picture-phone, located in the castle's tower. There is a direct line to the man himself in the afternoons during June, July, August and December. Not that a telephone line is entirely adequate for meaningful dialogue with one of the great figures of history. My search continued, with the options narrowing.

West of Rovaniemi, on the Swedish border, is the town of Pello and Santa Claus' Green Stop, home of the Green Elf, famed Salvia ceramics and a display of 2000 green plants. I had it on good authority that he hadn't been seen there for some time. Nor at Kemi, on the Gulf of Bothnia just below the Arctic Circle, where the jewel elf runs the Gemstone Gallery, with over 3000 precious stones committed to his care. There was a faint chance that he could have been in central Lapland at Luosto—the 8000 hectare Santa Claus' Ski and Vacation Resort, bordering the Phyatunturu Fell National Park.

As it eventuated, my hunt reached its conclusion at the very place it had begun—Santa Claus' Village at Rovaniemi. Led into his presence by a rather fetching blonde elf called Kirsi, I was put at ease instantly by an easy affability which, I was to discover, can be dispensed in some twenty languages. I'd hardly had a chance to assure him that I had indeed been a good boy all year and that I just happened to have a list of my computer hardware needs in my inside pocket, when he bravely plonked me down on his knee and handed me, of all things, a business card. Long and slender, it introduced him by his Finnish name, *Joulupukki*, neatly fashioned into a logo with the J appearing as a well-stuffed Christmas stocking.

Santa, as fatigued as he must have been by his December duties, was a gracious and illuminating host, with a quick wit and a ready recall of interesting statistics concerning his mail deluge. It seems that children of Finland send him the most letters, followed by those of Japan, Poland, Australia, West Germany and Italy, the United States and England. He had just received a single missive from Liberia and a scant fifty from Romania, though he expects that to rise following the political changes that have swept Eastern Europe. Most of the letter writers are around ten years old, although the British average is five to seven, and the Japanese spectrum ranges from infancy well into adulthood.

The tone of the letters varies dramatically from country to country. While the children of most western nations hopefully trot out a log of claims, others wouldn't dream of bothering him with their materialistic desires; they just want to transmit their greetings and even confide in him their fears of war and disaster and their hopes for a peaceful world. 'Japanese children don't want presents,' Santa revealed, 'they just want to tell me things about themselves and the world. They tell me they love me.'

(I probably would have too, if I had hung around there long enough. As it was, things were becoming a little sticky, what with his minions wanting to know about the possibility of their master picking up royalties from those songs about him by Michael Jackson, Elvis Presley, Madonna, Stevie Wonder, the Beach Boys, Sheena Easton, the Kinks and, of course, Ol' 55.)

Joulupukki is not unaware of his influence for good in the world. He has met with the Pope, spoken on Soviet television at the personal request of Mikhail Gorbachev, and personally greeted more starry-eyed children than a calculator could tally. In 1988 he welcomed to his headquarters a sixteen-year-old Australian girl called Trudy Davis who was soon to undergo intricate brain surgery in Switzerland. When I asked him about his effect on the young and more than a few of the not-so-young, Santa gave a humble smile, a momentary shrug and said, 'I hope I can do things that make people happy.' Well, *I* left with a grin.

*Santa's annual mailsack now exceeds a million pieces. It does not seem as if Boris Yeltsin is as big a fan of the jolly red gent as Mikhail Gorbachev but the Russian share of the letter deluge is growing steadily.*

# FLYING WRY

Unless the ghost of Oscar Wilde inhabits you, your truly best lines are invariably retrospective. It's a maxim for life that the most searing retorts to the inane and the offensive almost always occur after the culprit has escaped.

I don't recall the airline, the destination or even the class but I do recall the plastic tray spread with the substantial remains of a particularly indigestible meal. I had finished picking through it within ten minutes and for the next eighty minutes it sat before me, its glutinous mass congealing beneath an air vent I had employed to scatter its odour in the direction of those other passengers plainly less offended by the cuisine.

With my bile rising, my bladder bursting and my patience exhausted I was about to lunge toward the hostess call button when a representative of the cabin crew, on a rare reconnaissance mission, finally presented himself, beaming broadly and loudly enquiring: 'Would you like me to take your tray, sir?' All I could manage was a lame nod. It wasn't until he had disappeared into the galley that the range of possible replies presented themselves: 'No, I'd like to bronze it, so I can hang it on my office wall.' 'Why, is the captain still peckish?' 'Well, I was hoping to pack it away with my duty free so I can have a midnight snack in my hotel room.'

Although cabin crews are supposed to create a mood of calm security with their capable control of all eventualities, individual behaviour can become progressively unsettling. On a Royal Nepal Airlines flight I once witnessed otherwise demure cabin crew members skipping down the aisle giggling and tossing sweets at passengers with debilitating accuracy as the aircraft commenced its descent into the Kathmandu Valley. During the early days of airline deregulation in the United States, when competition between regional carriers was exceptionally fierce, I took an early morning Eastern Airlines service manned by a crew which delivered a polished stand-up comedy routine with the aid of lapel microphones. After the solid hour of banter I had learned the sexual orientation, domestic arrangements and mood swings of those serving me my juice and rolls. I found it amusing but then I wasn't a daily commuter on the route. At least it was a little more animated than the performance of an Air France economy class crew on a late-1970s flight from Bangkok to Paris who wheeled the drinks trolley into the centre of the section somewhere over India, announced 'Help yourselves' and disappeared until it was time to open the doors. Strangely, no one seemed to complain. Many didn't notice. It was economy after all.

Air travel just does not equate with dazzling cerebral agility. All mental faculties are slowed the moment the seat belt clicks and the pantomime lecture on how to tie a double scout knot on your life vest while the aircraft is plummeting sharply downward begins playing to an uninterested audience. Normal good taste in literature and cinema is suspended for the duration of the flight. One hour off the ground and you're prepared to watch the hostess paint her nails for entertainment. Without embarrassment, you have your seat upright and your headphones in place thirty minutes before the commencement of films that you wouldn't attend in a regular cinema if you were sent a free pass. The American screen formula of car chases and firearms suddenly seems inspired. You actually laugh at Mel Gibson and Danny Glover's swiped Three Stooges gags.

Likewise with literature. It is no accident that most of the paperbacks in airport bookstalls are garishly wrapped mounds of pulp. At home you may read Marquez, Matthiessen, Winton, Gordimer and Jacobsen—all of whom eventually become impenetrable at 30 000 feet. After a while the only words that don't seem to glaze your eyes over are written by men who claim to have once worked for the CIA, MI5 or Mossad, have remarkable intimate knowledge of female orgasm under extreme conditions and truly expect you to believe that there are working pay phones all over Moscow. Aircraft cleaners must have vast libraries of these bulky bestsellers in which the fate of the free world rests on the shoulders of a disillusioned Rhodes scholar with a talent for cryptography who is bequeathed a parchment that was written by Lenin and used to light Churchill's cigars, because anybody with the slightest regard for their public image leaves them deep in a seat pocket as soon as normal altitude and sanity are attained.

*Reassuring airport instruction, Bulawayo, Zimbabwe (Bob King)*

A return to sea level, though, is not always a guarantee of a return to sanity. At least not if you land at Singapore's squeaky clean Changi Airport where a very strange parlour game is played. They don't do it with mirrors but the effect would be the same. There is a block of shops near your exit gate, vending the usual array of overpriced books, electronics, toys, cosmetics, et al. Right beside the block is another block of exactly the same shops, then another one. Like Patrick McGoohan in the cult TV series *The Prisoner*, you're not sure if you're going where you've been, been where you're going or will ever find your way out of the maze. You usually make your way back to your aircraft by following the ankle-biter who sat behind you and metronomically kicked your seat from Sydney to Singapore.

Such an intrusion, I might just point out, is not likely to occur in the first-class cabins of Aeroflot aircraft assigned to prestige sectors (ie: not over Siberia). Whoever supplied the Russians with industrial espionage during the dark days of the cold war obviously overemphasised the spaciousness aspect of the expensive rows. In seat 1A it is possible for ballerinas and soccer players to practise their pursuits without disturbing other passengers; provided they do not wish to partake of nourishment. When my meal tray was placed atop the two spindly steel sticks attached to and lowered from the far distant bulkhead, it was necessary for me to balance precariously on the edge of my seat and lunge forward with a fork in the vain hope of spearing a pea. Whatever morsels I did capture invariably fell to the floor during the long journey back to my mouth.

But I was talking about airports and thoughts of Changi lead me to thoughts of Hong Kong's Kai Tak Airport which stands unchallenged for peak achievements in obstruction, pettiness and abrasive discourtesy on the part of every employee from cleaner to those who check in first-class passengers, and has done so for at least twenty years. I can't recall a single instance of getting through the place with my good humour intact. When I chew the fat with fellow travellers we swap Kai Tak horror stories.

Although it is not quite so stridently enforced these days, the airport authority has always had spotters stationed near immigration to ensure that carry-on baggage does not exceed rule-book limits by a centimetre or kilogram. Infringers, who may well have carried the same items onto planes at a dozen other airports, often find themselves, after furious blazing rows, lining up (if they haven't already been slugged at check-in) at the excess baggage window, one of the busiest in the world. Of course, safety is cited but if somebody in this odious chain of enforcement isn't getting a rake-off from the booty collected then I have a full head of hair and can still fit into my wedding suit.

I couldn't be bothered with the subterfuge any more but I do recall occasions when, having tumbled upon caches of rare albums in a Kowloon disc emporium which I was subsequently unable to accommodate in an already heavy suitcase, I would stroll past these inflexible centurions while casually whistling, broadly smiling and loosely swinging a piece of cabin baggage that appeared to be as difficult to tote as a rolled newspaper. However, once out of their sight, I would drop the dead weight, gasp violently for breath and try to massage some circulation back into my contorted fingers. It's a wonder my knuckles didn't drag along the ground for days afterwards.

Most other countries don't really care about this sort of nonsense, unless you try to tether the household goat to your seat leg. In a number of lands, France and Argentina among them, there often isn't even seat allocation on domestic flights. The prevailing rule is: if you can jam yourself and whatever you're carrying into and around whatever seats you can seize when the mad boarding scramble begins, and we can slam the doors shut when the dust settles, airline business is successfully carried on.

The increased sophistication of terrorism has come to result in airports caring less about the dimensions of your hand baggage than the contents. This is taken to alarming extremes at Heathrow, which joins Berlin's Tegel as the only two airports at which my accompanying photographers exhausted every known means of persuasion in a vain attempt to have professional photographic film hand-checked rather than sent through an X-ray machine. I shan't easily forget the security supervisor at Heathrow who, when questioned (indeed, implored), asked if we would prefer to have our bag of film taken outside and blown up, that being the only courtesy he was prepared to extend.

Admittedly, we were flying to Ireland at the time. Which is not unlike flying to Israel, or out of it again. I'd thought a body search was a cursory sweep around the perimeter of the person with a mobile metal detector until I found myself in a curtained cubicle at Tel Aviv Airport with a smart little *sabra* in chic khakis who managed to find crevices in my body with which my wife and doctor are unfamiliar.

There is a remarkably thin veneer of civility at most airports. Your compliance is counted upon because, let's be serious here, who is going to voluntarily delay oneself for innumerable hours just for the momentary satisfaction of pointing out the character failings of a uniformed klutz with Hitlerian tendencies and bad breath to boot? Better to acquiesce, even if it means chewing the inside of your cheek while you're doing it.

I tend to count to ten a lot at Heathrow, particularly upon arrival. England has formulated an interesting admissions policy for all citizens of European Community nations. Well, essentially there isn't one, beyond providing a dozen immigration desks where passports are merely glanced at while Eurocitizens romp past without breaking stride. Conversely, any residents of countries with the dubious fortune of having once been colonised by Britannia snake around steel barricades for a couple of kilometres on the way to the single desk bearing the notation 'Others'. There, as their passports are meticulously checked against voluminous listings of known felons, spies and job seekers, they are spot evaluated for individual worthiness.

Once, seeing the EC desks empty and the attendants slumbering, I deserted my bivouac and brazenly presented myself for processing. 'What makes you think you can come here?' the rubber stamp man asked. 'Oh well, we're all members of the Commonwealth, loyal subjects of the crown and all that, eh what?' I offered. 'Only when it suits you bastards,' he grunted with a grimace that threatened to break into a smile as he stamped my passport and tossed it at me with a movement of his head that unmistakeably suggested that I should scamper towards baggage collection, like quick. As I departed, my photographer presented himself, arguing 'Well, you let my mate through'. Thus was the empire unravelled.

When it comes to baggage misdirections I have, knock on wood, no real horror stories to relate. I've not sat in a Nadi hotel room while my luggage was buried beneath a snow drift on the tarmac in Anchorage. There was, however, a suitcase I checked onto a direct flight from Memphis to Los Angeles which was not there to greet me at LAX. It was found a full month later in a city I had never visited by an airline on which I had never travelled. What was particularly irritating was that I was back home in Australia, was emotionally adjusted to the loss, had replaced everything essential and was looking forward to an attractive compensation cheque, when I received word that Air Atlanta in Georgia had found my suitcase. Clearly labelled, it had managed to sit in a corner of Atlanta Airport for four weeks without anybody bothering to ask 'Hey, what's this doing here?' (Believe me, the south is *not* going to rise again.) Instead of getting to bank a fat cheque I got to unpack toxic underwear and irredeemably crumpled shirts that I never liked in the first place.

It could, as the maxim goes, have been worse. I could have been the poor schmuck standing next to me by the baggage conveyor belt at Moscow's Sheremetyevo Airport in 1989 who witnessed the appearance of his suitcase and wept. A long incision had been made—most likely with a razor—across its breadth and most of the contents had been removed. To compound his woes, dour and suspicious security guards then took him away for questioning, no doubt on the basis that a tourist's luggage is his own responsibility and this visitor had clearly failed to enter the Soviet Union in an orderly manner.

There is a lot to be said for orderly behaviour, particularly in the air—as anyone who has ever shared a plane with an intoxicated Australian body-contact sporting team will readily attest. Even if you never encounter airborne footballers, garden variety bronzed Aussies let loose with their duty-free allowance for a few hours can also persuade you to take your next holiday at a quiet caravan park. Two of them, clad fetchingly in stubbies, rubber thongs and Barnsie t-shirts, set to slugging out a disagreement by the baggage carousel at Denpasar airport the last time I was in Bali. They were immediately surrounded by worried uniformed men who didn't have the slightest idea how to separate the hairy, swearing brawlers. The fracas was still going strong as I lugged my bags out to the roadway, but obviously resolved itself while I was changing money. As I stepped into my hotel courtesy bus, I spotted the two pugilists, arms affectionately around each other's shoulders, wiping bloodied noses on their shirts and laughing as they climbed into an old Holden with surfboards on the top and shot off to Kuta Beach. It's a wonder an Australian passport will gain you admission to most neighbouring countries.

Still, there is worse. It just takes you more hours to get to it. Young Germans were the unrivalled hoons of Europe well before reunification. Large, loud and humourless, they are an intimidating presence on planes, trains and boats. By comparison, young Americans are merely stupid. Leaving aside the rampant and repugnant xenophobia which has come surging out of an unleashed East Germany like pus from a sore, there is a frightening amorality about the post-postwar baby boom produce of what was West Germany—a vacant cold-eyed disinterest which I first saw on the wan faces of Berlin's innumerable teenage street whores and junkies; the look of Christiane F. It's as if, in the rush to rebuild a conquered nation, a vital social component was lost—or abandoned.

Like British soccer hooligans, these Teutonic terrors have developed a taste for travel. A dozen or so occupied the back rows on my shuttle flight from Istanbul to Ankara, drunkenly yelling inanities and obscenities at each other as if there were no other passengers. The resigned Turkish businessman beside me dismissed them as 'Aryan arseholes'. It reminded me of parts of the BBC television play, *Caught On A Train*.

Talking of which, I was once caught on a plane for what I believe to be a record duration. Sydney to London during the infamous European winter of 1982, with fourteen hours stuck in a snowdrift on a Zurich tarmac. Time span from walking on board at Mascot to disembarking at Heathrow— 44 hours. My wife and I were convinced we would never be able to walk upright again.

I don't feel so bad about it now though. Not because of the obliterating passage of time but because of a recent news report I read about a Merpati Airlines sixteen-seater plane which crashed into the jungle on the Indonesian island of Sulawesi during a flight from cosmic Torajaland to the city of Ujung Pandang. There were no deaths but the passengers spent five days strapped in their seats and balancing precariously in treetops high above the forest floor before a rescue team reached them. I would probably have skipped over this snippet between bites of toast had I not, almost on the same day five years before, been in one of those sixteen seats. It fair sent a shiver through me.

Which, I suppose, is better than the near scalding I suffered on a full, daytime Philippines Airlines flight from Sydney to Manila when I was allocated a seat locked in permanent recline. The ceiling pattern had lost its novelty by the time we'd taxied out over Botany Bay so the remainder of the journey was spent trying to direct hot liquids and solids down my throat rather than my shirt front. I was able to watch the top half of the movie but any screen action conducted below the collar line was a bit of a blur. To make it worse, the errant seat was in economy class, enabling the man behind to ash his cigarette in my hair during the love scenes.

Economy class really is indefensible. It's not that you have to queue for three hours before departure to get a seat in the middle of a block of five that you can't occupy unless you fold yourself like a table napkin. And it's not that you are served tiny trays of tasteless, overcooked substances and have to plead for a bread roll, or even that the toilets are always scarce and putrid. It's that you become totally faceless and of minuscule importance. An economy hostess on a major airline, one that should know better, once walked past me and reached for a plastic cup which she no doubt presumed was empty. It wasn't, so I instinctively placed my fingers on it to denote continued ownership. Thus ensued a silent tug-of-war, which she eventually won. As she smugly marched off with her spoil of victory it did occur to me that they'd never do that up the pointy end.

# ONE FLEW OVER THE PENGUIN'S NEST

Colin Monteath was gazing at Smith Island with the sort of lust men usually feel guilty about as soon as the throbbing eases. We were two days out of Tierra del Fuego and it was our first Antarctic landfall. It emerged out of the mist as a series of steep, snow-scattered, grey mountains rising sheer out of the Antarctic Ocean, with no evident beach, bay or landing point.

With more than thirty Antarctic visits over the past twenty years and a reputation as a premier mountaineer, explorer, wilderness photographer and Antarctic scholar, this endearing innocent with the physique of a drinking straw was initially thought to be impervious to the sort of frozen delights that had us, his fifty or so eager charges, racing to the bridge of the *Akademik Sergey Vavilov* with loaded cameras and whirring videos every time anything white and high loomed in the distance.

A former field operations officer for New Zealand's Antarctic research programme, Monteath had always sailed down to the Antarctic Peninsula by other routes and had thus never laid eyes on this particularly severe-looking outcrop. He may have hauled himself up the Himalayas and the Andes, commanded dog sled teams over splintering glaciers, and made the first descent into the inner crater of the actively volcanic Mt Erebus, but he had never ascended any of the peaks on the unclimbed Smith Island in the South Shetlands. It was obvious from the intensity of his gaze that he soon would. We offered to wipe away his drool and then gave him some privacy.

Over the next two weeks, having snapped out of his momentary reverie, the dedicated devotee of all things physically remote had imbued in us a practical understanding of the complexities of a continent bigger than Europe and Australia and an affection for this white wilderness which we will carry with us for life. What we had all secretly feared might turn out to be a tedious expanse of ice garnished by even more ice unfolded before our eyes, ears and aroused senses as possibly the most commanding, overpowering and intimidating place on earth.

There is an ever-present sense of extreme privilege which comes from the realisation that, of the five billion inhabitants of the planet, only about five thousand of them set foot on Antarctica each year. That number may well double by the turn of the century as the tourism component increases but there are still not likely to be turnstiles at the penguin rookeries or handrails and walking tracks around the glaciers. Spread over 14 million square kilometres (and half as much again when the winter pack-ice sets in), that many people couldn't link hands and span a decent sized ice shelf. To place it into perspective: the numbers of the predatory leopard seals are believed to exceed half a million, yet in two weeks I encountered just one.

Few privileges, however, are as relatively easy to attain. The widely-held perception that the great lower continent is accessible only to the exceedingly rich or members of scientific expeditions is as puzzling as it is wrong. 'Green Tourism' in the Antarctic region began in 1958 and 20 000 people had visited for non-professional purposes by the early 1980s. There are now 70 regularly-used landing points for passengers from the dozen or so ships that move around the Antarctic Ocean during the brief 'window' of roughly six weeks from late December to early February.

Officially this is high summer, the halcyon days on the Antarctic calendar when the pack-ice has melted, the Picasso-conceived icebergs are afloat, light you can read by is present for 22 hours in the day and the temperature on the Antarctic Peninsula sits at around 0 degrees—a considerable improvement on the −89.6 recorded in 1983 at Russia's Vostock Station on the Polar Plateau. The Peninsula, under South America, is the continent's Cote d'Azur. Like most parts of the Antarctic coastline, it is twenty degrees or more warmer than the frigid mass of the continent proper, which sits more than 2000 metres above sea level, as opposed to the world average of 600 metres. Birds and seals come here to feed and breed on and around the thousands of irregular inlets, islands, channels, points and precipices which make the long hook of land the most diverse and visually spectacular portion of this awesome white world.

That is one reason why South America is the most logical departure point for ships. Another is that it is 3600 kilometres from South Africa to the Antarctic continent and 2250 from both New Zealand and Australia (Tasmania), but a mere 1000 kilometres from the Argentinian town of Ushuaia down to the tip of the Antarctic Peninsula. The crossing can be made in two fairly comfortable days, depending on the temperament of the seas in the Drake Passage.

Let us not forget that we are talking about Cape Horn here; two terrifying words seared into the fabric of many an old salt's worst nightmares. It can be a deceptive waterway. I struck a millpond going over and so decided to abandon the sticky medicinal patch behind my right ear (worn, I was relieved to discover, even by our hardy leaders who had climbed the north face of Everest without oxygen). The return leg was a rather rude shock and I found it prudent to be horizontal rather than vertical for a full day. Even with admirably effective stabilisers, the *Akademik Sergey Vavilov* accurately duplicated the motions of the tilt-a-whirl ride I was once press-ganged onto at Luna Park.

Fortunately, when it was not locked into buckling convulsions, the *Vavilov* was a warm, sociable and eminently functional refuge from the outside extremes, even if none of its passengers will ever again be able to look at a cold salad smorgasbord lunch with equanimity. Manned by a consummately capable 44-strong Russian crew headed by a serene, neatly bearded, hand-wringing captain of inestimable patience who never once blinked as his bridge was overrun by yelping hordes, the Finnish-built vessel had been provisioned, for reasons of intricate marine financing, out of Germany rather than the more logical Argentina. There were no steaks from the pampas but there was a stay in Buenos Aires at both ends of the expedition so that certain deprivations might be stoically borne.

Communal life aboard the meticulously maintained steel spear had unmistakable Keseyian elements (as in Ken Kesey, author of *One Flew Over The Cuckoo's Nest*). There wasn't a Nurse Ratched but there was a Chief—a silent towering Italian, constructed with the bones of a whale, who nearly made the boat tip when he descended the gangway. But even ignoring his lumbering omnipresence, the assortment was odd, to be sure.

I thought I knew the sort of folk who would go to Antarctica

. . . until I went there myself. To my surprise there were no strident eco-tourists surreptitiously measuring the depth of my footfalls and their displacement effect on the ice cover for their next action newsletter; no science students monitoring polar precipitation or seal secretions; no frostbitten explorers determined to follow in the footsteps of Smith, Weddell, Biscoe, D'Urville and Ross.

There was, however: a barrister from Melbourne whose most memorable case involved the tendering of purloined ladies underwear as exhibits before a judge who gazed so longingly at the selection that it was suspected he may have been intending to try them on for size during the first available recess; a clueless American photographer who did not understand a single punchline of a single joke or humorous aside but laughed a lot despite his impediment; a little, old, white-haired lady who, for three consecutive years, had checked herself out of a Sydney retirement village, waved goodbye to the geriatrics in the television room and headed off to Antarctica, which she found very clean; a well-travelled couple in the concrete pouring and card design business whose two young adult sons clambered to the top of every available mountain, video cameras clenched between their teeth; two elderly American social workers who had recently slipped under their government's embargo to visit and write about Cuba; a white-bearded Brazilian sculptor who sincerely preached a theory that Rio slum dwellers were at risk from AIDS-bearing fleas; and the deputy headmistress of a girl's high school who was the first to strip down to a swimming costume and bathe in what was touted as a thermal pool but ended up being minute amounts of steaming water seeping out of the coarse pebble sand at Pendulum Cove.

One of the quietest passengers, a divorced mother of teenage children who, toward the end of the journey, revealed herself to be a former prison officer, was actively courted by one of the Russian seamen, who was so besotted that he plied her with chocolates and champagne on the deck at 2 am and even took to singing his declarations of love in a Siberian dialect.

Notwithstanding some convincing pretensions there were no new-age Mawsons among the paying customers, although everyone politely sat through the documentary videos on the great, tragic polar expeditions each evening after dinner and paid due attention to Colin Monteath, Greg Mortimer and Margaret Werner's twice-daily, slide-illustrated tutorials on such essential

*Proselytising the penguins, Argentinian scientific base, Antarctic Peninsula (Glenn A. Baker)*

Antarctic topics as pinnipeds, catabatic winds, whales, icebergs, Gondwanaland and penguins. We certainly achieved simultaneous Antarctic orgasm as the knowledge swept over us in waves but what came to unite us all in a tensile bond of shared purpose and experience was our fragrance—*eau de penguine*. Indeed I can still catch a whiff of it as I leaf through my notebook.

I'm not sure of the collective noun for penguins, but might I submit that it should be a *lot* of penguins? In one rookery alone, set in a vast amphitheatre at Bailey's Head, there were a good half million of the gloriously absurd creatures, metronomically disappearing into the ocean and reappearing with fat bellies full of krill which they are obliged to regurgitate into the mouths of their greedy, grey-downed young who can devour the equivalent of their body weight in a few minutes.

You can watch penguins all day and sometimes I think we did. Watch them stand in groups on the beaches, nudge one of their number into the water to check for lurking leopard seals, then hit the deep with the precision of an Esther Williams aquatic ballet and 'fly' underwater at 30 kph in manic three-minute bursts. Watch them clamber up steep mountain sides with all the grace of drunken C3POs, squabble like soccer hooligans, defecate with the precision of archers and screech like incumbent politicians. All of which they will do while you are wandering about in their midst taking advantage of the fact that Antarctic wildlife has not yet had cause to view humans as predators and, apart from a potentially lethal elephant seal breath of fermented plankton and squid, offer no menace and expect none.

Cambridge University professor Bernard Stonehouse, who has been working as a biologist in the Antarctic for forty years and is grand company if you ever find yourself on Cuverville Island and get tired of trying to tell the Adelie penguins from the Gentoos, Macaronis and the irritating little Chinstraps, has written, 'I have often had the impression that, to penguins, man is just another penguin—different, less predictable, occasionally violent but tolerable company when he sits still and minds his own business'.

A fine theory, as is Colin Monteath's that this, contrary to popular opinion, is the 'new age of adventure'. That, although all the great lands have long been discovered and the maps drawn, it is now possible, with equipment and support beyond the dreams of a Scott, Shackleton or Mawson, to mount private expeditions not likely to result in the death or permanent disability of the participants. With greater sensitivity to dwindling resources and incomparable terrains, wondrous places are being actively protected and some species are inexorably restoring their numbers.

His argument was never more potently proved than the day three humpback whales were sighted on the port side and we all tumbled into the rubber Zodiacs used for the daily shore landings and set off in gleeful pursuit. For an hour we paced the three frolicking 40–50 tonne beasts and literally screamed with excitement as they effected deep dives and 'gave us the tail' on the way down, then shot out three-metre high jets of water from their spouts as they returned. Or the perfect day we cruised around the perimeter of the accurately named Paradise Bay beneath walls of blue glacial ice pockmarked with 'cathedral windows' and turned off the engines to better hear the wrenching, thunderous groans and exclamations of the glaciers as the jagged crevasses gave way and hundreds of tonnes of ice collapsed into the ocean to form floating domains larger than some European principalities.

I'd wondered how the mighty *Titanic* could have fallen foul of a Newfoundland iceberg until I saw some the size of a block of flats pass by the starboard bow. Tabular icebergs—those which fracture off ice shelf fronts—can be 200 metres thick and 100 kilometres wide, with 80 per cent of their mass beneath the water surface. Light planes can land on them (often catastrophically) and ships view them as their principal navigational hazard in polar waters and even beyond (they have been sighted drifting near the Tropic of Capricorn). Our otherwise fearless captain was not prepared to sail through the narrow Le Maire Channel because of their vast numbers. As the earth's largest source of freshwater, it has been proposed that icebergs be towed to arid regions for drought relief. A 10 kilometre by 10 kilometre block of ice will melt down to 10,000 billion litres of pure $H_20$.

The joy of icebergs, as I discovered when I accompanied Colin Monteath as he slipped away to photograph a few of the more charismatic ones for the second volume of his book *Wild Ice*, is that they are pliable and will maintain the bizarre deformities caused by pressures and dynamic glacial action long after they go floating away on their lonesome. They are also rarely all white. The infusion of light and water creates resonant greens, deep blues and lightly tinted pinks. They can bear uncanny resemblance to a gelati cone, a mushroom, a Scandinavian convention centre, chewed gum, a Cornwall cottage, a shrivelled scrotum and a toothless mutt. They can be absolutely anything you want them to be and a few things you'd rather they weren't.

Which can be said for Antarctica itself. The continent is still a blank canvas for the imagination. It is pristine, it is as the earth once was, it is the only real 'last frontier'. Still admirably protected by the surprisingly effective Antarctic Treaty of 1959, this harsh but fragile environment may well be the only unspoiled thing of true worth that this generation can hand on to the next. We can book the ceremony as soon as Colin Monteath gets around to scaling those enticing peaks on Smith Island.